International Macroeconomic Modelling for Policy Decisions

ADVANCED STUDIES IN THEORETICAL AND APPLIED ECONOMETRICS
VOLUME 5

International Macroeconomic Modelling for Policy Decisions

edited by

P. Artus and O. Guvenen
in collaboration with F. Gagey

1986 **MARTINUS NIJHOFF PUBLISHERS**
a member of the KLUWER ACADEMIC PUBLISHERS GROUP
DORDRECHT / BOSTON / LANCASTER

Distributors

for the United States and Canada: Kluwer Academic Publishers, 190 Old Derby Street, Hingham, MA 02043, USA
for the UK and Ireland: Kluwer Academic Publishers, MTP Press Limited, Falcon House, Queen Square, Lancaster LA1 1RN, UK
for all other countries: Kluwer Academic Publishers Group, Distribution Center, P.O. Box 322, 3300 AH Dordrecht, The Netherlands

Library of Congress Cataloging in Publication Data

Main entry under title:

International macroeconomic modelling for policy
    decision.

    (Advanced studies in theoretical and applied
econometrics ; v. 5)
    "Based on an international conference organised by
the Applied Econometric Association (AEA) ... which
was held in Brussels at the Commission of the European
Communities in December 1983"--Pref.
    Bibliography: p.
    1. International economic relations--Mathematical
models--Congresses. 2. Economic policy--Decision
making--Congresses. I. Artus, Patrick. II. Guvenen, O.
III. Gagey, F. IV. Applied Econometric Association.
V. Series.
HF1410.5.I577 1985   337'.0724   85-13698
ISBN 90-247-3201-8

ISBN 90-247-3201-8 (this volume)
ISBN 90-247-2622-0 (series)

Copyright

PRINTED IN THE NETHERLANDS

PREFACE

This book is based on an international conference organised by the Applied Econometric Association (AEA) on International Macroeconomic Modelling which was held in Brussels at the Commission of the European Communities in December 1983.

On behalf of the Applied Econometric Association, we would like to extend our thanks to all participants and contributors. This conference would not have been possible without the cooperation and support of the Commission of the European Economic Communities and of its Directorate General for Economics and Financial Affairs (DGII) staff, in particular M. Emerson, A. Dramais, and also H. Serbat of the Paris Chamber of Commerce and Industry.

Our thanks go also to J.P. Ancot for his constructive comments concerning the structure of this book.

We are grateful to M. Russo, R. Maldague and Y. Ullmo for opening the conference with their stimulating review and comments on the use of international macroeconomic models; and to R. Bird, A.M. Costa, A. Crockett, H. Guitton, J.C. Milleron, J. Paelinck, J. Waelbroeck for chairing the scientific sessions.

P. Artus
F. Gagey
O. Guvenen

INTRODUCTION

The main focus of this book is to present recent developments in the construction and use of international macroeconometric models.

Four main aspects are selected:

(i) analysis of trade linkages and exchange rate determination;

(ii) modelling and simulating the international economy;

(iii) international policy coordination;

(iv) the use of international macroeconomic models.

These four aspects are treated by theoretical and empirical studies to be used as research and forecasting tools at the universities, research institutes, and international organisations.

The Editors

TABLE OF CONTENTS

PART I

ANALYSIS OF TRADE LINKAGES AND EXCHANGE RATE DETERMINATION

CHAPTER 1

MODELLING BILATERAL SECTORAL TRADE FLOWS

A. Italianer* and G. d'Alcantara**
*Katholieke Universiteit Leuven, Belgium; **Katholieke Unviersiteit Leuven and CORE, Belgium

1. INTRODUCTION

The recession that has set in in the aftermath of the second oil crisis is taking such a shape that one is more and more tempted to compare it with the Big Recession that occurred about a long wave of 50 years ago.

Somewhat loosely speaking, one might say that Keynes' 'diagnosis' of underexpenditure and 'treatment' of government stimulation formed part of a macro-economic answer to the pre-war problems that proved to be right in the course of history.

The present recession, however, is of a much more complicated nature in several respects. It is dealing simultaneously with the financial problems and instability in general of the developing countries, and large government budget deficits (due to slackening growth, rigid expenditure patterns and expensive social security systems), low investment (due to high interest rates and uncertain expectations), high unemployment and numerous sectoral problems against a background of political instability, increasing protection and fierce international competition.

A common factor that applies to several items appearing on this list of sadnesses is the *interdependent* nature of things. Each *national* multiplier corresponding to a measure of *one* single government is confronted with a relatively high import leakage so to speak.

The complicated nature of the recession and the interdependencies that pull the world back and forth in the course of its development exclude a Keynesian one problem – one solution analysis of the state of affairs. And what is more, the increased validity of an economic law of communicating (and probably leaking) fusts prevents individual governments from taking effective action on their own.

The consequences of these conclusions for econometric modelbuilding are twofold. First, we cannot any longer rely on relatively simple macro-economic models to deal with questions that require anything but a macro-economic analysis. Second,

Artus, P. and Guvenen, O. (eds.): International Macroeconomic Modelling for Policy Decisions.
© *1986. Martinus Nijhoff Publishers, Dordrecht/Boston/Lancaster.*
ISBN 90-247-3201-8. Printed in The Netherlands.

any attempt at an integrated approach requires a model in which linkages between different countries or groups of countries are taken into account, at least in a rudimentary fashion.

The present paper tries to demonstrate, by way of a very simple exercise, how a refinement in the economic or econometric analysis may be achieved through a sectoral disaggregation of bilateral trade flows in a model that links several national models and zone models to a world model. The purpose is to show how different economic policies that *a priori* have the same macro-economic impact in fact generate differential macro-economic patterns because we have disaggregated the channels through which the policy measures are propagated.

The exercise will be applied to the European Economic Community (EEC) as an example of strongly integrated markets with differential sectoral developments and a scope for coordinated policy. A truly sectoral approach would require the dis-aggregated linkage of sectoral models for each of the EEC member countries. Although a project for the construction of such an integrated set of sectoral models is presently executed as a part of the HERMES modelling project,[1] cfr. d'Alcantara and Italianer (1982), its country models are not yet fully operational, and therefore we apply a disaggregated linkage to different macro-economic models in such a way that it is still possible to analyze the differential effects that may be expected from a sectoral approach. What we essentially do is disaggregating the bilateral trade flows of the COMET IV model, a world model that links 13 country models and 5 models that cover the rest of the world exhaustively.[2]

Disaggregating bilateral trade flows crucially hinges on data availability. The dataset we used was constructed from the most detailed OECD trade data that are available. These have the disadvantage that only trade data for OECD declarants are available, nevertheless these data permit to cover (in a disaggregated way) more than 80% of the world trade over the sample period.[3] The rest of world trade (i.e. trade between the five zones) is only covered in an aggregate way.

The disaggregation is in five categories of goods:

A – Agricultural, forestry and fishery products
E – Fuel and power products
Q – Manufacturing products : intermediate
K – Manufacturing products : equipment
C – Manufacturing products : consumption

The outline of the paper is as follows. In section 2 we give some historical evidence on trade developments for the five categories of goods that lead us to some *a priori* conclusions about what to expect from policy simulations. Section 3 gives a short description of the country and zone models of the COMET IV model, which is extended in Section 4 with some simple disaggregated import equations and their parameter estimates. In Section 5 we treat the modelling of disaggregated bilateral trade flow equations, after which we present the policy simulation results in Section 6. Conclusions, in Section 7, and a list of references conclude the paper.

2. EVIDENCE FROM THE PAST

Let X_i and M_j denote the value of exports of country i and imports of country j, in US dollars, respectively. Similarly, use $X_{i,EEC}$ and $M_{EEC,j}$ to denote exports to EEC countries by country i and imports from EEC countries by country j, respectively. Then the following two expressions are a possible measure for the integration of the EEC with respect to imports and exports, respectively, on a scale between 0 and 1

$$(\Sigma_i X_{i,EEC})/(\Sigma_i X_i) \qquad i = EEC \tag{1}$$

$$(\Sigma_j M_{EEC,j})/(\Sigma_j M_j) \qquad j = EEC \tag{2}$$

It is easy to see that both these 'integration ratios' may be derived from weighted percentages of total exports/imports with the EEC as destination/origin.

$$\Sigma_i v_i(X_{i,EEC}/X_i) \qquad v_i = X_i/\Sigma_k X_k \tag{3}$$

$$\Sigma_j w_j(M_{EEC,j}/M_j) \qquad w_j = M_j/\Sigma_k M_k \tag{4}$$

Integration ratios for total trade may be derived from a double-weighted similar expression

$$u_x \Sigma_i v_i(X_{i,EEC}/X_i) + (1 - u_x)\Sigma_j w_j(M_{EEC,j}/M_j)$$

$$u_x = \Sigma_k X_k/\Sigma_k(X_k + M_k) \tag{5}$$

which results in

$$(\Sigma_i X_{i,EEC} + \Sigma_j M_{EEC,j})/(\Sigma_i X_i + \Sigma_j M_j) \qquad i,j = EEC \tag{6}$$

The resulting integration ratios for imports, exports and total trade for the present 10 EEC members are given in Table 1 for representative years over the period 1963–1980.

On the *import* side the table shows that the largest intra EEC shift occurred for agricultural goods, which is not surprising of course in view of the heavy emphasis that is put on the Common Agricultural Policy. A large shift towards imports from the EEC also shows up for consumption goods, but the upward trend has gone downwards after 1975 under the influence of an increased market share for the Far East. The upward trend in intermediate goods is decreasing in speed but still present, while the stable pattern for equipment goods also was interrupted in 1975–1980, again in favour of Far Eastern countries. Regarding energy products,

Table 1. Integration ratios of the trade of the European Economic Community (incl. Greece), 1963—1980.

		A	E	Q	K	C	T
Imports	1963	18.7	22.4	50.8	67.2	38.3	42.3
	1970	28.0	20.3	53.1	67.2	48.8	50.5
	1975	34.8	18.5	60.9	66.1	54.0	51.1
	1980	35.2	21.9	61.6	60.7	51.4	49.9
Exports	1963	67.2	60.5	45.4	38.2	49.2	47.7
	1970	72.7	61.3	52.4	44.0	55.6	53.5
	1975	73.3	63.0	50.3	40.4	60.4	52.6
	1980	70.6	65.8	54.4	45.0	58.1	55.5
Total trade	1963	28.8	32.9	48.0	48.5	43.1	44.8
	1970	40.3	30.7	52.7	53.2	52.0	52.0
	1975	47.3	28.0	55.1	50.1	57.0	51.9
	1980	47.2	33.1	57.8	51.6	54.6	52.6

Percentages in value in US dollars.

the EEC slowly seems to be regaining its import share of the beginning of the 60s. The coal of that time is now of course mainly replaced by UK oil and Dutch natural gas.

The integration ratios for *exports* show that in the course of time an increasing part of export earnings for all categories of goods comes from the Common Market, with some exceptions for the recession year 1975 and turning tides for agricultural goods and consumption goods towards the end of the period.

For *total trade* the largest integration by 1980 is for intermediary goods, followed by consumption goods and equipment goods. The rapid agricultural integration seems to have come to a halt since 1975.

From the point of view of the EEC the most important integration ratio seems to be the one for imports because it gives an indication on the import leakage that we may expect for each category of goods in case of an increase in demand. As for 1980, the lowest leakage, and therefore the strongest effects on the EEC as a whole may be expected on the market for intermediate and equipment goods, followed by consumption goods.

A question that immediately raises after these general remarks is the relative importance of the five categories of goods on the import and export markets of the EEC as a whole and its member countries individually. These are given in Table 2 (for imports) and in Table 3 (for exports), not only for the EEC and its member countries, but also for the candidate member countries Portugal and Spain and the important trading partners, the United States and Japan.

Table 2. Shares of different categories of goods in total *imports* in *constant* 1975 US dollars.

		A	E	Q	K	C
BLEU	1963	11.3	18.1	21.7	27.2	21.7
	1970	8.4	18.0	24.2	28.1	21.3
	1975	7.9	14.6	22.0	30.1	25.3
	1980	7.1	12.7	21.9	27.4	30.9
Denmark	1963	10.0	21.7	18.2	28.1	22.0
	1970	6.4	21.8	20.8	28.2	22.8
	1975	6.4	18.6	19.7	32.7	22.6
	1980	8.1	15.1	21.9	27.7	27.1
W.-Germany	1963	18.9	17.8	17.9	14.5	31.0
	1970	12.3	21.0	21.5	19.8	25.4
	1975	11.3	17.9	20.3	21.4	29.0
	1980	9.4	13.9	20.8	26.0	29.9
Greece	1963	7.1	15.3	20.4	34.2	22.9
	1970	4.4	14.5	17.8	45.7	17.6
	1975	5.8	22.2	18.4	38.2	15.4
	1980	4.5	11.4	16.4	54.9	12.8
France	1963	16.4	27.4	18.9	19.6	17.8
	1970	9.7	26.3	22.3	24.7	17.6
	1975	8.2	23.2	21.1	26.7	20.8
	1980	6.4	21.1	21.2	28.7	23.1
Ireland	1963	13.2	15.9	14.4	26.1	30.4
	1970	8.0	15.2	16.3	32.0	28.6
	1975	7.5	14.1	19.3	30.0	29.5
	1980	4.9	8.8	20.4	35.5	30.5
Italy	1963	18.4	23.8	20.1	20.1	17.6
	1970	13.2	30.3	21.2	18.9	16.4
	1975	12.8	27.2	20.0	21.6	18.5
	1980	10.7	19.6	24.1	25.4	20.2
Netherlands	1963	11.5	20.5	16.1	29.8	22.1
	1970	8.2	23.3	18.3	28.5	21.7
	1975	10.3	18.0	18.7	28.8	24.2
	1980	9.2	15.9	20.1	26.9	27.9
United Kingdom	1963	19.3	21.9	12.3	7.6	38.9
	1970	11.7	24.5	16.1	14.2	33.4
	1975	9.7	18.4	16.2	22.6	34.0
	1980	7.1	10.1	17.7	32.1	33.1

Table 2 (continued)

		A	E	Q	K	C
EEC 10*	1963	16.5	21.5	17.2	18.2	26.6
	1970	10.6	23.6	20.3	22.1	23.3
	1975	9.7	19.8	19.6	25.1	25.7
	1980	8.2	15.4	20.8	28.3	27.4
Portugal	1963	20.5	20.4	20.4	26.6	12.1
	1970	15.0	15.6	21.9	29.9	17.6
	1975	18.2	15.2	20.4	28.6	17.5
	1980	18.3	14.5	22.3	31.4	13.5
Spain	1963	11.2	28.1	17.9	26.1	16.8
	1970	12.4	28.3	22.9	23.7	12.7
	1975	12.7	26.4	22.2	25.5	13.3
	1980	15.2	28.1	22.3	24.2	10.3
United States	1963	12.2	26.6	16.9	13.7	30.6
	1970	6.5	18.9	16.9	29.3	28.4
	1975	5.7	27.3	15.1	28.6	23.3
	1980	4.3	21.5	15.1	33.1	26.0
Japan	1963	27.2	38.4	17.0	7.9	9.5
	1970	20.2	44.3	17.9	7.5	10.1
	1975	18.2	44.5	14.9	7.8	14.5
	1980	18.7	38.0	18.3	8.8	16.7

*Includes intra-community trade

Table 3. Shares of different categories of goods in total *exports* in *constant* 1975 US dollars.

		A	E	Q	K	C
BLEU	1963	4.5	5.4	42.3	20.7	27.1
	1970	3.3	4.4	41.0	24.5	26.8
	1975	3.8	4.9	35.3	26.7	29.4
	1980	2.8	4.7	31.8	23.3	37.4
Denmark	1963	16.8	1.0	7.1	22.6	52.5
	1970	9.8	4.6	10.7	29.4	45.5
	1975	9.3	3.4	10.9	33.7	42.7
	1980	9.5	2.1	13.5	31.9	43.0
W.-Germany	1963	1.0	8.3	22.7	56.5	11.5
	1970	1.3	4.7	26.3	54.5	13.3
	1975	1.5	3.1	25.6	53.9	15.6
	1980	1.3	3.3	26.6	49.0	19.7

Table 3. (continued)

		A	E	Q	K	C
Greece	1963	68.0	1.4	8.7	2.3	19.6
	1970	36.4	2.5	31.2	1.6	28.4
	1975	20.9	11.1	28.2	5.7	34.2
	1980	15.8	8.3	30.4	5.9	39.6
France	1963	7.2	5.1	24.8	31.2	31.8
	1970	8.4	4.0	25.5	37.5	24.7
	1975	7.9	3.2	23.7	42.0	23.2
	1980	8.5	4.0	24.5	37.9	25.1
Ireland	1963	31.9	2.2	3.1	5.0	57.8
	1970	15.6	2.6	15.7	8.0	58.1
	1975	11.4	1.1	14.9	15.3	57.2
	1980	5.8	0.7	18.5	29.7	45.2
Italy	1963	9.1	13.2	13.9	35.7	28.0
	1970	6.1	12.3	15.5	40.6	25.6
	1975	5.3	5.8	19.6	42.2	27.1
	1980	3.9	3.6	19.1	43.1	30.3
Netherlands	1963	8.9	26.6	15.5	19.0	30.1
	1970	7.5	24.0	21.4	19.9	27.2
	1975	9.6	17.0	23.6	23.8	25.9
	1980	9.0	15.2	25.7	23.2	26.9
United Kingdom	1963	1.5	7.2	21.8	50.4	19.1
	1970	1.9	5.3	23.1	46.5	23.1
	1975	1.9	4.3	21.2	47.8	24.8
	1980	2.1	9.3	21.7	41.1	25.7
EEC 10*	1963	5.2	9.4	22.3	40.1	23.1
	1970	4.6	7.7	24.9	40.5	22.4
	1975	4.8	5.5	24.1	42.0	23.6
	1980	4.4	5.7	24.6	38.7	26.6
Portugal	1963	15.6	2.1	12.2	4.0	66.0
	1970	12.3	3.3	14.2	8.2	62.1
	1975	9.5	2.0	13.1	18.0	57.4
	1980	7.6	3.9	14.6	21.5	52.3
Spain	1963	48.2	8.8	13.3	6.6	23.0
	1970	30.2	11.9	12.4	18.0	27.5
	1975	16.1	3.3	19.0	31.2	30.5
	1980	12.7	2.9	30.2	30.1	24.1
United States	1963	22.4	7.4	18.1	32.1	20.1
	1970	17.3	7.1	20.8	39.3	15.4

Table 3 (continued)

		A	E	Q	K	C
	1975	17.0	4.6	15.1	48.6	14.6
	1980	17.7	3.9	16.2	46.4	15.8
Japan	1963	4.7	0.4	24.3	37.1	33.5
	1970	1.7	0.4	27.0	54.7	17.8
	1975	0.5	0.4	30.0	56.8	12.3
	1980	0.4	0.5	21.8	67.5	9.8

*Includes intra-community trade.

The figures, which are in constant prices, illustrate that for all 10 EEC member countries (except Italy), the import share of *agricultural* goods is now well below 10%, while this category of goods is relatively important as an export good only for Denmark, Greece, France and the Netherlands. This pattern seems to be stable except for Greece that typically emerges from its agricultural status, like Ireland, for that matter. For the United States the import share of agriculture has gone down to almost 4%, while Portugal, Spain and also Japan still rely on agricultural imports for 15–18%. The meaning of these goods for exports has strongly decreased in Spain and to a lesser extent in Portugal and the United States, although the share for the latter is still high in absolute value which confirms its position as the world's corn belt.

The dependency on *energy* imports shows a uniform picture for the EEC: a slight increase during the sixties and a decrease in the wake of the first energy crisis, probably reinforced by the events of 1979. The same signs show up for Japan although the decrease seems to have set in later. But whereas the EEC's energy import share approaches 15% on average, this figure is more than double for Japan. Also for Spain and the United Kingdom the share is rather high, while Portugal is more in line with the EEC.

The importance of energy as an export good is decreasing, but still considerable, for the Netherlands, while it increased for the United Kingdom recently, as well as for Greece.

The import share of intermediate goods varies rather stably and uniformly around 20% over the last decade for the EEC and its two candidate members, while being 2–5 percentage point lower for the United States and Japan. The export shares of intermediate goods are also rather stable for the EEC as a whole, but the only countries which confirm this pattern individually are established industrial nations such as France, Germany, the United Kingdom and the Netherlands. The other countries display quite some variations, ranging from the decrease from more than 40% to 32%, for the BLEU, to the increase, from 3% to almost 20%, for

Ireland. Given these developments, Portugal, the United States and Japan behaved rather stable although at different levels, while the acceleration for Spain during 1970–1980 is remarkable.

Imports of *equipment* goods have increased on average 10 percentage point for the EEC over the sample period. This increase was marked, however, only for Germany, Greece, France, Ireland, Italy to a minor extent and very strongly for the United Kingdom. For the other countries the import shares were rather stable around 28%. This same pattern held over the last decade approximately for Portugal and the United States, and was a bit lower for Spain. Japan's below 10% share speaks for itself.

For the EEC as a whole, exports of equipment goods are the main driving force behind total exports with a share of approximately 40%. As the examples of Denmark, Ireland, Portugal, Spain and notably Japan clearly show, industrial development goes hand in hand with the development of the equipment goods export sector as a growth stimulator.

Consideration of the imports of energy, intermediate goods and equipment goods as *production factors* leads to the tentative conclusion that intermediate goods seem to be rather complementary in the production process with respect to other factors, while energy seems rather substitutable. The share of capital goods in imports is relatively constant for the BLEU, Denmark, the Netherlands, Portugal and Japan and more volatile for the other countries. As far as these shares measure physical substitution possibilities capital goods are therefore complementary for the former countries and more substitutable for the latter. This does not take into account price developments, however. Import shares for consumption goods are around 25% for the EEC countries on average but with differing patterns over the member countries. As this category also contains manufactured food products it is hard to explain the divergencies among countries, for instance the relatively low shares for Greece, Portugal and Spain. For food they might indicate the development of domestic foodprocessing industries. The United States display about the same percentages as the EEC average, while there is a limited but increasing scope to gain Japan's import market for consumption goods.

Compared to the EEC average, the exports of consumption goods are relatively important for the BLEU, Denmark, Greece, Ireland and Portugal. Again, the occurrence of food products troubles the explanation of the diverging patterns. One would be tempted to say that the aforementioned countries rely more than others on food processing industry to the extent that food is part of this category. From the figures for Japan it is clear that consumption goods are a sharply decreasing source of export earnings.

What kind of *a priori* expectations may be inferred from these figures? Let us consider the following example. Suppose we perform two policy experiments, one in which we increase an exogenous part of investments and another in which we increase by the same amount an exogenous part of consumption, let us say in all ten EEC member countries simultaneously. First of all, if we take the 1980 situation as the prevailing circumstances, we expect that the resulting effect on average EEC exports relative to the resulting increase in imports will be larger for the former experiment than for the latter, given the first part of Table 1. Secondly, under the same assumptions, we expect that the first experiment will be more profitable for exports of countries with relatively high export shares of equipment goods, such as the United Kingdom and Germany, than for countries which are in an opposite position such as Greece and the Netherlands; and we would make a similar assertion regarding the second experiment, where we would expect the BLEU, Denmark, Greece, Ireland and outside the EEC; Portugal to profit at the expense of, say, Germany. These preliminary findings are however under the assumption that the share of the EEC in the exports of each country for each good are approximately equal. The ultimate test is therefore a model simulation, for which we refer to section 6.

3. THE COMET IV MODEL

The COMET IV model contains 13 models for the *countries* that already appeared in Tables 2 and 3. These country models have a *similar* structure, that is, they all describe the same variables and have — in principle — the same specification for the ± 50 behavioural equations. Differences in behaviour are therefore solely generated through differences in parameters. If the specifications are general enough to cover differences in economic behaviour for the countries under consideration, this approach has the advantages of comparability of results and an unequivocal inter-pretation of the causal structure of each country model, and therefore of the whole model.

Additionally the model contains separate, smaller models for five *zones* that divide the rest of the world exhaustively:

— rest of OECD;
— socialist countries;
— oil-exporting developing countries;
— fast-developing countries;
— rest of developing countries.

The main purpose of these zone models is to provide for a trade feedback mechanism that renders the whole world model closed. Their main equations therefore consist of an import equation that translates export earnings into a demand for imports, and an export price equation that indexes export prices to import prices.

The country models contain the following blocks:

- a factor demand system which translates input—output weighted final demand into demand for investments, energy, labour and imports of non-energy goods under the finluence of relative prices;
- equations for final demand components other than private non-residential investments;
- a wage—price block;
- a labour market block;
- the simplified accounts for the economic agents: households, firms and government;
- a monetary block;
- the degree of capacity utilization, which is crucial for the medium-term nature of the model;
- a trade block.

The trade block is similar for the country and zone models and contains the identities for the trade aggregates as well as the bilateral import equations that allocate imports over the 17 trading partners.

In the country models, imports of energy goods are derived as the difference between total domestic energy demand and (the exogenously given) production capacity for energy goods. The imports of non-energy goods form part of the factor demand system, like the domestic demand for energy. Both are therefore treated as production factors.

The disaggregation of bilateral trade flows is established through the creation of five different markets (for the five categories of trade A, E, Q, K and C) for the trade between the 13 countries and between the 13 countries and the five zones (the trade between the five zones is kept aggregate using the present bilateral import equations). As a consequence we have for each of the 13 countries five import allocation models that allocate imports of each particular category of goods over 17 trade partners. For the five zones this results for each zone in five import allocation models over the 13 countries and one import allocation model for aggregate imports from the four other zones. This process is depicted in scheme 1.

In section 4 we describe the five equations for total imports MO_s of each category s (s = A,E,Q,K,C), while the import allocation models over the partners are described in section 5.[4]

4. THE DISAGGREGATE IMPORT EQUATIONS FOR THE 13 COUNTRIES

The import equations for the five categories of goods may be given shape in two ways. A first possibility would be to start from an aggregate import equation and to

14

Scheme 1. Import allocation processes in the 13 countries and 5 zones

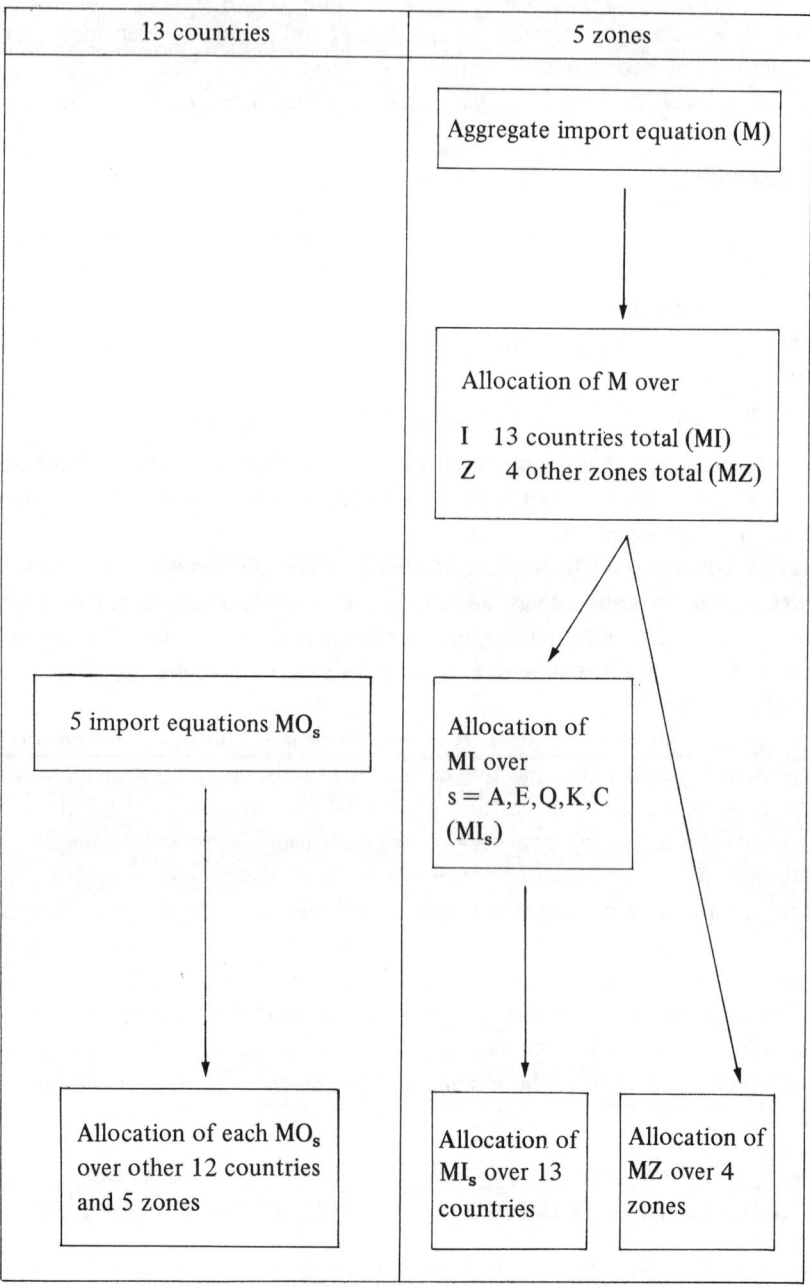

allocate aggregate imports over the five goods under a hypothesis of weak separability of the latter with respect to the components of domestic demand. This approach, however, would preclude the differential effects that we are trying to achieve by the disaggregation of trade. For if, say due to a price differential on the domestic market, there is a movement from energy demand away to capital demand or investments, this will certainly be reflected in the ratio between imports of energy and imports of equipment goods, or in other words: the hypothesis of weak separability no longer seems to be valid.

Therefore it seems more natural to link the imports of goods to corresponding domestic demand categories. The imports-of-energy equation as present in the COMET IV model and described in the previous section is therefore maintained, whereas the equation in the factor demand system for imports of non-energy goods is re-interpreted as the import equation of intermediate goods. A residual check on this equation revealed that this could be done without any harm to its explanatory power. This left us with three new import equations to be estimated per country: for agricultural goods (A), equipment (K) and consumption goods (C). The three equations were all estimated in logarithmic growth rates as a function of (1) a demand category in constant prices (GDP at market prices (YO) for A, total investments (IO) for K, and private consumption (CPO) for C) and (2) the import price concerned (PM$_s$ for s = A,K,C) relative to the corresponding price of the demand variable (PY, PI and PC, respectively). The influence of the relative price was assumed to come into effect according to a Koyck lag scheme for agricultural goods (A) and equipment goods (K), although the Koyck lag parameter turned out to be significant only for a few cases for equipment goods. If we denote the demand variable corresponding to category s by D$_s$ and its price index by PD$_s$, the estimated equation takes the general form:

$$\Delta \ln MO_{st} = \alpha + \lambda \ln MO_{st-1} + \beta [\Delta \ln D_{st} - \lambda \Delta \ln D_{st-1}]$$
$$+ \epsilon(1 - \lambda)\Delta \ln(PM_{st}/PD_{st}) \qquad (7)$$

with $0 \leqslant \lambda < 1, \beta > 0$ and $\epsilon < 0$, where PM$_s$ (s = A,K,C) is the import price of good s and $\lambda = 0$ for s = C.

The estimation results are presented in Tables 4–6. Between brackets are the standard errors of the estimated coefficients. An asterisk * indicates that the coefficient exceeded its *a priori* bounds and was fixed at the bound it exceeded. This is at the expense of explanatory power of the equation, and therefore the column 'F' gives in those cases the value of the following statistic

$$F = \frac{(SSR_R - SSR_U)/r}{SSR_U/(n-k)}$$

Table 4. Estimation results for imports of agricultural goods.

$$\Delta\ln MOA_t = \alpha + \lambda\Delta\ln MOA_{t-1} + \beta[\Delta\ln YO_t - \lambda\Delta\ln YO_{t-1}] + \epsilon(1-\lambda)\Delta\ln(PMA_t/PY_t)$$

	α	λ	β	ϵ	F	s	R^2	D.W.
BLEU	-0.015 (0.019)	0.0 *	1.387 (0.378)	-0.395 (0.168)	0.010 (4.75)	0.029	0.793	2.397
Denmark	0.0 *	0.0 *	0.905 (0.430)	-0.014 (0.200)	0.845 (3.89)	0.064	0.250	2.007
W.-Germany	-0.013 (0.012)	0.271 (0.253)	1.095 (0.352)	-0.479 (0.305)		0.032	0.707	1.825
Greece	0.0 *	0.0 *	0.479 (0.953)	-0.330 (0.684)	2.112 (3.89)	0.238	0.037	2.451
France	-0.012 (0.032)	0.0 *	0.808 (0.721)	-0.118 (0.124)	0.035 (4.75)	0.043	0.315	2.100
Ireland	-0.025 (0.042)	0.017 (0.316)	1.083 (1.011)	-0.158 (0.256)		0.074	0.161	2.272
Italy	-0.004 (0.030)	0.0 *	0.966 (0.547)	-0.375 (0.200)	0.009 (4.75)	0.066	0.461	2.266
Netherlands	0.0 *	0.274 (0.247)	0.544 (0.386)	-0.741 (0.368)	1.239 (4.75)	0.046	0.658	1.619
United Kingdom	-0.026 (0.016)	0.381 (0.233)	1.511 (0.407)	-0.299 (0.170)		0.032	0.570	1.679
Portugal	0.0 *	0.040 (0.270)	1.012 (0.372)	-0.266 (0.233)	2.609 (4.75)	0.092	0.449	2.079

Table 4. (continued)

	α	λ	β	ϵ	F	s	R^2	D.W
Spain	0.028 (0.080)	0.0 *	1.205 (1.476)	−0.290 (0.341)	0.002 (4.75)	0.126	0.421	1.731
United States	−0.042 (0.026)	0.0 *	1.972 (0.652)	−0.405 (0.132)	2.604 (4.75)	0.062	0.540	3.064
Japan	−0.048 (0.026)	0.0 *	1.526 (0.329)	−0.088 (0.097)	0.004 (4.75)	0.052	0.775	2.033

Sample period: 1965–1980.

Table 5. Estimation results for imports of equipment goods.

$$\Delta\ln MOK_t = \alpha + \lambda\Delta\ln MOK_{t-1} + \beta\,[\Delta\ln IO_t - \lambda\Delta\ln IO_{t-1}]$$
$$+ \epsilon(1-\lambda)\,\Delta\ln(PMK_t/PI_t)$$

	α	λ	β	ϵ	F	s	R^2	D.W.
BLEU	0.042 (0.021)	0.0 *	0.936 (0.566)	−0.179 (0.589)	0.289 (4.75)	0.064	0.658	2.165
Denmark	0.015 (0.022)	0.0 *	0.715 (0.241)	−0.807 (0.586)	0.072 (4.75)	0.079	0.544	2.516
W.-Germany	0.0 *	0.668 (0.212)	1.347 (0.399)	−0.559 (1.215)	7.619 (4.75)	0.074	0.771	1.868
Greece	0.015 (0.032)	0.519 (0.228)	0.985 (0.228)	−0.616 (0.477)		0.112	0.728	1.269
France	−0.011 (0.020)	0.633 (0.205)	3.359 (0.637)	−2.200 (1.621)		0.067	0.787	2.715
Ireland	0.009 (0.024)	0.092 (0.209)	1.101 (0.242)	−0.968 (0.379)		0.074	0.878	1.935
Italy	0.0 *	0.145 (0.336)	1.758 (0.329)	−0.084 (0.563)	7.876 (4.75)	0.078	0.793	2.101
Netherlands	0.0 *	0.312 (0.238)	0.664 (0.240)	−0.945 (0.704)	2.704 (4.75)	0.056	0.624	1.824
United Kingdom	0.051 (0.024)	0.269 (0.231)	2.448 (0.592)	−0.527 (0.356)		0.074	0.841	1.731
Portugal	0.017 (0.050)	0.0 *	0.732 (0.337)	−0.958 (0.606)	2.006 (4.75)	0.145	0.483	2.700

Table 5 (continued)

$$\Delta \ln MOK_t = \alpha + \lambda \Delta \ln MOK_{t-1} + \beta [\Delta \ln IO_t - \lambda \Delta \ln IO_{t-1}]$$
$$+ \epsilon (1 - \lambda) \Delta \ln(PMK_t/PI_t)$$

	α	λ	β	ϵ	F	s	R^2	D.W.
Spain	-0.020	0.350	1.550	-1.717		0.078	0.774	1.698
	(0.024)	(0.226)	(0.355)	(0.773)				
United States	0.100	0.074	1.348	-1.309		0.096	0.776	1.849
	(0.031)	(0.217)	(0.388)	(0.528)				
Japan	0.033	0.186	0.501	-0.870		0.130	0.589	2.382
	(0.047)	(0.257)	(0.456)	(0.572)				

Sample period: 1965–1980.

Table 6. Estimation results for imports of consumption goods.

	α	β	ϵ	F	s	R^2	D.W.
	$\Delta\ln MOC_t = \alpha + \beta\Delta\ln CPO_t + \epsilon\Delta\ln(PMC_t/PC_t)$						
BLEU	−0.031 (0.029)	3.296 (0.677)	−0.089 (0.297)		0.046	0.873	2.265
Denmark	−0.009 (0.018)	2.687 (0.486)	−0.050 *	1.903 (4.67)	0.056	0.771	1.835
W. Germany	−0.032 (0.032)	2.710 (0.736)	−0.191 (0.282)		0.052	0.799	2.656
Greece	−0.122 (0.040)	3.175 (0.668)	−0.175 (0.400)		0.068	0.711	2.110
France	−0.057 (0.065)	3.335 (1.425)	−0.110 (0.301)		0.073	0.694	2.343
Ireland	0.015 (0.025)	1.835 (0.547)	−0.653 (0.315)		0.068	0.735	2.824
Italy	0.001 (0.036)	1.737 (0.671)	−0.050 *	3.940 (4.67)	0.080	0.605	2.557
Netherlands	0.0 *	1.159 (0.369)	0.434 (0.358)	2.129 (4.67)	0.064	0.604	3.101
United Kingdom	−0.002 (0.013)	1.846 (0.421)	−0.050 *	0.436 (4.67)	0.036	0.714	1.604
Portugal	0.0 *	1.047 (0.427)	−0.106 (0.556)	0.650 (4.67)	0.137	0.305	2.395
Spain	−0.141 (0.055)	3.836 (1.015)	−0.976 (0.487)		0.089	0.648	2.084
United States	−0.052 (0.038)	3.295 (0.927)	−0.489 (0.283)		0.066	0.735	3.108
Japan	−0.046 (0.054)	2.583 (0.769)	−0.050 *	0.577 (4.67)	0.101	0.700	1.787

Sample period: 1965−1980.

which is assumed to follow an F (r,n−k) distribution. SSR_R is the sum of squared residuals with the coefficient(s) fixed, while SSR_U is the unrestricted sum of squared residuals. The number of observations is n, while k is the number of estimated parameters in the unrestricted equation and r the number of fixed coefficients. Between brackets below the values of the F-statistic are the critical values for a 95% confidence interval. The decrease in fit turns out to be significant in only 2 out of 22 cases.

The estimation results for imports of agricultural goods show high elasticities with respect to GDP for the United Kingdom, the United States and Japan, while they are around 0.5 for Greece and the Netherlands. The highest short-run relative price elasticity in absolute value is −0.5 for the Netherlands. The others are around −0.3 and close to zero for Denmark and Japan. The fit is poor for Greece, Portugal and Spain, countries of which the quality of the data is in general minor to that of the others.

For equipment goods, the volume elasticities are high for France, Italy and the United Kingdom, but also for the United States if one takes into account the trend of 10%. The short-run relative price elasticities are in general higher in absolute value than for agricultural goods, reaching about −1 for Ireland, Portugal, Spain and the United States. The fit of Greece and Portugal is again poor, now joined by Japan, whose imports of equipment goods are low relative to total imports, as was shown in Table 2.

For consumption goods we find volume elasticities ranging from about 1 for Portugal and the Netherlands to more than 3 for the BLEU, Greece, France, Spain, and the United States. There seems, however, to be a trade-off between a high elasticity and a negative trend. The relative price elasticities are below −0.5 in absolute value for most countries, except for Ireland and Spain. The fit for Portugal and Japan is poor: both equations have standard errors above 10%.

Despite the scope for improvement these equations are sufficient to establish a link between different demand components and the imports of different goods. It is this property that is of primary interest.

5. DISAGGREGATED BILATERAL TRADE FLOW EQUATIONS

In this section we concentrate on the allocation of the imports of goods, MO_s, for each of the 13 countries over its 17 trading partners. The adding-up that is required for the allocation to be true is established during simulations only with the use of a proportional adjustment factor, the bilateral import equations themselves do not satisfy the adding-up condition exactly.

The equations result from a bilateral import demand equation and a bilateral import supply equation, both written as double logarithmic equations. The bilateral import demand equation is equal to the equation proposed by Barten (1971), though we do not apply his proportionality constraint between the allocation elasticity and the relative price elasticity.[5] Furthermore we made the equation dynamic under the assumption that the relative prices follow a distributed lag according to a Koyck scheme. The resulting equation is

$$\ln M_{sijt} = \gamma_{sij} + \lambda_{sij}\ln M_{sijt-1} + \alpha_{sij}[\ln MO_{sjt} - \lambda_{sij}\ln MO_{sjt-1}]$$
$$+ \epsilon_{sij}(1 - \lambda_{sij})\ln(PM_{sijt}/PM_{sjt}), \tag{8}$$

with $0 \leqslant \lambda_{sij} < 1, \alpha_{sij} > 0$ and $\epsilon_{sij} < 0$, where

M_{sijt} = bilateral imports in constant prices for good s by country j from partner i

PM_{sijt} = corresponding bilateral import price index

MO_{sjt} = imports of good s by country j, in constant prices

PM_{sjt} = corresponding import price index.

The bilateral export supply equation takes the same form as (8) but the volume component is now export supply of good s XP_{sit} of country i, and the relative price is the one of the bilateral export price with respect to a domestic cost price index PB_{sit}.

$$\ln X_{sijt} = \eta_{sij} + \lambda_{sij} \ln X_{sijt-1} + \beta_{sij} [\ln XP_{sit} - \lambda_{sij} \ln XP_{sit-1}]$$
$$+ \pi_{sij} (1 - \lambda_{sij}) \ln(PX_{sijt}/PB_{sit}) \tag{9}$$

with $\beta_{sij} > 0$ and $\pi_{sij} > 0$, where

X_{sijt} = bilateral exports of good s from country i to country j, in constant prices

PX_{sijt} = corresponding bilateral export price index.

Note that we have used the same Koyck parameter in the distributed lag scheme for convenience. Furthermore we assume that the domestic price index PB_{sit} for sector s is proportional to a national index PB_{it} such that we may replace it by the latter and should re-interpret the constant as containing $-\pi_{sij}(1 - \lambda_{sij})$ times the logarithm of the proportionality factor (which is taken to be constant over the analyzed period).

Under the assumption of a market clearing mechanism through bilateral prices and a constant c.i.f./f.o.b. factor over the sample period, (8) and (9) may be solved to obtain the following two equations for bilateral imports and its price index

$$\ln M_{sijt} = \Psi_{sij} + \lambda_{sij} M_{sijt-1} + \frac{\pi_{sij}}{\pi_{sij} - \epsilon_{sij}} \alpha_{sij} [\ln MO_{sjt} - \lambda \ln MO_{sjt-1}]$$

$$- \frac{\epsilon_{sij}}{\pi_{sij} - \epsilon_{sij}} \beta_{sij} [\ln XP_{sit} - \lambda_{sij} \ln XP_{sit-1}]$$

$$- \frac{\pi_{sij} \epsilon_{sij}}{\pi_{sij} - \epsilon_{sij}} (1 - \lambda_{sij}) \ln(PM_{sjt}/PB_{it}) \tag{10}$$

$$\ln PM_{sijt} = \chi_{sij} + \frac{\pi_{sij}}{\pi_{sij} - \epsilon_{sij}} \ln PB_{it} - \frac{\epsilon_{sij}}{\pi_{sij} - \epsilon_{sij}} \ln PM_{sjt} \qquad (11)$$

$$+ \frac{\alpha_{sij}[\ln MO_{sjt} - \lambda_{sij}\ln MO_{sjt-1}] - \beta_{sij}[\ln XP_{sit} - \lambda_{sij}\ln XP_{sit-1}]}{(\pi_{sij} - \epsilon_{sij})(1 - \lambda_{sij})}$$

The logarithm of bilateral imports is equal to a weighted average of the volume components of the demand and supply equation, the weights being determined by the relative price elasticities. The latter also form a composite elasticity of bilateral imports with respect to the import price relative to the cost price index. The logarithm of the bilateral import price is a weighted average of the import price and the cost price with the same weights as for the volume equation. The difference between the volume component of demand and its equivalence for supply forms an indicator of shifts in equilibrium on the bilateral market.

The system (10)–(11) was estimated with two additional restrictions on the parameters, which were needed to ensure robustness of the estimations. The *first* restriction was to make the weights identical per exporting country

$$\frac{\pi_{sij}}{\pi_{sij} - \epsilon_{sij}} = \delta_{si}, \qquad \text{all } j \qquad (12)$$

which implies a proportionality between the relative price elasticities

$$\pi_{sij} = \frac{\delta_{si}}{\delta_{si} - 1} \epsilon_{sij} \qquad (13)$$

The weights δ_{si} were obtained from preliminary estimations of a discrete form of the Divisia export price index $\Delta \ln PXD_{si}$

$$\Delta \ln PXD_{sit} = \Sigma_j v_{sijt-1} \, \Delta \ln PM_{sijt}$$

$$= \tau_{si} + \delta_{si} \Delta \ln PB_{it} + (1 - \delta_{si}) \Delta \ln PW_{sit} \qquad (14)$$

$$+ \mu_{si} \{ \Sigma_j v_{sijt-1} [\Delta \ln MO_{sjt} - 0.4 \ln MO_{sjt-1}]$$

$$- [\Delta \ln XP_{sit} - 0.4 \ln XP_{sit-1}] \}$$

with $v_{sijt} = (PM_{sijt}M_{sijt})/(\Sigma_j PM_{sijt}M_{sijt})$ and

$$\Delta \ln PW_{sit} = \Sigma_j v_{sijt-1} \, \Delta \ln PM_{sit}$$

which may be derived from (11) with the aid of (13) and the simplifying assumptions

$\alpha_{sij} = \beta_{sij} = q_{si}\pi_{sij} = q_{si}\pi_{si}$ for all s, i and j and $\lambda_{sij} = 0.4$ for all s, i and j, while there is a trend τ_{si} added to capture sectoral differences in the effects of $\Delta \ln PB_{it}$ on $\Delta \ln PXD_{sit}$.

The Divisia export price index is therefore function of a trend, a weighted average of the logarithmic growth rates of the domestic cost price index and a competitors' price index PW_{sit}. The last expression in (14) represents the influence of shifts in equilibrium between export demand and supply on the formation of export prices. Because $\Delta \ln PX_{sit} \approx \Delta \ln PXD_{sit}$, where PX_{sit} is the observed export price, (14) was estimated with $\Delta \ln PX_{sit}$ as a dependent variable. The estimation results were reported in Italianer (1982b), and resulted for 58 out of 65 cases in estimates of δ_{si} between 0 and 1. For s = A a typical estimate of δ_{si} for agricultural nations was in the order of 0.5, while for s = E the general value was 0.1 with some exceptions. For intermediate goods the values were around 0.15, while for equipment goods they were in general the highest, say around 0.5 or 0.6. The consumption values were somewhat lower, around 0.3.

The *second* restriction on the parameters was the requirement that the ratio of the allocation parameters α_{sij} and β_{sij} should be inversely proportional to the ratio of long-run trends of import demand and export supply, approximated by their average growth rates over the sample period $\tilde{m}_{sj}$ and $\tilde{x}_{si}$

$$\alpha_{sij}/\beta_{sij} = \tilde{x}_{si}/\tilde{m}_{sj} \tag{15}$$

The rationale behind this restriction is that we assume that the economy is in a steady state or situation of balanced growth in the long run. In that case MO_{sjt} and XP_{sit} would both grow at the same rate and the last term in the bilateral price equation (11) would have to vanish to obtain a steady state path for the bilateral price, implying $\alpha_{sij} = \beta_{sij}$ which is tantamount to (15) with $\tilde{x}_{si} = \tilde{m}_{sj}$. Over the sample period, MO_{sjt} and XP_{sit} usually did not grow at the same rate. To account for this difference we may still induce a steady state effect on (11) by imposing (15) for estimation, and, ultimately, substitution of, say, β_{sij} by $\alpha_{sij}\bar{m}_{sj}/\bar{x}_{si}$ for simulation with $\bar{m}_{sj}$ and $\bar{x}_{si}$ average growth rates that adjust slowly over time. Inspection of (11) learns that the last expression will then vanish on average. This will, however, be the subject of further investigation, for the present (15) is only applied for the purpose of estimation.

The estimations of (10)–(11) under the restrictions (13) and (15) were described in Italianer (1982b), but are too numerous to report on. For small bilateral trade flows, they leaded usually to coefficients exceeding their a priori bounds but otherwise they were satisfactory. For simulation purposes we made the usual assumption made in bilateral trade flow models concerning bilateral prices, i.e. we replaced equation (11) by equation (14) with the indicator of shifts in equilibrium suppressed or $\mu_{si} = 0$ for reasons of stability of the simulation. This is tantamount to suppression of the corresponding term in (11) and introduction of the trend from (14).

6. POLICY EXPERIMENTS

If we apply a sectoral breakdown to international trade, the effects of this refinement will occur at two levels. The first level where we may distinguish the influence of a sectoral approach is formed by the total import equations of each good separately: where otherwise changes in the import shares of each good would not be visible, this is now the case. The second level is the allocation of total imports of each good over the trading partners. This determines the transmission of domestic impulses towards other countries and the extent to which, for each good individually, these impulses are more profitable for one country than for another.

This is why we have chosen to perform our policy experiments in two stages as well: for each experiment, we first simulate keeping the allocation over the partners equal to that of the last year before the simulation period in constant prices, and next we perform the same experiment, where we introduce the estimated equations (10), such that we allow for re-location effects and substitution effects due to changes in relative prices.

According to the dynamic and medium-run nature of the model, the resulting changes in the endogenous variables should be considered after a period of 3–5 years, when all effects have had the opportunity to exert their influences. This comprises the price effects in the total import equations of each good and equations (10) and (14), which were lagged with one year during simulations to decrease the simultaneous nature of the model. This increased on its turn the speed of convergence which is of importance for a model that contains almost 10,000 variables. For the policy simulations a maximum of ± 30 iterations over the whole model became therefore sufficient to obtain convergence for a single year.

6.1. The experiments

In section 4 we presented estimates for simple import functions for three types of goods: agricultural, equipment and consumption goods. The imports were related to GDP, investments and private consumption, respectively. This is why we have chosen to perform three experiments for each of these sources of import demand. In each experiment, we increase the element under consideration by the same amount in constant prices, i.e. 1% of GDP of the first year of the reference simulation. This shock is given in all EEC member countries simultaneously, as if it concerned a concerted action. The three experiments are performed twice: once with a constant import allocation over the partners (which therefore purely shows the 'first-stage' effect of a sectoral breakdown of imports), and once with the estimated bilateral import equations (10) introduced[6] (which displays the secondary effects of import demand, export supply and relative prices on bilateral flows). For each of the two series of experiments, therefore, a different 'reference' simulation or central projection was calculated.

The results, reported in Tables 7–9, should be interpreted with care for two reasons. The first matter that needs qualification is that the outcomes are in a sense 'local' results, determined by conditions of model specification, parameter estimates, values exogenous variables, time, etc. By reporting results in percentage difference form, we abstract however to a large extent from possible 'counter-intuitive' or anomalous results due to the local nature of the experiment. The second reason why the results should be considered as an illustration rather than a precise policy prescription is that we have exaggerated them through 'admission' of large elasticities in both the import functions that were presented in section 4 for the total imports of each good as for the bilateral import equations. Although such large elasticities may appear in the short run, it is unlikely that they are equally valid over a longer period, as a more careful specification certainly would have demonstrated. Nevertheless, they serve well for the purpose at hand, viz. a demonstration of the differential macro-economic effects of a sectoral breakdown of international trade.

In the following paragraphs we first discuss each of the three pairs of experiments separately with emphasis on the differential effects of the introduction of the estimated bilateral import equations (10). The comparison between the three experiments will be made afterwards.

Government non-wage consumption

The first experiment should increase GDP without increasing investments or private consumption directly. In this way we have a direct shock in the import equation for *agricultural goods*, while the others will only be affected indirectly through transmission processes. An increase in government non-wage consumption meets the requirement. Although the COMET IV model contains an equation explaining government consumption, we put its value exogenous over the simulation period and equal to the reference solution plus the value of the shock, while keeping government employment fixed. The results for the experiments with and without endogenous bilateral equations are presented in Table 7.

The introduction of the bilateral trade flow equations has a negative effect on the EEC average export change, which even turns negative in the last year of the simulation. The apparent cause for this result is the — almost uniform — increase in domestic cost that decreases the competitivity of the EEC with respect to the rest of the world. Whereas the percentage increase in the import price index does not exceed 1% in both the EEC and the rest of the world (not shown in the table), the average increase in domestic cost exceeds 2%. And indeed, the countries which have a relatively moderate cost increase (the BLEU, Ireland and Italy) are the only ones to keep a positive change in exports in the long run. That is, of course, if we abstract from the volume effects of import demand and export supply. Once they get stronger, they may dominate the relative price effects.

Government investment expenditure

An increase by 1% of GDP of year 1 of both reference simulations in government investment expenditure (which is an exogenous variable in the COMET IV model) goes directly into the equation for imports of *equipment* goods, and indirectly in the other import equations.[7] If we consider, in Table 8, the percentage differences in exports in year 5, we see that they range from 0.8% for Denmark to 2.5% for Ireland if we keep the import allocation over partners constant. If we introduce the endogenous allocation mechanisms the range expands dramatically to a minimum of −0.7% for Greece and 9.6% for the BLEU. Although the size of the increase in this range is possibly exaggerated due to the above mentioned reasons, it is at least an indication of the importance of introduction of an endogenous allocation mechanism.

Given the development of domestic cost and the import prices, where the latter again do not exceed an increase of 1% (also for the rest of the world, which is not in the tables), we would expect that there would be a deterioration of the average European increase in exports with respect to the experiment with fixed import allocation. This is however not the case in the long run. But the positive difference is based on the increase in three countries only: the BLEU, the Netherlands and W.-Germany. For the former two countries this is most probably due to their low absolute level of cost increase. For W.-Germany, which is the major West-European exporter of equipment goods, the volume effects of both import demand for German exports as export supply of Germany itself are stronger than the relative price effects, notably in the EEC market. Detailed inspection of the simulation results reveals that on the import markets of Japan and the five zones the loss of competitivity has a much larger effect than inside the EEC, where W.-Germany may permit itself some loss in relative prives.

Finally, the *a priori* expectations of section 2 are only partially confirmed in the fixed-allocation experiment: W.-Germany's export increase is more than average and Greece's the lowest, but the United Kingdom is lower than average and the

Table 7. Percentage differences between reference simulation and a sustained shock of 1% of real GDP of year 1 in government non-wage consumption for each country simultaneously.[a]

	Year	Exports			Imports			Domestic cost			Import price		
		1	3	5	1	3	5	1	3	5	1	3	5
BLEU[b]	I	0.6	0.6	0.3	0.6	0.4	0.3	-0.4	0.8	1.1	0.0	0.2	0.6
	II	0.4	0.5	0.7	0.5	0.4	0.4	-0.4	1.0	1.1	0.0	0.2	0.9
Denmark	I	0.2	0.3	-0.6	0.6	1.4	2.3	-0.7	2.3	4.0	0.0	0.0	0.3
	II	0.2	0.1	-1.5	0.6	1.6	0.8	-0.7	1.6	1.7	0.0	0.0	0.5
W.-Germany	I	0.4	0.2	-0.2	0.7	1.4	0.9	-0.3	2.2	3.2	0.1	0.1	0.5
	II	0.4	-0.3	-1.5	0.7	1.2	0.3	-0.3	2.6	3.9	0.0	0.1	0.7
Greece	I	0.2	0.5	0.3	0.7	1.3	0.7	-1.1	-0.2	0.3	0.0	0.0	0.4
	II	0.1	1.2	-0.7	0.7	1.3	0.8	-1.1	0.5	2.0	0.0	0.0	0.4
France	I	0.3	0.3	0.1	1.3	0.9	0.1	-0.2	1.3	1.9	-0.1	0.0	0.6
	II	0.3	0.0	-0.3	1.3	0.9	1.2	-0.1	1.2	1.9	-0.1	0.0	0.4
Ireland	I	0.2	0.5	0.4	0.4	0.9	0.3	-0.6	0.4	0.0	0.0	0.2	0.8
	II	0.2	0.4	0.7	0.4	0.8	0.2	-0.6	0.3	-1.6	0.0	0.2	1.0
Italy	I	0.4	0.5	0.3	1.0	0.6	0.3	-0.5	0.8	1.2	-0.1	0.1	0.4
	II	0.3	0.4	0.4	1.0	0.5	0.2	-0.5	0.8	1.3	-0.1	0.1	0.5
Netherlands	I	0.4	0.6	0.3	0.6	0.7	0.6	-0.7	0.8	1.9	0.1	0.2	0.6
	II	0.3	0.5	-0.8	0.6	0.6	0.3	-0.6	1.4	3.1	0.1	0.2	0.6
United Kingdom	I	0.3	0.3	0.0	0.4	0.7	0.7	-0.4	1.5	2.2	0.0	0.0	0.4
	II	0.3	0.3	-0.1	0.4	0.7	0.5	-0.4	1.4	2.0	0.0	0.1	0.8
EEC 10[c]	I	0.4	0.4	0.0	0.8	0.9	0.6	-0.4	1.5	2.2	0.0	0.1	0.5
	II	0.3	0.1	-0.7	0.8	0.8	0.5	-0.4	1.6	2.5	0.0	0.1	0.6

Table 7 (continued) NOTES

a   The figures concern total exports and imports of goods and services, as well as the corresponding total import price index. Domestic cost refers to an index of labour cost per unit of output.

b   I: The first row gives for each country the effects if, for each good, the bilateral import shares of the partners in constant prices are kept equal to the shares of year 0.

    II: The second row is the result if the estimated bilateral import equations (1) are introduced.

c   The results for the Europe of the Ten include intra-community trade and may be considered as EEC averages.

Table 8. Percentage differences between reference simulation and a sustained shock of 1% of real GDP of year 1 in government investment expenditure for each country simultaneously.[a]

Year		Exports			Imports			Domestic cost			Import price		
		1	3	5	1	3	5	1	3	5	1	3	5
BLEU[b]	I	2.5	2.3	2.3	2.5	2.0	1.7	-0.7	0.3	0.3	-0.2	-0.1	0.4
	II	2.6	5.0	9.6	2.5	3.0	3.9	-0.8	-0.6	-0.5	-0.2	0.0	0.7
Denmark	I	1.6	1.7	1.4	2.4	2.9	3.6	-0.8	1.0	1.8	-0.3	-0.3	0.2
	II	1.4	1.8	0.8	2.4	3.4	2.8	-0.7	0.9	0.8	-0.3	-0.3	0.2
W.-Germany	I	2.7	2.2	1.9	2.7	3.3	3.0	-0.6	1.6	2.5	-0.2	-0.2	0.3
	II	2.7	2.6	2.6	2.8	3.5	3.3	-0.6	1.8	3.0	-0.2	-0.2	0.3
Greece	I	0.7	0.9	0.8	3.2	2.7	1.9	-0.5	0.7	2.2	-0.2	-0.3	0.2
	II	0.4	0.6	-0.7	3.2	2.3	0.7	-0.4	1.0	2.5	-0.1	-0.1	0.4
France	I	2.0	1.8	1.6	5.5	4.2	3.3	-0.2	1.0	3.5	-1.1	-1.0	-0.2
	II	2.3	1.9	1.2	6.0	4.9	6.2	0.2	1.2	4.0	-1.1	-1.1	-0.9
Ireland	I	2.7	2.7	2.5	2.4	2.8	3.9	-0.8	0.6	4.9	-0.1	0.2	0.8
	II	1.7	1.3	-0.5	2.1	2.5	3.7	-0.5	1.3	10.5	-0.1	0.1	0.6
Italy	I	2.2	2.2	2.0	4.2	3.5	3.7	-0.3	1.0	3.3	-0.5	-0.5	0.0
	II	2.0	1.4	0.9	4.2	3.3	3.3	-0.3	1.1	3.4	-0.5	-0.4	0.1
Netherlands	I	2.1	2.1	2.0	2.1	1.7	1.6	-0.8	0.3	0.7	0.2	0.3	0.7
	II	1.7	2.3	2.8	2.0	1.9	2.0	-0.8	0.2	0.8	0.1	0.3	0.9
United Kingdom	I	1.6	1.2	1.0	6.0	5.3	5.2	0.7	2.3	5.8	-0.7	-1.0	-0.5
	II	1.4	0.8	-0.2	6.0	5.0	4.6	0.6	2.3	5.9	-0.5	-0.8	0.2
EEC 10[c]	I	2.2	1.9	1.7	4.0	3.6	3.4	-0.2	1.3	3.2	-0.5	-0.5	0.0
	II	2.1	2.3	2.2	4.0	3.8	4.0	-0.2	1.3	3.4	-0.5	-0.5	0.1

Table 8 (continued) NOTES

a The figures concern total exports and imports of goods and services, as well as the corresponding total import price index.
   Domestic cost refers to an index of labour cost per unit of output.

b I: The first row gives for each country the effects if, for each good, the bilateral import shares of the partners in constant
       prices are kept equal to the shares of year 0.

   II: The second row is the result if the estimated bilateral import equations (10) are introduced.

c The results for the Europe of the Ten include intra-community trade and may therefore be considered as EEC averages.

Netherlands even higher than W.-Germany. This is due to the fact that the Dutch share of exports to EEC countries is more than average (around 70%), while the contrary is true for the United Kingdom (around 40%). The assumption made in section 2 of equal shares is not met, therefore.

Private consumption

The shock in private consumption is performed, like the first experiment, by adding 1% of real GDP of year 1 to the two reference paths and keeping the variable exogenous, which precludes the influences of second-round effects but ascertains that the increase is effectively what it should be. This time the import function for *consumption* goods is affected directly and the others only indirectly.

From the results in Table 9 it is again clear that introduction of the estimated bilateral import equations (10) widens the range of the effects on exports, although to a minor extent than for the previous experiment.

Again the introduction of the bilateral import equation causes a loss in export gains due to loss of competitivity. The only countries which are able to escape this fate are Denmark and the Netherlands, while the loss for Ireland is moderate because of its cost decrease in the long run. For Denmark the volume effect on its important export market W.-Germany is strong, while for the Netherlands this holds not only for W.-Germany but also for France, and to a minor extent the BLEU and the United Kingdom.

The *a priori* considerations of section 2, which predicted a more than average export increase for the BLEU, Denmark, Greece and Ireland and the converse for Germany, are confirmed in the long run for the experiment with constant shares, except for Denmark which exports more than 40% of its consumption goods to non-EEC countries and is therefore dependent on an increase of those import markets which is only second-round for this experiment and negative.

6.2 Comparisons

Let us first compare, for the three experiments, the effects of the same shock if we keep the allocation over partners *fixed* in constant prices. Then we see that both for exports and for imports the percentage difference after 3–5 years increased with the following order of the shocks: 1) government non-wage consumption, 2) private consumption and 3) (government) investment. The only exceptions are Greece for exports (Greece hardly exports equipment goods, cf. Table 3) and again Greece, and the BLEU for imports (the latter effect is probably due to the BLEU's high import elasticity for consumption goods, cf. Table 6). If we abstract from these few exceptions, we therefore reach the conclusion that if the import allocation over partners is kept fixed, the order of the trade effects of the same stimulus in the three different final demand components that were analyzed is *uniformly the same* over all EEC member countries. We will see below whether this conclusion changes if we introduce the bilateral import equations.

The effects on average European exports and imports (which include intra-EEC trade) follow of course the same order as for the individual countries. Notice, furthermore, that in the long run a 1% increase of imports increases exports in the same order as the absolute increases. And this corresponds exactly to the import leakages that could be derived from Table 1, and which led us to the *a priori* consideration that the relative increase of exports with respect to imports, or empirical 'export elasticity', would be the largest for that category of goods of which the EEC countries import most from each other.

Another point of interest is the relative distribution of the export gains in each of the three experiments. A look at the signs of the percentage differences in exports in year 5 with respect to the European average reveals that the sign pattern, and therefore the pattern of relative gains and losses is stable if the import allocation is kept fixed. The exceptions are W.-Germany, Greece and France for the government investment experiment. W.-Germany, which has a strong equipment goods industry, and France are close to the average, however, while it was already mentioned that the exports of equipment goods are small for Greece and therefore second-round effects will dominate the first round impact on these exports. Otherwise, the countries whose exports are in general below or equal to the average are Denmark, W.-Germany and the United Kingdom.

Summarizing until so far we have seen that if the import allocation is kept fixed in constant prices:

— the effects on exports and imports are, practically uniformly, the largest for an increase in (government) investment expenditure, followed by private consumption and government non-wage consumption; otherwise said, equipment goods are the strongest trade locomotive;
— the empirical export elasticity of the EEC with respect to its imports follows the same order, which could be predicted from the fact that the average share of intra-EEC imports follows this order (Table 1),[8] and from the constant import allocation;
— the relative distribution of export growth is almost equal for the three experiments, i.e. the countries exporting more or less than the EEC average for each experiment are lamost identical.

The first of these conclusions could be predicted on the basis of a comparison of the import elasticities that were estimated in Section 4, the import contents of the volume components appearing in the estimated equations (not presented here)

Table 9. Percentage difference between reference simulation and a sustained shock of 1% of real GDP of year 1 in private consumption for each country simultaneously.[a]

Year		Exports			Imports			Domestic cost			Import price		
		1	3	5	1	3	5	1	3	5	1	3	5
BLEU[b]	I	1.7	1.4	1.1	2.3	2.1	2.1	-0.2	1.5	2.8	-0.1	0.0	0.6
	II	0.8	0.5	-0.3	2.1	1.9	2.0	0.1	1.7	3.3	-0.1	-0.1	0.6
Denmark	I	1.3	1.0	0.0	2.4	2.5	2.9	-0.6	3.0	5.9	0.0	0.1	0.5
	II	1.2	1.6	0.6	2.4	2.8	2.3	-0.5	2.1	2.6	0.0	0.0	0.5
W.-Germany	I	1.1	0.8	0.3	2.1	2.1	2.1	-0.5	1.6	2.8	0.0	0.1	0.6
	II	0.6	0.4	-0.4	2.0	1.9	1.8	-0.4	1.7	3.1	-0.1	0.0	0.5
Greece	I	1.5	1.5	1.5	1.1	1.2	0.8	-0.8	0.1	0.0	0.0	0.0	0.4
	II	0.5	1.2	0.3	1.0	1.2	1.0	-0.7	0.6	1.3	0.0	0.0	0.3
France	I	1.0	0.9	0.8	2.8	1.8	0.1	-0.3	1.2	2.3	-0.2	0.1	1.1
	II	0.5	0.5	0.2	2.8	2.2	2.7	-0.2	1.1	2.4	-0.2	-0.2	0.2
Ireland	I	1.5	1.4	1.4	1.4	1.4	1.0	-0.6	0.3	-0.1	0.0	0.2	0.9
	II	0.9	1.1	1.2	1.2	1.2	0.7	-0.4	0.1	-1.2	0.0	0.1	0.9
Italy	I	1.3	1.1	0.7	1.9	1.7	1.7	-0.5	1.4	2.6	0.0	0.0	0.4
	II	0.5	0.5	0.3	1.7	1.5	1.5	-0.4	1.3	2.5	-0.1	0.0	0.4
Netherlands	I	1.6	1.4	1.3	1.6	1.3	1.3	-0.8	0.9	2.1	0.2	0.3	0.7
	II	1.0	1.9	3.0	1.4	1.5	2.0	-0.6	1.2	2.5	0.1	0.3	0.9
United Kingdom	I	1.0	0.8	0.4	1.8	1.6	1.7	-0.5	1.7	2.8	0.4	0.1	0.6
	II	0.6	0.7	0.3	1.7	1.5	1.4	-0.6	1.4	2.4	0.4	0.1	0.8
EEC 10[c]	I	1.2	1.0	0.6	2.1	1.8	1.4	-0.5	1.5	2.6	0.0	0.1	0.7
	II	0.6	0.7	0.3	2.0	1.8	1.9	-0.4	1.4	2.6	0.0	0.0	0.5

Table 9 (continued) NOTES

[a] The figures concern total exports and imports of goods and services, as well as the corresponding total import price index. Domestic cost refers to an index of labour cost per unit of output.

[b] I: The first row gives for each country the effects if, for each good, the bilateral import shares of the partners in constant prices are kept equal to the shares of year 0.

II: The second row is the result if the estimated bilateral import equations (10) are introduced.

[c] The results for the Europe of the Ten include intra-community trade and may therefore be considered as EEC averages.

and on the fact that the import allocation was kept constant. The latter circumstance is also an explanation for the other two conclusions.

It becomes therefore interesting to look at the same subjects after an endogenous explanation of the import allocation through (10) has been introduced. The effects on bilateral trade of import demand and export supply and the relative price developments are a potential source of disruption of the stable, predictable conclusions reached at above.

For the EEC as a whole, then, equipment goods remain the strongest trade locomotive, but this is no longer true for the *exports* of all countries individually. Apart from the Greek case, also Irish, Dutch and British exports grow stronger — in the long run — after the shock in private consumption than after the shock in investment. For the exports of Italy and the BLEU the same assertion holds for the shock in government non-wage consumption compared to the shock in private consumption. For *imports* the order of the effects of the shocks remains uniformly equal in the long run.

The empirical elasticity of the average European exports with respect to imports increases slightly for the shock in investment if we introduce endogenous bilateral trade flow equations, but for the two other shocks it goes down and becomes even negative in the long run for the shock in government non-wage consumption. The general cause for this development seems to be loss of competitivity due to increased domestic cost for the EEC with respect to the rest of the world.

The relative distribution of export growth changes substantially upon the introduction of the estimated bilateral trade flows. Close inspection of the tables reveals that for each EEC country there is at least one policy experiment where its percentage difference for exports with respect to the reference solution is at least as good as the EEC average. The implications of these results for a coordinated European economic policy would, for instance, be that one might choose a stimulus that relatively favours some weak countries and vice versa, a European export distribution policy as it were.

7. CONCLUSIONS

In this paper we have analyzed the effects of a sectoral disaggregation of trade in a macro-economic model, with emphasis on the macro-economic trade effects of such a refinement. The disaggregation was performed in two stages.

In the *first stage*, non-energy imports were no longer treated in a holistic way, but disaggregated in four types of goods, for three of which new, simple, estimates of the sectoral import equations were presented. The resulting model was simulated keeping all the allocation of sectoral imports over the partners fixed in constant prices. Three experiments were performed, each time a sustained increase of 1% of

GDP in one of the three volume measures corresponding to the three estimated sectoral import equations: GDP, investments and private consumption. It was shown that due to the size of the import elasticities of imports of equipment goods and the import contents of investments, the investment shock generated the highest increase in trade for all countries. Because the average share of the EEC in the imports of equipment goods is higher than for other goods, this leaded to the highest empirical export elasticity with respect to the generated import demand in the long run. For each experiment the relative distribution of export growth is almost the same and has in general detrimental effects on Denmark, W.-Germany and the United Kingdom, with the important exception for W.-Germany in the case of an investment chock.

In the *second stage*, the assumption of a constant import allocation pattern was deleted and sectoral bilateral import equations were derived that contain the combined effect of import demand, export supply and domestic cost relative to import prices. In particular the influence of relative prices was shown to have a negative effect on the competitive position of the EEC countries with respect to the rest of the world, which resulted in general in a decrease of the empirical average EEC export elasticity with respect to imports, certainly if one disregards the German result for the investment shock. Furthermore the assertion that equipment goods are the largest 'trade generator' for all countries individually no longer proved to be true: the volume and relative price effects in bilateral trade served to demonstrate that in individual cases (Ireland, the United Kingdom and the Netherlands to a minor extent) also stimulation of private consumption may have the strongest effects on exports, although as a whole investments have to be preferred from this point of view.

Finally, it was shown that the pattern of countries whose exports grow more (or less) than the average, i.e. the relative distribution of export growth, varied among the experiments, which is another demonstration of the refinements in the analysis that already may be achieved by a simple disaggregation of international trade on its own.

This is however but a foretaste of the ultimate situation in which a complete disaggregation of the national models and their linkage will have to be established.

NOTES

The authors gratefully acknowledge the financial support of the Commission of the European Communities which made it possible to prepare this contribution as a part of the HERMES modelling project. They also express their gratitude to Karin Julliard for her efficient typing.

1) The construction of the HERMES model is presently being carried out by groups located in each European country with the coordination of a Central Group. It is followed by a coordinating group of representatives of the Directorates General involved, in particular the Directorate General for Eonomic and Financial Affairs, the Directorate General for Science, Research and Development, the Directorate General for Energy and the Statistical Office of the European Communities.

2) The COMET IV model was constructed at the Katholieke Universiteit Leuven for the Directorate-General of Economic and Financial Affairs of the Commission of the European Communities (DG II). The model was regularly documented in reports submitted to DG II, while a monograph is presently being prepared. A description of a previous version of the model – on which COMET IV builds further – may be found in Barten *et al.* (1976)

3) Cf. Italianer (1982a), also for a complete description of the construction of disaggregated bilateral trade flows in value and their price indices.

4) For the time being, the allocation of MI over MI_s and the allocation of MI_s over the 13 countries is kept simple: previous year's shares (in constant prices) are applied (cf. scheme 1 for the symbols).

5) This prportionality is implied by the additivity of the 'aggregator' function from which Barten's equation was derived; if we delete it we therefore assume a more general underlying aggregator function.

6) Flows smaller than 1 million US dollars in current value were recalculated with the constant shares assumption for reasons of stability of the simulation.

7) We assume that the increase is not of specific government nature, but equal to the average composition of total investment.

8) Because imports of agricultural goods were related empirically to GDP in section 4, we relate government non-wage consumption to these imports.

REFERENCES

d'Alcantara, G. and A. Italianer (1982), 'European Project for a Multinational Macrosectoral Model', *Commission of the European Communities, DG XII, Reference MS 11*, Brussels, March 1982.

Barten, A.P. (1971), 'An Import Allocation Model for the Common Market', *Cahiers Economiques de Bruxelles*, 50, pp. 3–14.

Barten, A.P., G. d'Alcantara and G. Carrin (1976), 'COMET, A Medium-Term Macro-economic Model for the European Community', *European Economic Review*, 7, pp 63–115.

Italianer, A. (1982a), 'Bilateral Trade Data for the European Project for a Multinational Macrosectoral Model', *Commission of the European Communities, DG XII, Reference MS 13*, Brussels, October 1982.

Italianer, A. (1982b), 'Towards a Disaggregated Bilateral Trade Flow Model', *Commission of the European Communities, DG XII, Reference MS 14*, Brussels, November 1982.

CHAPTER 2

PRODUCT AVAILABILITY, PRICE DISCRIMINATION AND INTERDEPENDENT IMPORT FLOWS

Jean-Marie Viaene
Erasmus University, Rotterdam, The Netherlands

1. INTRODUCTION

In international trade each commodity is completely specified by its physical characteristics, the location of its supply, the location of its demand and the date of which it is available. Each price and value of the traded commodity are characterized as commodity flows by the same dimensions. Supply and demand prices will differ at their equilibrium levels by two varying factors, namely, the tariffs and the per unit freight and insurance costs. Prices are slow to adjust to their equilibrium levels and in the short-run non-price variables (waiting time for orders, trade credits) predominantly clear markets (see Gregory (1971)). There is considerable theorizing yet to be done to specify the dynamics of these non-price variables and the empirical estimation of the equilibrium path of prices requires a full market theory not yet available. Therefore we set the limited goal of estimating a set of import demand functions.

In trade theory demand for imports is explained as the difference between the demand for and the supply of importables. It should thus be determined on the basis of the domestic demand price- and supply price- and output-elasticities of importables but it is almost conventional to assume that in developed countries demand is the overwhelming effect. The existence of product differentiation both in terms of physical characteristics and in terms of sales conditions (see Kravis and Lipsey (1978)), makes it difficult to have perfect substitutes in international trade and extends the list of traded commodities which, however, we assume to remain finite. All traded commodities were treated, until a few years ago, as if only consumed. Knowing that the bulk of international trade is in intermediate products which are solely used as inputs in the production of other products many pointed out this departure from conformity to reality (see Van Bochove (1982)). A lack of microeconomic foundations in constructing testable propositions was also deplored (see, e.g. Gregory (1971), Burgess (1974)).

Artus, P. and Guvenen, O. (eds.): International Macroeconomic Modelling for Policy Decisions.
© *1986. Martinus Nijhoff Publishers, Dordrecht/Boston/Lancaster.*
ISBN 90-247-3201-8. Printed in The Netherlands.

A minimum requirement is the use of a model of trade flows which offers both the supply and the physical characteristics dimensions to vary. A model of bilateral trade flows with commodity disaggregation is a good candidate to fulfill such requirement and in addition, has the advantage of solving all adding up inconsistencies of other types of import models and allows for a theorization along the line developed in demand theory.

In this paper we intend to generalize an alternative functional form of bilateral trade flows, whose groundwork was discussed elsewhere (Viaene (1982)), by allowing for commodity disaggregation. It bridges a gap between previous studies by focusing on the role of both consumption goods and production inputs in international trade and as a result, many new properties and interpretations can be given. Bilateral imports of a given market from the set of suppliers will be considered as a system of demand equations for inputs and consumption goods derived from very general cost and direct utility functions. For a given commodity bundle there is the possibility of (weak) positive or negative interdependency between flows coming from various suppliers which in turn, may give rise to inferior and Giffen consumption goods, and to inferior factors in international trade. Also, among different input bundles there may exist (strong) positive or negative interdependency dictated by properties of the underlying cost function. Under certain conditions, it permits efficient estimation. The generality of the model, which we call the System of Interdependent Import Functions, is not without problems since it requires estimation of a large number of parameters.

In Section 2 of the paper we discuss the mathematical specification of the system and justify the claims in the previous paragraph. In Section 3, the weak version of the model is estimated on quarterly German data covering the period 1970.1– 1979.4.

2. SPECIFICATION OF THE SYSTEM

2.1. The mathematical model

A well-known approach in production theory is that firms choose a set of inputs $y' = (Y_1, Y_2, \ldots, Y_r)$ in such a way that it minimizes a cost function $G = G(Q, p')$ subject to a given level of output $Q = \rho(y')$, where $p' = (P_1, P_2, \ldots, P_r)$ are the prices of factors. The factor demand equations resulting from this maximization procedure are

$$Y_i = Y_i(Q, p') \qquad i = 1, \ldots r. \tag{1}$$

Utility maximization by consumers under budget constraint would lead to demand equations for commodities Y_i of a similar form with p' interpreted now as prices of commodities and Q the level of income. In an open economy a subset of y contains factors or commodities which are imported from the set of foreign suppliers. In a multicountry world the demand for imports theoretically depends on all domestic and competitors' prices.

Imagine $(n + 1)$ regions in the world in trade relation with each other. Let $Y_{\gamma ijt}$ represent the trade flow of commodity γ from exporting region j to the import market i at time t, for $i = 1, \ldots n + 1, j = 1, \ldots n + 1$ and $j \neq i, \gamma = 1, \ldots G$ and $t = 1, \ldots T$. To proceed with this analysis we fix the i dimension to focus on the demand pattern for bilateral imports of the e.g. $(n + 1)$th and domestic import market. From the optimization behaviour of firms or households we can derive the following set of import demand functions[1]

$$y_t = Bx_t + u_t \qquad (2)$$

$$(nGx1) \quad (nGxm) \, (mx1) \, (nGx1)$$

where y is the vector of import demands, x a vector of m predetermined explanatory variables (output, domestic and foreign bilateral prices) and $B = [b^1_{\gamma j}]$ a matrix of parameters $(1 = 1, \ldots m)$. The vector of disturbance terms u_t has been introduced to represent all factors that affect bilateral trade flows other than the m explanatory variables. Their combined effects will be considered as a random variable. Variables are labeled according to the time frame to which they belong with

$$T > m \qquad (3)$$

to perform single equation estimation and

$$T > m + nG \qquad (4)$$

for system estimation (Klein (1974)).

Econometric estimation of (2) would lead to inconclusive results given the large number of parameters to be estimated and the multicollinearity of prices. To go about these difficulties let us first assume that, for each traded commodity γ, the flow between regions j and $n + 1$ depends only on variables pertaining to j and $n + 1$ and not to those of any third region $h(h = 1, \ldots n, h \neq j)$ and any other traded commodity $\delta(\delta = 1, \ldots G, \delta \neq \gamma)$. In terms of the model above this is equivalent to imposing zero restrictions on elements of B. This assumption implies sole substitution between imports and domestically produced commodities and the response of imports to variation in domestic income. So far only flow creation or destruction is permitted and the possibility of substitution or complementarity among the sources of supply is excluded *a priori*. Allowing for interdependency between the flows the system becomes

$$y_t = Bx_t + Ay_t + v_t \qquad (5)$$

where $A = [a^{\delta h}_{\gamma j}]$ is a $(nG \times nG)$ matrix of interdependency parameters whose diagonal elements obey[2]

$$a_{\gamma j}^{\gamma j} = 0 \qquad j = 1, \ldots n; \gamma = 1, \ldots G. \tag{6}$$

This is the so-called normalization rule, which asserts that each equation can be written with an endogenous variable having a unit coefficient. Equation (5) states that each flow $Y_{\gamma j}$ is related not only to variables of x which pertain to γ, j or $n + 1$ but also to disaggregated trade flows from the n remaining regions to the domestic market. Interdependency can take several forms depending on the variability of the commodity and/or supplier dimension. Weak interdependency occurs if $a_{\gamma j}^{\gamma h} \neq 0$ and $a_{\gamma j}^{\delta h} = 0$. Strong interdependency arises when $a_{\gamma j}^{\gamma h} \neq 0$ and $a_{\gamma j}^{\delta h} \neq 0$. If the effect of a change in $Y_{\gamma h}$ or $Y_{\delta j}$ on $Y_{\gamma j}$ is positive (negative) then interdependency is said to be positive (negative). If the effects are null $Y_{\gamma j}$ is independent of all other flows and region j can behave independently of other regions in its supply of commodity γ to the home country.[3]

Negative interdependency between flows of the same commodity results from competition among the various sources of supply. Any loss of competitiveness of region j with respect to region h will increase $Y_{\gamma h}$ at the expense of $Y_{\gamma j}$. However, the existence of product differentiation makes difficult any price comparison and possible the practice of price discrimination. Positive interdependency has no rationale between flows of a same homogenous commodity and is only a product of aggregation. The concept, however, becomes relevant if we are talking, as usual, about flows of commodity bundles composed of non-homogenous commodities and about relations between flows of different commodity bundles. It arises since (1) commodities cannot be used as inputs or consumed independently of certain other commodities and (2) suppliers cannot produce the whole spectrum of goods, either temporarily or permanently. Positive interdependency may exist between imports of manufactures and of raw materials. Also, any increase in car imports of the domestic market from region h may increase imports of tires from region j in which case we observe positive interdependency within the bundle of manufactured products.

For the domestic market we have a set of nG equations in nG unknowns which can be represented in reduced form as follows

$$y_t = (I - A)^{-1} B x_t + (I - A)^{-1} v_t \tag{7}$$

We shall break up matrix $(I - A)$ into $n \times n$ submatrices through partitioning both by sets of rows and by sets of columns according to the commodity index

$$(I - A) = \begin{bmatrix} A_{11} & A_{12} \ldots & A_{1G} \\ A_{21} & A_{22} \ldots & A_{2G} \\ \cdot & \cdot & \cdot \\ \cdot & \cdot & \cdot \\ \cdot & \cdot & \cdot \\ A_{G1} & A_{G2} \ldots & A_{GG} \end{bmatrix} \tag{8}$$

Each diagonal matrix which has unitary diagonal cells carries the weak interdependency parameters while the off-diagonal matrices contain parameters representative of the interdependency between commodity bundles.

2.2 Restrictions

The generality of the system has been achieved at a certain cost, however. There is a large number of parameters. The constants to be estimated are $b_{\gamma j}^l$'s and $a_{\gamma j}^{\delta h}$'s. If $m_{\gamma j}(m_{\gamma j} < m)$ is the number of predetermined variables explaining $Y_{\gamma j}$ there will be $(m_{\gamma j} + nG)$ coefficients to estimate with

$$T > m_{\gamma j} + nG - 1 \tag{9}$$

If the number of regions and/or traded commodities increase, (9) may be binding and most data samples may not be able to support conclusive results. It is important to find a procedure to eliminate a few parameters while keeping the basic properties intact. To this end three types of restrictions can be imposed.

First, we can assume that $A_{\gamma\delta} = 0_n$ which means that all forms of interdependency between commodity bundles disappear. Under certain circumstances this is justified on the ground that interdependency between two commodity groups hardly exists (food products and raw materials or energy). Under this first constraint, matrix $(I - A)$ degenerates into a block diagonal matrix whose inverse simplifies to

$$\begin{bmatrix} A_{11}^{-1} & 0 & \dots & o \\ 0 & A_{22}^{-1} & \dots & 0 \\ \cdot & & & \cdot \\ \cdot & & \cdot & \cdot \\ \cdot & & \cdot & \cdot \\ 0 & 0 & \dots & A_{GG}^{-1} \end{bmatrix} \tag{10}$$

Second, another constraint still allows for interdependency between commodity bundles but the extent being the same for all n suppliers. Each submatrix $A_{\gamma\delta}$ consists then of rows of equal parameters. Third, by imposing both constraints, more sensible analytical properties can be derived. Each diagonal submatrix becomes

$$\begin{bmatrix} 1 & & -a_{\gamma 1} \dots -a_{\gamma 1} \\ -a_{\gamma 2} & 1 & \dots -a_{\gamma 2} \\ \cdot & \cdot & \cdot & \cdot \\ \cdot & \cdot & & \cdot & \cdot \\ \cdot & \cdot & & \cdot & \cdot \\ -a_{\gamma n} & -a_{\gamma n} & \dots & 1 \end{bmatrix} \tag{11}$$

the inverse of which is

$$
\begin{bmatrix}
\dfrac{1}{d_{\gamma 1}}\left(1+\dfrac{a_{\gamma 1}/d_{\gamma 1}}{\widetilde{D}_\gamma}\right) & \dfrac{a_{\gamma 1}/d_{\gamma 1}}{\widetilde{D}_\gamma d_{\gamma 2}} & \cdots & \dfrac{a_{\gamma 1}/d_{\gamma 1}}{\widetilde{D}_\gamma d_{\gamma n}} \\[3ex]
\dfrac{a_{\gamma 2}/d_{\gamma 2}}{\widetilde{D}_\gamma d_{\gamma 1}} & \dfrac{1}{d_{\gamma 2}}\left(1+\dfrac{a_{\gamma 2}/d_{\gamma 2}}{\widetilde{D}_\gamma}\right) & \cdots & \dfrac{a_{\gamma 2}/d_{\gamma 2}}{\widetilde{D}_\gamma d_{\gamma n}} \\[3ex]
\vdots & \vdots & \cdots & \vdots \\[3ex]
\dfrac{a_{\gamma n}/d_{\gamma n}}{\widetilde{D}_\gamma d_{\gamma 1}} & \left(\dfrac{a_{\gamma n}/d_{\gamma n}}{\widetilde{D}_\gamma d_{\gamma 2}}\right)\cdots & \dfrac{1}{d_{\gamma n}}\left(1+\dfrac{a_{\gamma n}/d_{\gamma n}}{\widetilde{D}_\gamma}\right)
\end{bmatrix} \tag{12}
$$

where

$$
\widetilde{D}_\gamma = 1 - \sum_{s=1}^{n}\left(\frac{a_{\gamma s}}{1+a_{\gamma s}}\right)
$$

and

$$
d_{\gamma s} = 1 + a_{\gamma s} \qquad s = 1, \ldots n
$$

The Jacobian of the matrix is positive if $a_{\gamma s} > -1$ and $\widetilde{D}_\gamma > 0$. $\widetilde{D}_\gamma$ is the measure of overall interdependency for each commodity group γ. When greater than 1 it indicates that, for all trade flows of that commodity to the domestic import market, negative interdependency outweighs positive interdependency. When less than 1 the reverse holds. When equal to 1 then either there is no interdependency or the negative one is offset by the positive.

2.3 Economic properties

A first property of the system is that it generates general demand functions for commodities of the type $Y_{\gamma j} = Y_{\gamma j}(Q, p^1)$, derived from the optimization of a very general utility and cost function. We are thus freed from the *a priori* representation of the technology of the firm and/or of preferences of individuals. Even though they have been constrained to respond only to activity and to their own relative price in the structural form, the system allows for cross-price effects through all interdependency parameters and any change in any supplier's price (belonging to the same or different commodity group) will affect all flows.

In addition the system allows for complementarity between flows and offers the possibility to detect inferior and Giffen goods which is, as far as we know, a new property in international trade models. In fact, there is no reason why we should not expect to find Giffen effects in international trade if it is accepted that over certain price ranges and defined situations of satiated characteristic, Giffen goods occur and are a valid part of demand theory (Lipsey and Rosenbluth (1971)). This is best illustrated using the third restriction of the previous paragraph. Assume, for a given commodity group γ, that X^1 is domestic activity, X^2 and X^3 are country j's and country h's bilateral relative export prices, respectively. The reduced-form output elasticity of imports from j is[4]

$$\epsilon_Q = \frac{1}{d_{\gamma j}}\left[b_{\gamma j}^1 + \frac{a_{\gamma j}}{\widetilde{D}_\gamma}\left(\frac{b_{\gamma 1}^1}{d_{\gamma 1}} + \frac{b_{\gamma 2}^1}{d_{\gamma 2}} \ldots + \frac{b_{\gamma j}^1}{d_{\gamma j}} \ldots + \frac{b_{\gamma n}^1}{d_{\gamma n}}\right)\right] \tag{13}$$

The first parameter in the bracket is the rate of change of $Y_{\gamma j}$ in response to the rate of change in domestic activity in a world of no interdependence. The second term represents the induced rate of change brought by the interdependence between trade flows. The greater the positive interdependency between flows, the smaller $\widetilde{D}_\gamma$ becomes and the bigger the contribution of the second term. If the contribution is positive ($a_{\gamma j} > 0$) it augments the output elasticity of the bilateral trade flow. If $a_{\gamma j} < 0$ the second term offsets the first one and the output-elasticity can become negative, allowing for inferior goods and factors in international trade. The own-price elasticity of imports from j and the cross-price elasticity of region h are similarly derived

$$\epsilon_{jj} = \frac{1}{d_{\gamma j}}\left[b_{\gamma j}^2 + \frac{a_{\gamma j}}{\widetilde{D}_\gamma}\left(\frac{b_{\gamma 1}^2}{d_{\gamma 1}} + \frac{b_{\gamma 2}^2}{d_{\gamma 2}} \ldots + \frac{b_{\gamma j}^2}{d_{\gamma j}} \ldots + \frac{b_{\gamma n}^2}{d_{\gamma n}}\right)\right] \tag{14}$$

$$\epsilon_{jh} = \frac{1}{d_{\gamma j}}\left[b_{\gamma j}^3 + \frac{a_{\gamma j}}{\widetilde{D}_\gamma}\left(\frac{b_{\gamma 1}^3}{d_{\gamma 1}} \ldots + \frac{b_{\gamma j}^3}{d_{\gamma j}} \ldots + \frac{b_{\gamma h}^3}{d_{\gamma h}} \ldots + \frac{b_{\gamma n}^3}{d_{\gamma n}}\right)\right] \tag{15}$$

Given that X^2 is only present in the (γ, j) equation it implies that $b_{\gamma p}^2 = 0$ for p = 1, 2, ... n and $p \neq j$. Using this simplification we can show from (14) that the own-price elasticity can lie anywhere between 0 and $-\infty$ when $a_{\gamma j} > 0$ but can become positive if

$$\frac{a_{\gamma j}}{\widetilde{D}_\gamma d_{\gamma j}} < -1 \tag{16}$$

which can only occur if $a_{\gamma j} < 0$. This condition defines Giffen goods in consumption only and is of no relevance in production where factor demands are always downward sloping (Hicks (1946)). Similarly X^3 is only present in the (γ, h) equation yielding $b_{\gamma g}^3 = 0$ for g = 1, 2, ... n and $g \neq h$. Accordingly the cross-price elasticity becomes

$$\epsilon_{jh} = \frac{1}{d_{\gamma j}} \frac{a_{\gamma j}}{\widetilde{D}_\gamma} \frac{b_{\gamma h}^3}{d_{\gamma h}} \tag{17}$$

and is positive when $a_{\gamma j} < 0$. This is an interesting result since substitution or complementarity between flows of a given commodity from the set of suppliers can be readily detected at the structural level when negative or positive interdependency occurs. Slutsky symmetry $\epsilon_{jh} = \epsilon_{hj}$ is satisfied if and only if

$$a_{\gamma j} b_{\gamma h}^3 = a_{\gamma h} b_{\gamma j}^2 \tag{18}$$

Symmetry involves the imposition of $n(n-1)/2$ cross-equation restrictions but this is an unnecessary task since it has been shown in consumption theory that, with general preferences, market demand functions need not satisfy in any way the classical restrictions which characterize consumer demand functions (Shafer and Sonnenschein (1982)).

2.4. Estimation

It is a well known proposition that under linear restrictions on structural coefficients, the necessary but not sufficient condition for identification is that the number of excluded predetermined variables $(m - m_{\gamma j})$ is greater or equal to the number of included endogenous variables minus one $(nG - 1)$. It is not difficult to find a specification such that

$$m - m_{\gamma j} = nG - 1 \tag{19}$$

in which case exact identification is achieved. In that case and if structural errors are normally distributed and serially uncorrelated then 3SLS reduces to 2SLS and efficiency in the estimation of the system is attained.

3. APPLICATION TO GERMAN IMPORT DATA

In this section we estimate the model using quarterly data from 1970.1 to 1979.4 for German imports. All traded commodities are aggregated into a consumption bundle, food products (SITC 0 + 1), and three groups of production inputs: raw materials (SITC 2 + 4), energy (SITC 3) and manufactures (SITC 5 − 9).[5] The set of suppliers is limited to France, Italy, UK, USA and the rest of the world (ROW).

Previous empirical studies have shown that imports gradually adjust to relative price and activity changes justifying an inherent dynamics in the form of a decision lag. A simple way of approximating these dynamics is the well-known partial adjustment model

$$Y_t - Y_{t-1} = \theta(Y_t^* - Y_{t-1}), \qquad 0 < \theta < 1 \tag{20}$$

where $Y^*(Y)$ denotes the desired (actual) level of bilateral imports and θ is an adjustment coefficient which will differ for each country pair. The desired level of each variable is given by the model of bilateral import demand of equation (5) imposing the third restriction of section 2.2. Each of the five equations for bilateral imports of consumption goods include as independent part real food consumption expenditures as income, domestic price of food and the bilateral export price of the foreign supplier corrected for tariffs and cif-fob margins. Similarly the specification of the independent part of each import demand function for imported inputs contains GDP in manufacturing, the corrected bilateral export price of the foreign supplier and the domestic supply price of the relevant input which is a mark-up over all cost components.

The availability of bilateral price indices reconciles our analysis with the persistent evidence of price discrimination, that is, that the export price of any country j is dependent of the destination of its exports (Kravis and Lipsey (1978)). This same evidence is confirmed by our sample. For each product group, the bilateral export price of a supplying source to Germany was regressed on the average export price of the same supplying country. Price discrimination was assumed to exist when the estimated parameter was different from unity at the five percent significance level. Following this method our sample carries ten cases (out of twenty) of positive price discrimination of which four occur in group 5–9 (all countries except France), three in group 2 + 4 (Italy, UK, USA), two in group 3 (France, ROW) and one in group 0 + 1 (France). This rough measure is not without drawback since it is not feasible at this level of aggregation to distinguish effective price discrimination from varying grades of quality and technology in imports.

The system is specified in log-linear form and estimated by applying 3SLS to each commodity group separately since this is a test of weak interdependency with thus overidentified structures. The first results of estimation are very satisfactory. All estimated coefficients of the income/output and price elasticities are of the expected signs while the sign of $a_{\gamma j}$'s is observed as an empirical question. Of the 76 parameters 71% is statistically significant at the 5% level and no serious serial correlation is detected. The coefficient of determination adjusted for degrees of freedom provided by the OLS equivalent ranges from 0.96 to 0.99.

The long-run income/output, own- and cross-price elasticities are reported in Table 1 and 2 respectively.[6] Among the major empirical findings a few come forth. Substitution between flows is the rule in commodity group 0 + 1 ($\widetilde{D}_{0+1} = 8.694$) and group 3 ($\widetilde{D}_3 = 10.063$). So far the statistical picture is familiar enough. Where the statistics begin to break some new ground is in their indication that complementarity is the overwhelming effect in group 2 + 4 ($\widetilde{D}_{2+4} = 0.444$) and group

Table 1. Long run income/output elasticities.

	France	Italy	UK	USA	ROW
SITC 0 + 1	0.571	0.523	0.258	0.509	0.735
SITC 2 + 4	0.971	0.720	1.122	1.256	1.597
SITC 3	0.299	0.324	0.223	0.293	0.647
SITC 5 − 9	0.652	0.634	0.533	0.592	0.784

Table 2. Own- and cross-price elasticities.

Price change in	France	Italy	UK	USA	ROW
SITC 0 + 1					
France	−2.550	0.050	1.003	0.842	0.044
Italy	0.072	−1.035	0.575	0.483	0.025
UK	0.955	0.380	−13.680	6.369	0.332
USA	1.202	0.478	9.553	−9.830	0.418
ROW	0.012	0.005	0.100	0.084	−0.926
SITC 2 + 4					
France	−1.103	−0.301	−0.585	0.0	−0.141
Italy	0.004	−1.390	0.013	0.0	0.003
UK	−0.306	−0.471	−3.635	0.0	−0.220
USA	−0.391	−0.601	−1.169	0.0	−0.281
ROW	−0.249	−0.382	−0.744	0.0	−0.833
SITC 3					
France	−0.376	0.020	0.066	0.015	0.002
Italy	0.052	−3.462	1.792	0.402	0.062
UK	0.253	2.682	−4.315	1.946	0.302
USA	0.031	0.326	1.054	−2.677	0.037
ROW	0.003	0.035	0.112	0.025	−0.448
SITC 5 − 9					
France	−0.956	−0.305	−0.442	0.0	−0.119
Italy	0.005	−1.869	0.018	0.0	0.005
UK	−0.056	−0.129	−2.916	0.0	−0.051
USA	−0.233	−0.532	−0.772	0.0	−0.209
ROW	−0.154	−0.352	−0.511	0.0	−0.875

5–9 ($\widetilde{D}_{5-9} = 0.590$). These findings, when drawn together, paint a fairly consistent picture. Consumption goods and energy products are often available with a high degree of qualitative homogeneity in most supplying countries (except for ROW), therefore leading to substitution between flows. Raw materials include a broader class of products, each showing a high degree of homogeneity but whose availability depends on each country's endowments. By virtue of their basic nature in the productive process and the fact that primary inputs cannot be produced in all countries German bilateral imports of these products are complementary. Within manufactures the most natural explanations of complementarity are product heterogeneity and the division of the production process in a large number of domestic and foreign distinct operations. The latter has the use of international returns to scale (Ethier (1979)) while the former is a result of the search for some temporary monopoly over the world market for a particular product. Producers are then able to sell in distinct markets at different prices and thereby increase profits.

No case of Giffen consumption goods or inferior factors is observed, which is a reassuring evidence for growth prospects of exporting nations. The income/output elasticities are all positive and vary more across our four commodity groups than across our five countries within a group, at the exception of the ROW. They range, on arithmetic average, from low 0.357 for SITC 3 to 1.133 for SITC 2 + 4 with 0.519 and 0.619 for SITC 0 + 1 and 5–9 respectively, which, if they had been weighted, would give rise to a smaller aggregate elasticity than previously found (Geraci and Prewo (1982)). The measures in Table 2 tell us more however. The own-price elasticities in all groups are relatively high for UK and relatively low for the ROW. Imports of 2 + 4 and 5–9 from the USA are not surprisingly inelastic since the highest degree of positive price discrimination has been found in both cases. The cross-price elasticities of Italy are non-negative indicating a steady pattern of substitution w.r.t. all other suppliers even in the groups with characterized complementarity. Finally, in moving to the symmetrical estimates no cross-equation restrictions were imposed but a check of the closeness seems, however, instructive. The Pearson correlation coefficients between rows and columns of the matrix of price elasticities belonging to each commodity group are 0.99, −0.45, 0.86, −0.64 for SITC 0 + 1, 2 + 4, 3 and 5–9 respectively. Hence, symmetry tends to hold only for commodity groups with characterized substitution between flows.

4. CONCLUSIONS

This paper deals with the theoretical underpinning of three stages of country interdependence: (1) the usual interdependence between the importing country and the supplying nations through the trade flows of various commodity groups, (2) within a commodity group, the possibility of substitution or complementarity between the supplying countries and (3) among commodity groups, the substitutive or complementary relationships which are based upon the characteristics of the underlying domestic cost and utility functions.

Our application of the system using German data provides a test for the second type. The results support the evidence of substitution between sources of supply of food products, and of energy. In contrast, they support the hypothesis of complementarity between bilateral flows of raw materials, and of manufactures. A first implication of complementarity between bilateral trade flows of the same commodity bundle for international trade is that it fosters interdependence among nations in the conduct of economic policy-growth. Also, referring to the recent wave of protectionism, a discriminatory increase in trade barriers for a particular commodity group against a supply source will also tax imports from other sources. A second consequence is that the trade diversion effects or, in general, the negative welfare effects of the formation of customs unions are much less significant in practise than stressed in the theory.

NOTES

I would like to thank M. Dell and G. Hommes for research assistance, and P. de Boer, P. de Grauwe, H. Glejser, R. Harkema, J. Paelinck, T. ten Raa and C. G. de Vries for very useful comments and suggestions. I am also very grateful to P. Ranuzzi of the European Community, Brussels, for permission to use the trade data as processed by him. An earlier version of the paper appeared under the title 'A System of Interdependent Import Functions'.

1) The analysis is confined to the class of linear or log-linear import demand functions.
2) Subscripts of $a_{bj}^{\delta h}$'s and $b_{\gamma j}^{1}$'s give the coordinates of the independent variable. Superscripts of the former parameters are indicative of the coordinates of the interacting flow in that equation with, δ, the commodity index and, h, the region index. Exogenous variables are associated with the superscript 1 of the latter parameters.
3) It is shown below the equivalence between positive interdependency and complementarity on one hand and between negative interdependency and substitution on the other hand.
4) To simplify expressions parameters represent elasticities.
5) Final capital goods are lumped in manufactures and thus considered as inputs of production.
6) These are obtained from the reduced-form of our estimated structural relationships.

REFERENCES

Burgess, D.F. (1974), 'Production Theory and the Derived Demand for Imports', *Journal of International Economics*, 4, pp. 103–117.
Ethier, W. (1979), 'Internationally Decreasing Costs and World Trade', *Journal of International Economics*, 9, pp. 1–24.
Geraci, V.J. and W. Prewo (1982), 'An Empirical Demand and Supply Model of Multilateral Trade', *Review of Economics and Statistics*, 64, pp. 432–441.
Gregory, R.G. (1971), 'U.S. Imports and Internal Pressure of Demand 1948–68', *American Economic Review*, 61 pp. 28–47.
Hicks, J.R. (1946), *Value and Capital*, Oxford University Press.
Klein, L.R. (1974), *A Textbook of Econometrics*, Prentice-Hall, Englewood Cliffs, N.J.
Kravis, I.B. and R.E. Lipsey (1978), 'Price Behavior in the Light of Balance of Payments Theories', *Journal of International Economics*, 8, pp. 193–246.

Lipsey, R.E. and G. Rosenbluth (1971), 'A Contribution to the New Theory of Demand: a Rehabilitation of the Giffen Good', *Canadian Journal of Economics*, 4, pp. 131–163.

Shafer, W. and H. Sonnenschein (1982), 'Market Demand and Excess Demand Functions', in *Handbook of Mathematical Economics*, Vol. II, ed. by K.J. Arrow and M.S. Intriligator, North-Holland.

Van Bochove, C.A. (1982), *Imports and Economic Growth*, Martinus Nijhoff Publishers.

Viaene, J.M. (1982), 'A Customs Union Between Spain and the EEC: an Attempt at Quantification of the Long-term Effects in a General Equilibrium Framework', *European Economic Review*, 18, pp. 345–368.

CHAPTER 3

EXCHANGE RATE EXPECTATIONS AND CURRENT BALANCES IN THE OECD INTERLINK SYSTEM

Paul Masson and Peter Richardson*
*Department of Economics and Statistics, OECD, Paris, France

1. INTRODUCTION

The proper treatment of expectations in large-scale empirical macro-models is an area of considerable controversy. The traditional, adaptive expectations formulations have rightly been subject to much criticism. Adaptive expectations imply that agents are systematically wrong in their forecasts — that is, arrival of a piece of new information will usually cause them to be consistently wrong in one direction or another from that moment on. Furthermore, the adaptive scheme precludes allowing for the future values of any variables in expectations. This is unrealistic, as there are clearly some events that can be anticipated. For instance, some policy changes are announced in advance, and, to the extent that the latter are believed, they will affect behaviour from the time of announcement. A properly constructed model should allow for this possibility.

The alternative of rational expectations has become widely preferred to adaptive expectations, at least in theoretical and small empirical models,[1] because it meets the above objections. To the extent that agents know the future values of variables, they will correctly use this information in a way that is consistent with the model's structure. This has the advantage in the context of an *ex-ante* forecast that the agents whose behaviour is being modelled act on 'expectations' that are the same as the forecast produced by the model itself, assuming that these agents have the same advance 'knowledge' of the exogenous variables that the forecaster does. Viewed in this light, a better name would perhaps be 'consistent' expectations — indeed this term was proposed early on[2] — rather than the word 'rational' with its normative connotations.

Unfortunately, rational, or consistent, expectations are difficult to implement in large-scale macroeconomic models. Some attempts have been made, but their cost in terms of computing time and their lack of flexibility, e.g. restrictions on the

Artus, P. and Guvenen, O. (eds.): International Macroeconomic Modelling for Policy Decisions.
© *1986. Martinus Nijhoff Publishers, Dordrecht/Boston/Lancaster.*
ISBN 90-247-3201-8. Printed in The Netherlands.

length of the horizon, have so far made them impossible to use routinely.[3] The non-linearity of most macro-models makes an analytic rational expectations solution impossible, so that simulation must be employed. The simulator, however, must not only iterate over the current values of endogenous variables, but also forwards and backwards over all the periods of the simulation until convergence is achieved. The cost of simulation rises accordingly. In addition a compromise has to be made with the forward looking nature of behaviour: some sort of terminal condition must be imposed and the infinite horizon truncated. The resulting rational expectations' solution is thus approximate for two reasons: it has had further terminal conditions imposed on it, and the solution procedure is accurate only to within a certain tolerance (assuming that the neighbourhood of the true solution has in fact been located).

The alternative which forms the subject of this paper is a more tractable way of implementing rationality. It proceeds in two stages. First, each of the INTERLINK country models is reduced to a much smaller, linear model, and a model of the rest of the world is also created, by aggregating together the relevant foreign variables. In some cases key equations are taken directly from INTERLINK. In others partial simulations are performed in order to compress whole sectors into single equations — for instance, for income determination and for price formation. These models have as exogenous variables two domestic variables — money supply and government spending — for both the home country and the aggregate foreign country. Second, an explicit consistent solution to this two-country model is calculated using the formula derived by Blanchard and Kahn.[4] The solution for next period's value of a given variable provides its rational expectation, provided the values of the exogenous variables are known at the time expectations are formed, and it can be coded into INTERLINK wherever one-period-ahead expectations are required. There are several advantages to this procedure. What results is an explicit, compact equation for the expected value of a variable, which has considerable interest in its own right. It will be seen below in the context of exchange rate expectations that this equation shows how short-run financial variables and longer-run real forces — that is, competitiveness — combine to influence the exchange rate. The procedure avoids the need for special algorithms for solving INTERLINK; once the equation is coded in, the model can be simulated in the usual way.

The expectations of main concern here are those for the exchange rate. Because exchange market participants respond quickly to new information, and transactions costs are low, the exchange rate is likely to reflect all current information. The assumption of rationality seems especially relevant to this case. It is also useful because it makes it possible to work through the interaction of a short-run, asset market view of exchange rate determination with a current account response to changes in competitiveness that feeds back on to the level of asset stocks. Exchange market participants must somehow weight together these various forces, and the forward solution of the model provides a way of replicating this.

The plan of the paper is as follows. The next section briefly describes the INTER-LINK model and describes some alternative specifications for exchange rate expectations. Section 3 describes the structure of the mini-model for a small open economy, with emphasis on the dynamic adjustment of the exchange rate and the current balance. This conceptual model serves as a prototype for the empirical mini-model which is described in Section 4. This section also details the simulations performed to derive its coefficients from INTERLINK. Section 5 then discusses the method of finding the explicit rational solution to the mini-model, and presents coefficients for the resulting expected exchange rate equation.

2. ALTERNATIVE SPECIFICATIONS FOR EXCHANGE RATE EXPECTATIONS

The INTERLINK model is a world model designed to study the international linkages between various countries and regions of the world.[5] it contains individual country models for each of the 24 OECD members, with up to 150 equations per country, as well as more rudimentary models for eight non-OECD regions grouping the remaining countries. The model includes a framework for making export and import prices and volumes consistent across the world; developments in individual countries have repercussions on other countries through these trade linkages. In addition, a financial linkages model has recently been implemented. Designed to be operated either in fixed or in floating exchange rate modes, it determines capital flows on a consistent world basis, as well as their implications for either money supply or exchange rate movements.[6] The concern here is with use of the model in floating rate mode; conceptually, then, the capital flow equation for each country, or rather the underlying asset stock demand, can be thought of as determining the exchange rate.

The resulting exchange rate equations are similar to other portfolio balance models in that they assume that investors holding assets denominated in different currencies will exert pressures on interest rates and exchange rates that will tend to equalize expected returns, after allowance for risk premiums. In INTERLINK, the risk premium is made a function of the net international claim position of the country in question, that is, its cumulated current account. Because of the necessities of international consistency, INTERLINK uses weighted bilateral exchange rates and weighted interest rates; constraints are imposed on the system so that capital outflows from one country or region show up as inflows elsewhere, after allowing for an estimate of the world statistical discrepancy.

Exchange rate determination in the short-run thus results from financial factors. Because the current account can be thought of as essentially predetermined in the short run, the exchange rate must move to equate asset demands with given asset supplies,[7] that is, given net claims positions. Exchange rate models usually introduce longer-run considerations through a specification of the determinants of *expected* exchange rates. Typically, some form of purchasing-power-parity is used to condition expectations.[8] It can be argued that real exchange rate movements away from some equilibrium level tend to reverse themselves, and that in the long run purchasing-power-parity is re-established.[9] The assumption is often made that investors expect a gradual return to PPP, with the speed of adjustment usually estimated as a parameter in the equation. There is, however, a broad consensus among economists that PPP is a very poor predictor of short-run exchange rate movements.[10]

It seems unlikely that investors forming expectations about the exchange rate would not also use what information they had about the financial factors affecting relative rates of return. The dichotomy between long-run competitiveness factors affecting exchange rates through expectations and financial factors entering directly into the structural exchange rate or asset demand equation seems artificial and unconvincing. The link between the two is provided by the current account. The current account responds gradually to competitiveness factors and over time contributes to asset accumulations. Eventually the economy achieves a level of net claims on foreigners that permits attainment of equilibrium in goods markets as well as in financial markets. Expectations of market participants surely acknowledge this linkage; and concern with competitiveness factors in forming expectations is consistent with it. Furthermore, it may imply a tradeoff, in long-run equilibrium, between stocks of net claims and the real exchange rate. Suppose the current balance is written as the sum of net interest receipts (rNFA), which depend on the level of net claims on foreigners (NFA), and the trade balance, made a negative function of the log of the real exchange rate, $(e + p - p^*)$, as well as of domestic (y) and foreign (y^*) outputs:

$$CB = rNFA + t(e + p - p^*, y, y^*) \qquad (1)$$

Suppose that in steady state the output variables take their full employment values, and the current balance satisfies the condition that foreign assets grow at a rate (g) that keeps portfolio shares balanced, *i.e.* at the rate of growth of wealth.

Now $NFA = CB$,

so if $NFA/NFA = g$

then $CB = g\,NFA$,

and from equation (1),

$$(r - g)NFA = -t(e + p - p^*, y, y^*)$$ (2)

Provided the interest rate exceeds the rate of growth of wealth, equation (2) gives a positive long-run relationship ($\partial t/\partial e$ is negative) between the level of net claims and the real exchange rate: a wealthier country can afford to be less competitive as it finances goods trade deficits from services receipts.

The relationship depicted in (2) has been used to provide a basis for expectation formation, notably by Hooper and Morton.[11] However, without a fully specified model the variables of interest cannot be determined. NFA will be affected by the entire path of future current account balances; it is impossible to infer from its current level what it will be in the long run. Indeed, with a J-curve phenomenon, the value of net claims may be responding perversely in the short run, and expectations that do not 'see through' the J-curve will clearly be destabilizing. In addition, domestic and foreign income will be different in steady state depending on the level of net claims, and this may affect the trade balance between them. The outcome depends on the specification of expenditure equations.

More generally, the method of trying to use long-run equilibrium conditions in the formation of expectations provides no means of weighting the importance of these long-run considerations relative to purely short run, temporary, disturbances, such as temporarily tighter monetary policy. In practice the current stance of monetary policy and views about its continued credibility seem to be among the major influences on exchange rate expectations. It seems essential to find a way of integrating these various factors into a specification for expectations.

One solution is to estimate a sort of 'unrestricted reduced form' for the exchange rate, including past, current and future values of relevant variables, or their determinants, and impose a weak form of rationality that says that investors were aware of this historical, reduced-form relationship. This procedure was tried in early versions of financial INTERLINK, but there are several difficulties with it. As a practical matter, the list of candidates for inclusion as explanatory variables is so long that the point is quickly reached where there are few degrees of freedom, and arbitrary choices have to be made. And the properties of the model can be very sensitive to the choice made. Second, the variables that appear will include those in the 'structural' exchange rate equation; because they have been fitted to the same data, exchange rate expectations not being observable, it is hard to distinguish one equation from the other.

Hence the choice was made to build a 'mini-model'[12] of the INTERLINK model and to derive a closed-form expression for the rational expectation of the exchange rate, given future information about the exogenous variables. This mini-model is linear, permitting an analytic solution for next period's exchange rate, whose equation can then be coded into the INTERLINK model. Its coefficients are complicated functions of the coefficients of the mini-model; the latter summarize the behaviour embodied in INTERLINK. Foreign influences are modelled endogenously, through equations that determine output, inflation and interest rates for the rest of the world. The mini-model, is not, however, a reduced-form of INTERLINK. It is a structural model of manageable size. In fact, the proposed model embodies some structural information that is not currently imposed in INTERLINK, such as homogeneity of excess demand functions and proper accounting for the wealth accumulations and decumulations implied by current balances, and the corresponding services payments. Because of its relative simplicity, however, it can be used to calculate a reduced form expression for the expected exchange rate, with known coefficients, that can be coded into the full structural model. The structure of this mini-model and its long-run properties are discussed in the next section.

Of course this equation will not give a value which will be exactly that calculated by INTERLINK in the next period. The mini-model has cut through some of the detail and non-linearity. In addition, some of the exogenous variables have been omitted. The main advantage, however, is that it does incorporate future values of exogenous variables, and allows for dynamic adjustment of endogenous variables to be accounted for in expectations formation. Since the expected exchange rate equation is coded only for a one period horizon, and it depends on current values of state variables produced by INTERLINK, discrepancies between the two models tend to be corrected as the simulation proceeds.

3. EXCHANGE RATE AND CURRENT BALANCE INTERACTION IN A SMALL, TWO-COUNTRY, MACRO-MODEL

We are interested in the expected effective exchange rate for each of the major OECD countries. Our strategy is to condense INTERLINK into a series of two-country models, one each for the OECD countries of interest. The 'domestic' country model is a small model reflecting the properties of the (much larger) INTERLINK country model. The 'foreign' country model has the same structure as the domestic one, but aggregates not only sectors but also countries: it reflects the aggregate behaviour of all the remaining countries in INTERLINK. Thus in the mini-model INTERLINK is reduced to a series of partially-overlapping two-country models. Table 1 puts down the structure of these two-country models. This prototype is in fact a stylized version of the mini-model that is described in the following section because the dynamics here are simplified: only the essential asset stock dynamics and those related to sticky prices are put down explicitly. The mini-model introduces additional lags, related to the lagged response of expenditure, and hence also the current account, to competitiveness and real interest rates.

A short description of the mini-model follows. The parameters for equation (1)

Table 1. Prototype model of INTERLINK.

(1)	e	$=$	$e(+1) + a_0 + a_1(R - R^*) + a_2 NFA$
(2)	TB	$=$	$b_0 + b_1(e + p - p^*) + b_2 y^* + b_3 y - b_4 rNFA$
(3)	$NFA(+1)$	$=$	$NFA + TB + rNFA$
(4)	y	$=$	$c_0 + c_1(R - \hat{\pi}(+1)) + c_2 gov + c_3 rNFA$
			$+ c_4(e + p - p^*) + c_5 y^*$
(5)	(a) π	$=$	$\hat{\pi}(+1) + d_2 y$
	(b) $\hat{\pi}(+1)$	$=$	$\hat{\pi} + d_1(\pi - \hat{\pi})$
(6)	R	$=$	$(-m + p)/f_1 + f_2 y/f_1 + f_2 \bar{y}/f_1 + f_0/f_1$
(7)	y^*	$=$	$c_0^* + c_1^*(R^* - \hat{\pi}^*(+1)) + c_2^* gov^* - c_3^* rNFA$
			$- c_4^*(e + p - p^*)$
(8)	(a) π^*	$=$	$\hat{\pi}^*(+1) + d_2^* y^*$
	(b) $\hat{\pi}^*(+1)$	$=$	$\pi^* + d_1^*(\pi^* - \hat{\pi}^*)$
(9)	R^*	$=$	$(-m^* + p^*)/f_1^* + f_2^* y^*/f_1^* + f_2^* \bar{y}^*/f_1^* + f_0^*/f_1^*$

*Variables**

e	= effective exchange rate
R	= short-term interest rate
NFA	= real net claims on foreigners, divided by world wealth
TB	= trade balance plus non-factor services balances, divided by world wealth
P	= price level
π	= rate of inflation $= p - p(-1)$
gov	= real government spending, divided by capacity output
m	= money supply
y	= actual GDP, divided by capacity output
$\bar{y}$	= capacity output

*Lower case letters are logarithms of the respective variables. An asterisk signifies a variable or parameter for foreign countries taken as a whole, and a hat over a variable refers to its subjective expectation formed at t. Parameters are a_i, b_i, c_i, d_i, f_i and r.

are taken directly from a similar equation in INTERLINK though here the expected exchange rate will be replaced by the actual rate the following period, $e(+1)$. The equation implies that the interest differential is equal to the expected depreciation plus a risk premium, which depends on the net claims position of the country divided by world wealth. This formulation is appropriate if wealth transfers do not take the form of financial investment but rather real transfers; the problem of choosing an exchange rate at which to value foreign claims does not arise.

Equations (2) and (4), for the current balance and gross domestic product, respectively (and equation (7), for foreign GDP), are linearised versions of the trade linkages and income-expenditure blocks of INTERLINK. Equation (2) expresses the trade balance as a function of the real exchange rate, domestic and foreign GDP, and net claims on foreigners. The aggregate demand equations, (4) and (7) are quasi-reduced form equations, that are functions of both domestic and foreign GDP, the real exchange rate, net foreign claims, and domestic real interest rates and government spending. These equations can be derived from the national accounts identity and individual expenditure functions.

For instance, suppose that both the trade balance and expenditure at home and abroad depend on gross *national* product, as well as the real exchange rate in the first case and real interest ratesand government spending in the latter two cases. Because GNP is equal to the variable Y, that is GDP, plus net interest recepts from abroad, we can write these functions as follows (upper case letters are used here, denoting the levels, not logs, of variables and both lags and expectations are omitted):

$$TB = T(Y + rNFA, Y^* - rNFA, e + p - p^*) \tag{10}$$

$$E = E(R - \pi, Y + rNFA, GOV) \tag{11}$$

$$E^* = E^*(R^* - \pi^*, Y^* - rNFA, GOV^*) \tag{12}$$

If (10) and (11) are solved with the corresponding national accounts identity, namely

$$Y = E + TB \tag{13}$$

then GDP can be expressed as a quasi-reduced form:

$$Y = Y(R - \pi, GOV, NFA, e + p - p^*, Y^*) \tag{13}$$

Similarly, (10) and (12) can be solved with the national accounts identity for the foreign country,

$$Y^* = E^* + TB \tag{15}$$

yielding

$$Y^* = Y^*(R^* - \pi^*, GOV^*, NFA, e + p - p^*, Y) \tag{16}$$

Equations (14) and (16) appear in Table 1 in linearised form as equations (4) and (7). Equation (2) is a linearised version of equation (10) above.

The definitions of some of the variables appearing in these three equations merit further explanation. Potential output is exogenous in the min-model, and actual output is expressed as deviation from capacity. Similarly, government spending is expressed as a ratio to capacity output. The trend in output is not modelled, but is assumed equal to the sum of exogenous labour force and productivity growth. Turning to the balance-of-payments variables, both the current balance and the net claims variables can take positive and negative values. It is therefore inappropriate to take the logs of these variables. Instead, they are scaled by world wealth, which is exogenous to the mini-model, as the accumulation of domestic claims is not modelled. The accumulation of foreign claims is, however, and equation (3) relates the accumulation in foreign claims of the home country to its current account surplus. In effect, this equation determines the distribution of world wealth between the two countries. Because the current balance and net claims variables are scaled by world wealth, the appropriate interest rate (r in equation (3)) is a real interest rate net of the real growth of world wealth. It appears as a parameter here so that the model can be linear in variables.

Equations (5a) and (8a) make the rate of inflation depend on the anticipated value for the rate of inflation next period, and on a demand pressure variable. Such an equation could result from wage bargaining that was forward-looking because of multiperiod contracts, and mark-up pricing of normal unit labour costs. Equations (5b) and (8b) specify how these anticipations of inflation are formed. In contrast to the exchange market, where exchange rate expectations are assumed equal to next period's value, we presume that participants in labour markets form their inflation expectations adaptively. Labour markets and goods markets are seen as behaving differently from financial markets. In the latter, because of the sophistication of participants and low transactions costs, prices reflect all available information, while in the former price stickiness and adaptive expectations are the rule.[13] The equations embody the natural rate hypothesis, and there is a vertical long run Phillips curve, though this is not strictly the case for INTERLINK itself.

Equations (6) and (9) are standard transactions demand for money equations renormalized on the nominal interest rate. The parameters f_1 and f_1^* are interest semi-elasticities of money demand (with positive sign), and f_2 and f_2^* are income elasticities. An equation similar to (6) appears in INTERLINK for each of the countries with financial blocks.[14] However, a different aggregate is modelled, depending on the country, and for some countries a simple specification such as (6) or (9) is not adequate. In particular, if a broad aggregate is chosen as being most relevant to the country in question, then the demand function might well include wealth as an argument, as well as an own-rate of interest. Equations (6) and (9) are more appropriate for a narrowly-defined monetary aggregate.

The last three equations are simply identical aggregate demand, inflation and interest rate equations for the foreign countries treated as a group. For these countries, the effective exchange rate, in logs, is simply the negative of the rate for the home country. Similarly, their current balance is the negative of the latter's. The two-country model is thus perfectly symmetric. In particular, if the parameters are identical for the domestic and foreign countries (and hence also $b_2 = -b_3$), then it can easily be verified that the model can be transformed into a set of equations explaining the exchange rate, the current balance, and deviations between domestic and foreign output, prices, and interest rates as functions of relative money supplies and relative government spending. As is shown below, such a relationship among the parameters does not prevail, however.

Now consider the long-run properties of the model, when expectations are realized and all variables settle down to constant rates of growth, or, as in the case of interest rates, inflation rates, and net claims divided by world wealth, constant values. It is assumed that the money supply grows at some constant rate for the home country and a possibly different, but constant, rate for the foreign country. Capacity output, which is exogenous in the model but in principle depends on the size of the labour force, is assumed to grow at rate g in both countries. This same growth rate is also assumed to apply to world wealth and government spending in the two countries.

Now the real exchange rate is constant in steady state, so the nominal exchange rate rises to the extent that foreign inflation exceeds domestic inflation,

$$e - e(-1) = \pi^* - \pi \tag{17}$$

From (1) then, provided $a_1 = 1$ (as it should be in principle for an annual model), the real interest rate at home will be lower than that abroad to the extent that net claims on foreigners exceed some 'normal' level (captured by the constant term a_0):

$$(R - \pi) = (R^* - \pi^*) - a_2 NFA - a_0 \tag{18}$$

The equilibrium levels of net claims on foreigners (NFA) and of the real exchange rate, $(e + p - p^*)$, come from the conditions for external and internal balance. Equations (2) and (3), and the condition that net claims divided by world wealth are constant in steady state, imply a relationship between the two variables of interest that must hold for a sustainable balance of payments position:

$$r(1 - b_4)NFA = -b_0 - b_1(e + p - p^*) - b_2 y - b_3 y^* \tag{19}$$

The last two variables, y and y^*, are zero in steady state. The sign of $(1 - b_4)$ is positive as b_4 is the sum of the two countries' marginal propensities to import. It captures the partial offset on the trade balance resulting from the home country spending some of its foreign interest earnings abroad, as well as effects, with opposite sign, on foreign spending. Hence, equation (19) implies that for given values of domestic and foreign income, a higher real exchange rate must be accompanied by higher net foreign assets (b_1 is negative), because a lower trade balance must be offset by higher interest receipts, unless either the interest rate minus the growth of world wealth (r) is zero or the sum of marginal propensities to import (b_4) equals unity.[15]

Similarly, equation (4) and the condition that actual output must equal potential output in the two countries gives a relationship between the real exchange rate and net foreign assets that must hold for internal balance. It depends only on exogenous variables, after the two real interest rates in (18) have been replaced by their determinants using the two countries' aggreate demand equations, (4) and (7), with y, y^* equal to zero. This yields

$$(c_3/c_1 + c_3^*/c_1^* - a_2)NFA = -(c_4/c_1 + c_4^*/c_1^*)(e + p - p^*)$$
$$- (c_2/c_1)\,gov + (c_2^*/c_1^*)gov^* \qquad (20)$$

(The constant term has been omitted.) This is a positive relationship between the level of net claims and the real exchange rate, c_1 and c_4 being negative in both countries. It captures the effect of higher government spending at home leading, via higher real interest rates, either to a higher real exchange rate or lower net foreign claims, or some combination of the two. The opposite effect occurs when foreign government spending increases.

Equations (19) and (20), describing long-run equilibrium, can be written more compactly as follows:

$$e + p - p^* = B(NFA) \qquad (19')$$

$$e + p - p^* = Y(NFA, gov, gov^*) \qquad (20')$$

The signs of the partial derivatives are Y_2, $Y_2 > 0$, $Y_3 < 0$. As mentioned above, the derivative of B is ambiguous. If the expenditure effects of higher net claims worsen the current balance more than the resulting interest earnings improve it, then it could be downward sloping in $(NFA, e + p - p^*)$ space, It should be possible to rule out this case, as it implies propensities to spend on imports summing to more than unity. Figure 1 plots likely positions for the two curves, where what is termed here the BB curve, corresponding to equation (19') is positively sloped, but less steep than the YY curve corresponding to equation (20'). In such a case, an increase in government spending at home has the long-run effect of raising both the real exchange rate and foreign claims. It is also possible to have a BB curve that is steeper than the YY curve, and where a government spending increase lowers both the real exchange rate and net claims on foreigners. This could happen if the home country's output were very little affected by the home real interest rate, but greatly affected by the real exchange rate. A government spending increase would produce little real exchange rate movement but would open up a large positive real interest

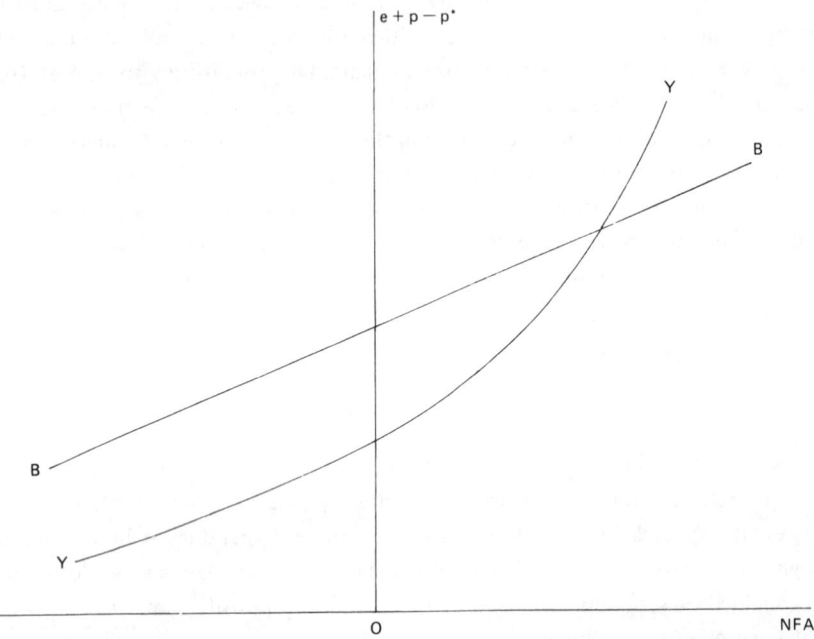

Figure 1. Long-run equilibrium of real exchange rate and net foreign claims

rate gap with respect to the foreign country, which would be consistent with portfolio balance only if foreigners acquired a large stock of claims on the home country.

The determination of the other endogenous variables is straightforward. The price level is determined by the condition that money supply equals money demand [equations (6) and (9)] because the home interest rate R has already been determined by financial arbitrage, and income is equal to its potential level. Given the two price levels and the real exchange rate, the nominal exchange rate is also determined. The inflation rate is just equal to the rate of money growth minus $f_2 g$, as can be seen from differentiating equation (6). A similar relationship holds for the foreign country.

4. QUANTIFICATION OF THE MINI-MODEL

The derivation of parameter values for the mini-model described in the previous section is considered next, along with a number of related practical issues. At the prototype stage the empirical analysis has been confined to a single case, one where the United States is treated as the 'home' country with the 'Rest of the World' aggregated as single group. It should be noted that the latter group is in fact made up of models which fall into two distinct classes within the INTERLINK system — those for OECD countries, which include full domestic income-expenditure equations and those for non-OECD regions which are semi-reduced form trade equations, with imports determined essentially as a function of export earnings. For the purpose of simulation analysis the non-OECD group was allowed to operate fully as an integral part of the 'Rest of the World' although the variables corresponding to domestic income, inflation and real interest rate are defined wholly in terms of OECD countries less the United States.

For several equations — those for the exchange rate and interest rates — the mini-model specifications for the United States are consistent with those already contained within the INTERLINK financial blocks (FINLINK) so that, subject to appropriate measurement conventions, parameter values can be directly taken from the existing equations.[16] For the more aggregative items — trade balances, output and inflation — a series of partial model simulations was carried out over a period of 5 years for each equation, shocking in turn each of the respective independent variables, whilst holding the remaining independent variables constant. Given the structure of the INTERLINK system, in particular its international consistency properties, this proved to be a relatively straightforward process. Solved in linkage mode any combination of countries or variables can be fully or partially exogenised without interfering with the cross-country consistency of results. With appropriate choice of exogenisation for unwanted feedbacks, therefore, it was possible to administer separate controlled shocks for each independent variable in turn, on the United States and the 'Rest of the World' models, with the latter treated as a cohesive group (referred to as ROW in what follows).

Before discussing the quantified system in any detail a word about model dynamics is in order. The model characterised in Table 1 is clearly abbreviated in terms of dynamics compared with the average quarterly or semi-annual macro-econometric model. In practice many of the influences summarised in the model are expected to have their effects distributed over time and this is no less the case for the INTERLINK model. The influence of competitiveness, for example, on demand and the trade balance (c_4 and b_1) will reflect a combination of distributed lag functions contained in the trade equations, which have a maximum lag of up to 3 years. The dynamics of the consumption and investment equations are equally important with the influence of interest rate changes being relatively slow to feed through for some countries. In the context of the rational expectations solution for the system, described later in section 5, the presence of extended lags in the system can pose problems. The complexity of the solution and its programing requirements increase directly with the number of variables defined in the system which, expressed as it is in first-order linear dynamic form, is required to contain additional 'state' variables for each lagged term included. To constrain the problem within manageable proportions the dynamics of the system have been summarised as parisomiously as possible using, where necessary, rational lag approximations to the various lag distributions in the system. In effect, where significant dynamics were present in the INTERLINK simulation results these were subsequently modelled in transfer function form with numerator and denominator terms of up to second order, by applying normal estimation techniques to the actual simulation results.[17] That this method was found to be reasonably robust reflects the relatively low order dynamics present in a semi-annual model of this type, compared with one of greater frequency.

Table 2 sets out the overall results for the summary two country model after taking account of individual variable dynamics. In writing the model down, we found

Table 2. The coefficients of a two-country model, of the United States and the Rest of the World.*

(1)	e	$= e(+ 1) + 0.5(R - R^*) + 0.0006395$ NFA
(2)	NFA(+ 1)	$= 1.00$ NFA $- 0.04121$ COMP $+ 0.1125$ $y^* - 0.18625$ y
(3)	COMP(+ 1)	$= 0.8560$ COMP $- 0.2151$ COMP($- 1$)
		$- 1.5772(e(+ 1) + p(+ 1) - p^*(+ 1)) + 1.9362$
		$(e + p - p^*)$
(4)	y	$= -0.25$RR$(+ 1) + 0.285$gov $+ 0.1265$NFA
		$- 0.1274$TT$(+ 1) + 0.1575y^*$
(5)	RR(+ 1)	$= 1.30$RR $- 0.42$RR($- 1$) $+ 0.12(R - 2^*$INHAT$(+ 1))$
(6)	TT(+ 1)	$= -1.4127$ TT $- 0.6572$TT($- 1$) $+ 0.2445(e + p - p^*)$
(7)	IN	$=$ INHAT$(+ 1) + 0.1029$y
(8)	INHAT(+ 1)	$=$ INHAT $+ 0.0769($IN-INHAT$)$
(9)	m $-$ p	$= 0.114$y $- 0.428$R $+ 0.806(m(- 1) - p + IN)$
(10)	y^*	$= -0.2687$RR$^*(+ 1) + 0.285$gov$^* - 0.00765$NFA
		$+ 0.1244$TT$^*(+ 1) + 0.1400$y
(11)	RR*(+ 1)	$= 1.1023$RR$^* - 0.2225$RR$^*(- 1)$
		$+ 0.1202(R^* - 2^*$INHAT$^*(+ 1))$
(12)	TT*(+ 1)	$= 1.1941$TT$^* - 0.4473$TT$^*(- 1) + 0.2532(e + p - p^*)$
(13)	IN*.	$=$ INHAT$^*(+ 1) + 0.1026y^*$
(14)	INHAT*(+ 1)	$=$ INHAT$^* + 0.3438($IN*-INHAT$^*)$
(15)	$m^* - p^*$	$= 0.3555y^* - 0.6606R^* + 0.6917(m^*(- 1) - p^* + IN^*)$

*For information on the definitions of variables, see the Appendix.

it convenient to use additional, synthetic variables for the rational lag functions. This way of writing the model accords with the state space representation necessary for finding its rational expectations solution, as described below, except that for that purpose further variables are also necessary when a rational lag polynomial exceeds first order. The rational lag functions reported in Table 2 are applied to the real exchange rate (or the terms of trade — in this model the two are the same since traded and non-traded goods are not distinguished) and to real interest rates at home and abroad. The real exchange rate variables are labelled COMP, TT and TT*; three are necessary because the lagged response to the real exchange rate differs for the current account, domestic output and foreign activity respectively. The lagged functions of real interest rates are labelled RR and RR*, for real rate effects on output in the two countries. In each case the rational lag variables are written in such a way that in the long run they take on the value of their driving variable, whether the real exchange rate or the real interest rate. (The reader can verify that the sum of the coefficients on the right-hand side of each of these equations is unity.) Consequently, the coefficients applied to these variables, where they appear in Table 2, correspond to long-run effects of the real exchange rate or the real interest rate. For instance, the long-run effect of 1% increase in the real exchange rate is a decine in the United States current balance (divided by world wealth, and multiplied by 1000) of 4.1%.

Constant terms are omitted from all the equations. The expected exchange rate equation is to be used in counter-factual simulation, not for forecasing. The constant term would be calculated such that a base case value was replicated. Similarly, trend output has been omitted from the money demand equation. Changes in m and m* are to be taken relative to a value that allows for real growth.

Equation (1) in Table 2 is taken directly from Financial INTERLINK. The coefficient estimated there for the interest differential was insignificantly different from 1.0, as expected; since here R and R^* are at annual rates but the time period is semi-annual, the coefficient was divided by two. A similar adjustment has been made in the calculation of real interest rates in equations (5) and (11).

Equation (2) summarizes current balance responses to relative prices and activity at home and abroad and was obtained by partial simulations of INTERLINK. The lagged response to competitiveness was best captured by the rational lag reported in equation (3). There is a strong J-curve effect, as evidence by the large negative coefficient on current relative prices in (3). The unit coefficient applied to NFA in (2) reflects the imposed value for b_4 of 1. The reason for this is discussed below. Equation (2) embodies some asymmetry in the effects of home and foreign activity, with the United States variable having a larger effect on its current account. To some extent this may simply be the result of the relative size of GDP in the United States and in the 'Rest of the World'. Simulations of INTERLINK produced a response of the current balance that was nearly complete in the current half-year, and hence lags were not needed here.

The aggregate demand equation (4) for the United States, and its counterpart for the ROW, equation (10), explain deviations of GDP from its potential level by real interest rates, real government spending, net foreign assets, competitiveness and foreign output. Real interest rates and competitiveness produced lagged responses of GDP and are modelled as rational lags.

In equation (10), the parameters of the rational lag were actually obtained by OLS fitting of the model to simulation results. For the United States, however, this method produced implausible long-run effects of real rates on y, and the rational lag was manually fitted to the simulation output. The simulation response of output to changes in real rates gave quite similar long-run results for the two countries but the initial effects were somewhat larger for the United States. Other variables also have similar coefficients, except NFA. Indeed, the government spending variable produced exactly the same effect for the two countries, when averaged over 4 half-years. Since all other variables in equations (4) and (10) are in logs or are rates of return, except NFA, the coefficient of the latter may well differ because of the relative size of the two countries. As for lags, all shocks to the variables appearing in equations (4) and (10) produced some dynamic response in INTERLINK, no doubt resulting from the interaction of multiplier and accelerator, as well as other factors. However, fluctuations were quite small compared to their ultimate effect, and only real interest rates and competitiveness exhibited a long, slow build-up of response.

The coefficients in equations (7) and (8) were derived by shocking domestic activity and observing lagged effects on prices. As mentioned above, a vertical long-run Phillips curve of this type does not appear in INTERLINK itself; however, such a simple model does fit the simulation results quite well. Both USA and ROW equations have quite similar impact coefficients, but the speed of adjustment of expectations to actual inflation is substantially higher in the latter.

The demand for money functions, equations (9) and (15), are inverted to endogenize the interest rates R and R^*. The United States equation was obtained directly, for the M1 aggregate, using data over the period 1973Q2 to 1983Q1; the coefficients were then converted to their rough semi-annual equivalents by squaring the adjustment parameter. For the ROW, coefficients were obtained by aggregating demand for money functions for individual countries, in particular for the remaining six biggest countries in the OECD. The coefficients were averaged using as weights those that serve for calculating the effective exchange rate for the United States, though here the weights were rescaled to sum to unity over these six countries. Thus the resulting demand for money function, equation (15), mimics the demand for a weighted average monetary aggregate for the six countries, provided their income, prices and interest rates move together. This equation is further assumed to describe how the interest rates of the remaining countries of the world would respond to income and price fluctuations; hence the variables that appear in the equation apply to an aggregate of all countries, excluding the United States.

As the above description no doubt suggests, the assumptions behind the use of (14) to describe the demand for money function for the rest of the world are heroic. The reader should keep in mind, however, that the purpose here is not to try to model realistically the world demand for money, or even to construct a proper measure of world monetary expansion, but rather to construct a feedback rule for interest rates, if the authorities did strictly target some monetary aggregate. What is assumed here, somewhat arbitrarily, is that the smaller countries follow the big countries in moving their rates. As it is, the variable m^*, if data for it were to be calculated, is a hybrid, as it is comprised of a different component aggregate for each of the big seven countries, chosen on the basis both of the stability of its demand function and its relevance for official targets. The aggreagates chosen are the following: Japan, M2; Germany, M3; France, M2; United Kingdom, M1; Italy, M2; and Canada, M1. Trend output has been omitted from the equation (compare Tables 1 and 2): it is netted out from the exogenous money supply variable, for both USA and ROW.

The form of the money demand equation, and especially its interest ealsticity, is quite important for the dynamics of the model. Since the money supply is exogenous, inflation shocks induce movements in the same direction of nominal interest rates to prevent money demand from rising. However, if the interest elasticity is too high, the nominal interest rate does not match the rise in inflation, and real interest rates fall, leading to an expansion in output, and, via the Phillips curve, to a further increase in inflation. The potential for instability is evident, and, in fact, an early version of thc mini-model incorporated a money demand equation that implied a pair of complex unstable roots corresponding to this interaction of money demand and the Phillips curve. The values for the coefficients in Table 2 do not imply instability, however.

5. CALCULATING THE RATIONAL EXPECTATIONS SOLUTION FOR THE EXPECTED EXCHANGE RATE

The method of solution of the mini-model under the assumption of rational expectations is due to Blanchard and Kahn.[18] The model is first written as a matrix equation for the state variables, partitioned such that endogenous variables that are predetermined are distinguished from those which are functions of contemporaneous expectations of future endogenous and/or exogenous variables.[19] The non-predetermined variable set, in this model, includes only the current value of the exchange rate.

Specifically, the model must first be written in the following form:

$$
\begin{bmatrix} X_{t+1} \\ {}_tP_{t+1} \end{bmatrix} = A \begin{bmatrix} X_t \\ P_t \end{bmatrix} + \gamma Z_t
\tag{21}
$$

where X_{t+1} is an n-vector of predetermined endogenous variables, ${}_tP_{t+1}$ is an m-vector of agents' expectations of the non-predetermined endogenous variables, held at t for period $t + 1$, and Z_t is a k-vector of exogenous variables. A and γ are matrices of constant coefficients. In the model, $m = 1$, and P equals e, the logarithm of the effective exchange rate.

The rational expectations solution to the model given by (21) requires that

$$
{}_tP_{t+1} = E(P_{t+1} \mid \Omega_t)
$$

that is, agent's expectations are identical to the mathematical expectations of the model, given their information set Ω_t. Ω_t includes at least past and current values of X, P and Z, and may include future values of the exogenous variables as well. A condition for a solution to exist is that exogenous variables must not grow too fast; exponential growth is ruled out. Because the exogenous variables are in log form, they grow arithmetically, not exponentially, in steady state. The rational expectations solution is subject to two boundary conditions. For the predetermined variables the boundary condition is that these variables are equal to their initial values. For the non-predetermined variable, there is a terminal or transversality condition that forces it to remain bounded at all times and the system to converge to a steady state.

The solution for predetermined and non-predetermined variables, for all future periods, is given in Blanchard and Kahn. It will not be repeated here. What is of interest here is the solution for the sole non-predetermined variable, the log of the exchange rate, for the following period. If the present — that is, the time when expectations are formed — is period 0, then what is wanted is the solution for $t = 1$. On the assumption that there are as many unstable eigenvalues as non-predetermined variables, but no more, this solution will be as follows:[20]

$$
\begin{aligned}
e_1 = {} & -B_{21}(B_{11}^{-1}B_{12} - J_1 B_{11}^{-1} B_{12} J_2^{-1}) \\[6pt]
& \times \sum_{i=0}^{\infty} J_2^{-i}(C_{21}\gamma_1 + C_{22}\gamma_2)E(Z_{+i} \mid \Omega_0) \\[6pt]
& - \sum_{i=0}^{\infty} C_{22}^{-1} J_2^{-i-1}(C_{21}\gamma_1 + C_{22}\gamma_2)E(Z_{1+i} \mid \Omega_1) \\[6pt]
& + B_{21}B_{11}^{-1}\gamma_1 Z_0 + B_{21}J_1 B_{11}^{-1} X_0
\end{aligned}
\tag{22}
$$

The solution of the model for the exchange rate next period will depend on initial values of the predetermined variables (X_0) and of the exogenous variables (Z_0), and on expectations of future values of these exogenous variables held currently and in the next period. The weights to be applied to these variables are complicated functions of the model parameters, as described below.

The matrices J and C are the result of transforming A into Jordan canonical form:

$$A = C^{-1}JC \tag{23}$$

where J is a diagonal matrix of eigenvalues and C is a matrix of corresponding eigenvectors. J is partitioned so that the stable eigenvalues appear in J_1, and the one unstable eigenvalue in J_2

$$J = \begin{bmatrix} J_1 & 0 \\ 0 & J_2 \end{bmatrix}$$

As noted above it is assumed that there is only one eigenvalue outside the unit circle: this is verified below for this model. By implication, then, the number of stable eigenvalues corresponds to the number of predetermined variables (let this number be n). The matrices, C, C^{-1} and γ are partitioned conformably:

$$C = \begin{bmatrix} C_{11} & C_{12} \\ C_{21} & C_{22} \end{bmatrix}, \qquad C^{-1} = \begin{bmatrix} B_{11} & B_{11} \\ B_{21} & B_{22} \end{bmatrix}$$

$$\gamma = \begin{bmatrix} \gamma_1 \\ \gamma_2 \end{bmatrix}$$

The dimensions of these submatrices are as follows: C_{11} (n × n), C_{12} (n × 1), C_{21} (1 × n) and C_{22} (1 × 1); B_{ij} the same as C_{ij}; and γ_1 (n × k), γ_2 (1 × k).

Equation (22) is a quite general form that allows any future path for the exogenous variables, and does not require the information set at time 1 to be the same as that at time zero. Therefore exchange market participants may well find their anticipations falsified by subsequent news. In the first implementation of the model, however, its generality was deliberately limited thereby simplifying the calculations. In the context of a forecast, it seems reasonable to give investors in the exchange market the same information as has the forecaster himself. If the forecaster now expects some change in exogenous variables to occur later in the forecast, then it will not be a surprise for him when it does occur. There is similarly no reason to think that the exchange market participant will be surprised by these developments either, unless the forecaster considers himself to have superior divining powers. So the first simplification imposed on the simulation is that the information set available next period is the same as available now, and both include the subsequently realized values of the exogenous variables, Z_{+i}. The second simplification concerns the way of describing the future paths of exogenous variables. Any arbitrary values for the first four periods of the forecast are allowable; from then on, however, exogenous variables must grow at a constant growth rate (which may be zero): because variables are in logs, growth is arithmetic. The choice of four periods coincides with the forecast horizon: the semi-annual forecast made at OECD looks ahead 4 half-years, and data on exogenous variables therefore exist for that period. Asking area specialists to specify constant growth rates for those variables from then on is not too demanding.

The two assumptions mentioned above allow a considerable simplification of equation (22) and elimination of the infinite sums. First define new coefficient matrices for notational simplicity. Let

$$R_1 = C_{21}\gamma_1 + C_{22}\gamma_2$$

$$R_2 = B_{21}(B_{11}^{-1}B_{12} - J_1 B_{11}^{-1}B_{12}J_2^{-1})R_1$$

$$R_3 = C_{22}^{-1}R_1$$

$$R_4 = B_{21}B_{11}^{-1}\gamma_1$$

$$R_5 = B_{21}J_1 B_{11}^{-1}$$

Further, replace the expectation of Z_{+i}, whether held at time 0 or 1, by the variable itself. Then (22) can be rewritten as

$$e_1 = (R_4 - R_2)Z_0 - (R_2 + R_3) \sum_{i=1}^{\infty} J_2^{-i}Z_i + R_5 X_0 \qquad (24)$$

If, further, we specify that

$$Z_t = Z_{t-1} + g \quad \text{for} \quad t = 4, 5, \ldots \qquad (25)$$

where g is a k-vector of arithmetic growth rates, then (24) can be written solely as a function of the variables Z_0, Z_1, Z_2, Z_3, g and Z_0:

$$e_1 = (R_4 - R_2)Z_0$$

$$- (R_2 + R_3)J_2^{-1}Z_1$$

$$- (R_2 + R_3)J_2^{-2}Z_2$$

$$- (R_2 + R_3)[J_2^{-2}/(J_2 - 1)]Z_3$$

$$- (R_2 + R_3)[J_2^{-2}/(J_2 - 1)^2]g + R_5 X_0 \qquad (26)$$

The coefficients in (26) can be calculated as described above. The discount factor

J_2 is a real scalar that is greater than 1 in absolute value, and is equal to the unique unstable eigenvalue of the A matrix. The individual matrices that appear in equation (22) can be complex, though the final results of the calculations that appear in equation (26) are necessarily real. A program has been written in the RAL language to manipulate the matrices of complex numbers and to calculate the coefficients of (26).

The eigenvalues for the model presented in Table 2 are given below in Table 3. There is only one unstable root, corresponding to the non-predetermined, 'jump' variable, the exchange rate. Its size means that the future is discounted at a fairly high rate (12% per half year or a 25% annual rate), so the distant future is not very important. Depending on the values of a_2, b_1, b_4, c_3 and c_3^* (see Table 1), there can be a real root slightly greater than 1.0 corresponding to the accumulation of net claims on foreigners. Though we have not proved it formally, it seems likely that the conditions discussed in Section 3 for the YY curve to be steeper than the BB curve must hold for this source of instability to be absent. Given the small effects of NFA on e and on y and y^*, for this to be so, with a value of r of 0.01, b_4 must be quite close ot unity. It is in fact set to that value, giving a horizontal BB curve. Thus the real exchange rate is unaffected, in the long run, by the levels of exogenous variables.

Table 4 presents the expected exchange rate equation in the form of equation (26). Interestingly enough, the coefficients on home and foreign variables are almost equal in magnitude and opposite in sign. This is an indication of the degree of symmetry between the two countries.

The coefficients indicate a very strong impact of the exogenous policy variables, in particular of money supply levels and expected growth rates. A 1% permanent level change in the United States money supply starting three periods hence would cause an 1.7% lower level to be expected for the exchange rate next period. (Hence

Table 3. Eigenvalues for USA — Rest of World model.

Root	Modulus (if complex)
1.1212	
0.9965	
0.9904 ± 0.0420i	0.9913
0.9626 ± 0.0933i	0.9671
0.6994 ± 0.3985i	0.8050
0.8028	
0.5878 ± 0.3022i	0.6610
0.6439 ± 0.0501i	0.6458
0.4286 ± 0.1779i	0.4641
0.2688	

Table 4. The Coefficients of the expected exchange rate equation E(+ 1), assuming constant growth in exogenous variables starting three periods hence.

State variables		Exogenous variables	
Variable	Coefficient	Variable	Coefficient
NFA	0.0800	gov	0.1516
COMP	−0.0078	gov(+ 1)	0.0669
COMP(− 1)	0.0015	gov(+ 2)	0.0597
RR	−0.2805	gov(+ 3)	0.4924
RR(− 1)	0.1362	gov*	−0.1027
TT	−0.0677	gov*(+ 1)	−0.1791
TT(− 1)	0.0663	gov*(+ 2)	−1.1597
INHAT	13.0288	gov*(+ 3)	−1.3776
P	0.4660	m(− 1)	−0.1708
RR*	0.7806	m	0.8888
RR*(− 1)	−0.1967	m(+ 1)	−0.2361
TT*	−0.1885	m(+ 2)	−0.2106
TT*(− 1)	0.1156	m(+ 3)	−1.7373
INHAT*	−8.5338	m*(− 1)	0.1654
P*	−0.2002	m*	−0.5482
		m*(+ 1)	0.1711
		m*(+ 2)	0.1526
		m*(+ 3)	1.2592
		subsequent growth in:	
		m	−14.3329
		m*	10.3885

also a large change in *today's* exchange rate). If the permanent change occurs in period t + 1, the effect is larger, roughly 2.2%. The size of the effect on next period's rate indicates the degree of overshooting in the model resulting from price stickiness, as the long-run effect of a level shift in money is a one-for-one depreciation of the currency (see Table 5). A contemporaneous one-shot change in money tends to appreciate the exchange rate. This counter-intuitive result comes about for the following reason. The money increase lowers interest rates this period, and since this change in relative rates of return on domestic and foreign assets is anticipated, it must be compensated by an expected *appreciation* of the currency. However, since money demand adjusts with a lag, money demand will be higher next period, while the money supply will return to its normal level. These effects combine to give higher interest rates next period, hence a depreciation from period 1 to period 2, and by an amount that requires E(+ 1) to be higher than in the base case.

A comparison of the short-run and long-run effects of government spending in Tables 4 and 5 also shows the danger of forming expectations on the basis of steady state results and assuming that the exchange rate will move smoothly to the long

Table 5. Long-run effects of exogenous variables.

Endogenous variable	Exogenous variable			
	gov	m	gov*	m*
NFA	−14.1880	0	13.2006	0
$(e + p - p^*)$	0	0	0	0
$(R - IN)$	0.4221	0	0.6680	0
$(R^* - IN^*)$	0.4039	0	0.6848	0
P	0.9312	1	1.4736	0
P*	0.8655	0	1.4674	1
e	−0.0657	−1	−0.0062	1

run. Here the signs of short- and long-run effects are opposite for the United States. The mechanism is quite straightforward. In the long run the increased government spending leads to a decumulation of net foreign claims and an increase in the price level. In the short run, however, its effect falls mainly on output. Higher output raises the domestic interest rate and appreciates the currency in the short run, given the monetary target.

The coefficients applied to the state variables in Table 4 are also instructive. Given the persistence in asset stock behaviour, the higher the net foreign claims variable is now, the higher one expects the exchange rate to be next period. For the real interest and exchange-rate variables, current and lagged values have opposite coefficients, reflecting the complicated dynamics. The inflation and price level variables seem at first sight to have perverse signs. However, they capture some of the effects of the nominal interest rates, which are not themselves state variables. For given money supply, a higher price level implies higher rates, *ceteris paribus*. Similarly, high inflation rates now, because of inertia, will imply high inflation rates for some time to come and continuing pressure on money demand, leading to higher interest rates.

6. CONCLUDING REMARKS

The results are only preliminary, and are available for only one exchange rate, the United States effective rate. Work on other big-seven countries is underway. Nevertheless, the United States results have shown the feasibility of the method, and coefficient values indicate that simple adaptation to long-run effects is not a realistic exchange-rate forecasting tool.

76

NOTES

1) Among the latter are Patrick Minford, 'A Rational Expectations Model of the United Kingdom under Fixed and Floating Exchange Rates', in K. Brunner and A.H. Meltzer, eds., *On the State of Macro-Economics* (Amsterdam: North-Holland, 1980) and John Taylor, 'Estimation and Control of a Macroeconomic Model with Rational Expectations', *Econometrica*, September 1979.

2) A.A. Walters, 'Consistent Expectations, Distributed Lags, and the Quantity Theory', *Economic Journal*, June 1971.

3) Some examples include: Paul Anderson, 'Rational Expectations Forecasts from Nonrational Models', *Journal of Monetary Economics*, January 1979, and Peter Spencer 'The Effect of Oil Discoveries on the British Economy – Theoretical Ambiguities and the Consistent Expectations Simulation Approach', mimeo.

4) Olivier Jean Blanchard and Charles M. Kahn, 'The Solution of Linear Difference Models under Rational Expectations', *Econometrica*, July 1980.

5) Earlier versions of the model have been described in various Occasional Studies accompanying the OECD *Economic Outlook*. See 'The OECD International Linkage Model', January 1979; 'Fiscal Policy Simulation with the OECD International Linkage Model', July 1980; 'International Economic Linkages', November 1983, and 'The OECD Interlink System', forthcoming.

6) Described in a forthcoming OECD Department of Economics and Statistics Discussion Paper, 'Financial Interlink'.

7) In the absence of official intervention, which changes the prive sector's holdings of net claims.

8) See Jacques Artus, 'Exchange Rate Stability and Managed Floating: The Experience of the Federal Republic of Germany', *IMF Staff Papers*, July 1976.

9) There is an extensive literature on purchasing-power-parity. For a survey see Lawrence Officer, 'The Purchasing-Power-Parity Theory of Exchange Rates: A Review Article', *IMF Staff Papers*, March 1976.

10) See Rudiger Dornbusch and Paul Krugman, 'Flexible Exchange Rates in the Short Run', *Brookings Papers on Economic Activity* 3: 1976, and Peter isard, 'How Far Can we Push the 'Law of one Price'?', *American Economic Review*, December 1977.

11) Peter Hooper and John Morton, 'Fluctuations in the Dollar: A Model of Nominal and Real Exchange Rate Determination', *Journal of International Money and Finance*, April 1982.

12) The use of scaled-down versions of macroeconomic models –called 'maquettes' – in order to understand their properties has been proposed, in another context, by Michel Deleau, Pierre Malgrange and Pierre-Alain Muet, 'Une maquette representative des modeles macroeconomiques', *Annales de l'INSEE*, No. 42-1981, pp. 53–92. A recent application in the context of policy control is described by David Vines, Jan Maciejowski and James E. Meade in *Stagflation, Vol. 2 – Demand Management*, London, Allen and Unwin, 1983.

13) This distinction is quite common in the literature. See, for instance, William Poole, 'Rational Expectations in the Macro Model', *Brookings Papers on Economic Activity*, 2:1976. For an open economy model similar to this one, but does not account for net claims on foreigners, see Willem Buiter and Marcus Miller, 'Monetary Policy and International Competitiveness: The Problems of Adjustment', *Oxford Economic Papers*, July 1981.

14) See 'Demand for Money in Major OECD Countries', OECD *Economic Outlook*, Occasional Studies, January 1979.

15) Provided the effects on r, which is a parameter, are ignored. Otherwise the results are ambiguous, and depend on whether the contry is a net creditor or debtor.

16) Although the FINLINK capital flow system is defined on a consistent world basis only the exchange rates of 17 main OECD economies matter for this portfolio allocation.

17) A more sophisticated approach adopted for a non-linear economic model is described in Jan Macjiewski and David Vines, 'The Design and Performance of a Multivariable Macro-economic Regulator' *Proceedings of IEEE Conference on Applications of Adaptive and Multivariate Control*, Hull, United Kingdom, July 1982.

18) See Blanchard and Kahn, *op. cit.*

19) For a rigorous discussion of the distinction, see Willem Buiter, 'Predetermined and Non-predetermined Varaibles in Rational Expectations Models', *Economics Letters* 10(1982), pp. 44–54.

20) Blanchard and Kahn, *op. cit.*, p. 1308, equation (5) evaluated at t O 1.

APPENDIX

Definition of variables in Table 2

Endogenous variables

e   = the log of the effective exchange rate
NFA   = net foreign assets divided by world wealth (the latter divided by 1000)
COMP   = a synthetic competitiveness variable (equals the real exchange rate in the long run): captures J-curve.
y   = log of the ratio of actual GDP to its potential level
RR   = a synthetic variable in output equation (equals the real interest rate in the long run)
TT   = a synthetic variable in output eqation (equals the real exchange rate in the long run)
IN   = semi-annual rate of inflation (change in log of prices)
INHAT   = expected inflation, with expectation formed in previous period
p   = the log of GDP deflator
R   = nominal short-term interest rate, as annual decimal fraction

Exogenous variables

gov   = the ratio of real government spending (CGV) to potential output
m   = the log of the money supply net of real growth of potential output times its money demand coefficient

Note: variables followed by an asterisk refer to the ROW, others to the United States.

CHAPTER 4

THE STERLING-DOLLAR EXCHANGE MARKET 1973–1982: SURPRISES AND EXPECTATIONS

Andy Murfin* and Paul Ormerod**
*London School of Economics, U.K.
**Henley Centre for Forecasting, London, U.K.

1. INTRODUCTION

It is a characteristic of linked systems of national models which are linked only by the trade sector, to have a weak degree of interdependence. Fromm (1979) quotes results from the DESMOS and LINK systems to illustrate this point. Deflationary fiscal and/or monetary policy carried out in any one country, for example, will lead the level of that country's real output to fall. Other things being equal, this implies a lower demand for imports. This is then translated via the trade linkage model into a lower demand for exports of the other countries in the system, with subsequent contractionary effects upon real output in these countries. This latter reduction feeds through the individual country models to trace out the effects on employment, prices, etc. The second round effects are, however, typically small, even for rather large initial shocks to the system.

The aim of this paper is to develop an operational system which allows more direct and more powerful effects of a change in the domestic monetary policy of any of the countries on the economies of other countries in the system, than those which are obtained indirectly from the trade linkage model.

The domestic monetary base of every major Western country is made up of the domestic liabilities of the central banking system, plus international reserves. Interest rates and the domestic liabilities of the central bank are usually determined simultaneously as the monetary authorities attempt to manipulate domestic interest rates and/or the growth rate of some specified monetary aggregate at some desired level. The balance of payments on both current and capital account will respond to the current policy stance, and will in turn affect that stance.

Ideally, monetary linkages should take account of all these linkages between the various economies. A fully specified structural model of current and capital international flows would then trace the effects of a change in the domestic monetary

Artus, P. and Guvenen, O. (eds.): International Macroeconomic Modelling for Policy Decisions.
© 1986. Martinus Nijhoff Publishers, Dordrecht/Boston/Lancaster.
ISBN 90-247-3201-8. Printed in The Netherlands.

policy in any one country, through the economies of the other countries in the system. However, such a solution is very difficult to implement in practice. Apart from any theoretical difficulties which may exist in attempting to specify such a complete structural system in a consistent manner, there are very substantial practical problems and in particular the almost complete absence of data on bi-lateral capital flows.

The underlying model developed in this paper to deal with monetary linkages investigates the role of 'surprises' or 'news' inboth domestic monetary and exchange rate determination. Such models have become increasingly widespread with the advent of the 'monetarist counterrevolution' of the 1970s and 1980s. This issue has been considered in the 'efficient markets' literature, for example Frenkel (1981) who suggests that short run movements in exchange rates are dominated by the effect of unanticipated changes in the relevant exogenous variables.

The paper considers four central issues within the foreign exchange market:

1) the estimation of anticipated and unanticipated variable components through the application of rational expectations;
2) the imposition of non-linear constraints in the estimation of rational expectations within a simultaneous equation model;
3) the role of 'surprises' in the exogenous variables which determine the spot exchange rate (in the model) and the difficulties experienced in attempting such a specification;
4) the role of the forward exchange rate as the implicit market forecast of the spot rate is considered, and in praticular its use as the benchmark from which to measure any 'errors' in the market's anticipation of the future spot rate.

The paper begins with a theoretical specification, first of the 'surprise' element in a general rational expectations model and then of the structural forecasting equations which determine the predicted values of the exogenous variables. The model is complex but it cannot, of course, be taken as a definite representation of 'surprises' model of the exchange rate. It is, however, intended both as a demonstration of the simplicity with which direct non-linear estimation of a simultaneous system can be applied, and as a fairly full and detailed example of a 'surprises' specification. The alternative estimation procedures are then outlined before we proceed to an analysis of the results.

2. THEORETICAL SPECIFICATION

The guiding principle behind a 'surprises' specification of the exchange rate is the explanation of *'errors'* in *forecasts* of exchange rate movements, rather than the *actual* movements themselves. The objective must first be to separate the effects of anticipated and unanticipated movements in the exogenous variables which are presumed to determine movements in the exchange rate. The anticipated and unanticipated movements in the exogenous variables which are presumed to determine movements in the exchange rate. The anticipated and unanticipated components of changes in the exogenous variables should prompt corresponding anticipated and unanticipated fluctuations in the exchange rate.

Following Bean (1982) and, particularly, Hartley (1982), the underlying rational expectations formulation can be written as follows (see also Lucas and Rapping (1969), Hall (1978) and Muellbauer (1982)). Let us assume

S = the level of the spot exchange rate
V = the error in the forecast of the one period ahead spot rate.

The error in the one period ahead spot rate forecast may be written as

$$V_{t+1} = S_{t+1} - E(S_{t+1} | \phi_t) \tag{1}$$

where ϕ_t is information relevant to the price of foreign exchange at time $t + 1$, available at time t, and E indicates the conditional mathematical expectation in accordance with the rational expectations hypothesis (see Muth (1961)). Now let economic theory tell us that

$$S_{t+1} = X_{t+1} B + u_{t+1} \tag{2}$$

where X is a matrix of observations on the variables which are presumed to determine the exchange rate, S_{t+1}. It is then assumed that the X variables follow a stochastic process

$$X = Z\alpha + e \tag{3}$$

where the Z matrix of observations is of past information only. Then from (1) and (2).

$$\begin{aligned} V_{t+1} &= [X_{t+1} - E(X_{t+1} | \phi_t)] \beta + [u_{t+1} - E(u_{t+1} | \phi_t)] \\ &= [X_{t+1} - X_{t+1}^*] \beta + \epsilon_{t+1} \end{aligned} \tag{4}$$

where (following Hartley (1982))

ϵ_{t+1} = vector of errors with $E(\epsilon_{t+1} | \phi_t) = 0$
X_{t+1}^* = matrix of one period ahead optimal forecasts of X

Thus, if expectations are indeed rational then agents will use (3) to form expectations in (4). This gives us the 'surprise' specification

$$V = (X - Z\alpha)\beta + \epsilon \tag{5}$$

so that the 'error' or 'surprise' in the actual (from predicted) exchange rate, V, is determined by the 'error' or 'surprise' in the forecasts of the exogenous variables $(Z - Z\alpha)$, plus a further random error, ϵ.

In terms of estimation, essentially two alternatives are available, both of which were recognised by Bean (1982) and Hartley (1982). The first procedure is to estimate either by non-linear three-stage least squares or non-linear full information maximum likelihood with cross-equation restrictions on the α parameters. The second is to first estimate (3) and then use the resulting error as a data series input into equation (5).

Our concern is to show how easily such a model can be estimated as a system with cross-equation restrictions. In addition, we follow Backus (1982) and allow the data to be of more assistance in determining the final specification, than the theory of equations (1)–(5) above would warrant. In particular, we allow both *predicted* and *actual* values to enter the appropriate equations, rather than the *error* as such. We follow two basic approaches to estimation which can be indicated from an analysis of a simplified version of part of the model.

In the monetary sector, let us presume that interest rates (R) are determined by the *expected* change in the Money Supply $(\overset{o}{M})$. We may then have a two-equation model where

$$\overset{o}{M}_t = \theta_0 + \theta_1 Z_{t-i} \tag{6}$$

$$R_t = \delta_0 + \delta_1 \overset{o}{M}_t^e \tag{7}$$

From the discussion above, it is apparent that we may either estimate (6) by OLS and then use the *fitted* value for $\overset{o}{M}_t$ (*ie* $\overset{o}{M}_t^e$) as an exogenous variable in (7) and estimate that by OLS. A next step might be to estimate (6) and (7) as a system but with no cross-equation restrictions. A further step, however, is to substitute (6) into

$$R_t = \delta_0 + \delta_1(\theta_0 + \theta_1 Z_{t-i}) \tag{8}$$

and then jointly estimate (6) and (8) as a system embodying the non-linear cross-equation restrictions on the parameters. We pursue all three approaches for our model below.

To return to the general specification of equations (1)–(5): if we are to implement this system empirically Hartley (1982) lists our requirements as an observable proxy for $E(S_{t+1}|\phi)$, a theory of exchange rate determination (2) and a forecasting equation (3) for the right-hand side variables in (2).

As regards the observable expected value of the exchange rate, Frenkel and Razin (1980) show that if traders in the forward foreign exchange market are not risk averse, and future prices are known with perfect foresight, or are not correlated with the future level of the exchange rate, then

$$_tF_{t+1} = E(S_{t+1}|\phi_t) \tag{9}$$

where $_tF_{t+1}$ is the one period ahead forward rate at time t. Under these assumptions the forward rate can then be used as an observable proxy for the expected value for the spot rate in the next period.

3. THE STRUCTURE OF THE ECONOMIC MODEL

From the above, it remains for us to specify a theory of exchange rate determination and forecasting equations for the relevant explanatory variables. Our concern is to explain the 'surprises' in the exchange rate movements, where the 'surprise' is the difference between the spot rate of period t and the one period ahead forward rate in the previous period. Empirically, we are seeking an explanation of the 'surprises' in the monthly average sterling-dollar exchange rate, 1972–82. The first 17 months of data are, however, made available for the generation of forecast values of the explanatory varibles and so the exchange rate actually considered is for the period 1973.06–1982.12.

Two channels of influence are examined in the structural economic model: the monetary sector and the current account of the balance of payments. This is such that *actual* and *forecast* values of interest rates and current accounts in the two countries are allowed to feed into the final exchange rate equation. As regards the current account, previous attempts at discerning the impact of 'news' have used exogenous OECD forecasts of current account imbalances as the expected values (Dornbusch (1980)), but this is available only at a six-months frequency. The inclusion of current account variables can be justified by Dornbusch and Fischer (1980) type risk reasons, where the state of a country's current account contains some information regarding future asset flows. In our model a simple expectations generating mechanism for each current account is derived from the data, in which the present value is related to lagged endogenous values and price effects:

$$CA = g(CA_{-i}, p_{-i}, p^f_{-i}) \tag{10}$$

$$CA^f = g^f(CA^f_{-i}, p_{-i}, p^f_{-i}) \tag{11}$$

where CA denotes the current account imbalance in dollar terms, p denotes the consumer price index, and superscript f denotes values for the USA. In many ways, the external account component is the most unreliable section of the model. The original data are notoriously unreliable and also subject to many revisions. Furthermore, they are only available on a quarterly basis and so have been interpolated, using the trade imbalance as the related series (see Edison (1981), Chow and Lin (1971) and Liu (1969)). The Chow and Lin method, which involves a redistribution of the residuals, was adopted. Income variables have not been used as explanatory variables in (10)–(11), since this itself involves further interpolation and 'surprises' in the relevant variables would then seem even more remote and unreliable. This remains an area for further development of the model in both current account and the money supply equations below. A further role for the current account is permitted along traditional lines in which price *changes* are related to the *level* of excess demand (see McCallum (1970)). This implies that it may be the accumulated level of excess demand, as given by the accumulated current account imbalances between the countries, which will determine the change in the spot rate. This sort of variable has been examined previously in the exchange rate literature (see Ormerod and Walshe (1981)).

The model might be described as Keynesian owing to its treatment of the monetary sector. First, the money supply is presumed not to follow a random walk (unlike, for example, Driskill (1981)). Secondly, expected changes in the money supply are seen to feed into interest rates which then feed into the exchange rate. As regards the former point, it is of course very difficult to deny that a variable, such as money supply, does not follow a random walk (see Shiller (1982) for a related discussion). For the rational expectations monetarist, such a proposition derives from their belief that money does not matter unless its stock is changed randomly, while for a Keynesian money matters to the extent that it determines the equilibrium interest rate (see Hahn (1980)). For our purposes, it is assumed that the respective money supplies are not random and that, therefore, a better expectation of next period's money supply (change) can be derived than just using today's value. Furthermore, while our model admits a separation between the effects of anticipated and unanticipated money supply changes (and indeed for other variables), fully anticipated changes are permitted to have *real* effects.

In the monetary sector of the model, *predicted* changes in money supply feed into the *predicted* interested rate equations. These in turn feed into the exchange rate equation. The M1 money supply equations are given as:

$$\Delta_3 M = h(\Delta_3 M_{-i}, p_{-i}, \Delta p_{-i}, M_{-i}, R_{-i}, R^f_{-i},$$
$$\text{Seasonal factors)} \tag{12}$$

$$\Delta_3 M^f = h^f (\Delta_3 M^f_{-i}, p^f_{-i}, \Delta p^f_{-i}, M^f_{-i}, R^f_{-i},$$
$$\text{Seasonal factors)} \tag{13}$$

in obvious notation. These equations are intended to capture money 'supply' adjustment rather than demand or supply in particular. The corresponding interest rate equations are:

$$R = j(\Delta_3 M^*, R_{-i}, R^f_{-i}, S_{-i}, \Delta R_{-i}) \tag{14}$$

$$R^f = j^f(\Delta_3 M^{f*}, R^f_{-i}, S_{-i}, \Delta R^f_{-i}) \tag{15}$$

where * denotes forecast value and S denotes the spot dollar-sterling exchange rate.

It should be noted that lagged values of the US interest rate are allowed to determine both UK and US interest rates and money supply, while UK rates only affect domestic variables. A further estension of the model would be to allow *anticipated* rather than *lagged* US rates to enter the UK interest rate equation, but this is not examined here. These interest rate equations may be interpreted as reaction functions, rather than structural equations, and are intended primarily to model government responses to money supply charges. It should be noted that our expectational variables are all formed *ex post* and no 'multiple viewpoint' approach is feasible within our estimation procedure. For a recent approach to this sort of estimation, see Fair and Taylor (1983). Equations (12)–(15) are estimated in logarithmic form, while the current accounts are left in levels terms. Money supply is examined in quarterly difference terms. The above equations feed into the following equation for the 'surprise' in the spot rate:

$$\ln S_t - \ln_{t-1} F_t = \lambda_0 + \lambda_1 \text{LQBPD} \qquad (16)$$
$$+ \lambda_2 CA_t^{t\,*} + \lambda_7 CA_t^{*}$$
$$+ \lambda_8 (CA^{f\,*} - CA^f)_t$$
$$+ \lambda_9 (CA^{*} - CA)_t$$
$$+ \lambda_3 (\ln S_{t-1} - \ln_{t-2} F_{t-1})$$
$$+ \lambda_4 R_t$$
$$+ \lambda_5 R_t^{f}$$
$$+ \lambda_6 (R_t - R_t^{*})$$
$$+ \lambda_{10} (R_t^{f} - R_t^{f\,*})$$

where $\lambda_0 - \lambda_6$ and $\lambda_7 - \lambda_{10}$ are so numbered only because $\lambda_0 - \lambda_6$ remain significant within the estimated model, and the lagged dependent variable (λ_3) remains, after longer lags proved insignificant and so are omitted. LQBPD is the cumulative sum of the US–UK balance of payments differential.

$$\sum_{i=1}^{\eta} (CA_{t-i}^{f} - CA_{t-i}) \text{ where } \eta \text{ begins at 1972.01.}$$

To close the model, an equation is needed for the forward exchange rate, since the use of $_{t-1}F_t$ as the rational expectation of S_{t+1} has shifted the basis for forecasting onto the forward rate rather than the spot. Arbitrage is presumed to create the link between spot and forward exchange markets, essentially because arbitragers always cover their forward commitments by reverse spot transactions. Following Ormerod (1980) it can be argued that the forward exchange rate will equal the so-called interest-parity spot exchange rate. From Frenkel and Razin (1980), this may be written as:

$$\frac{{}_{t-1}F_t - S_t}{S_t} = \frac{R_t^f - R_t}{1 + R_t} \tag{17}$$

and so

$${}_{t-1}F_t = \left[1 + \frac{(R_t^f - R_t)}{(1 + R_t)}\right] S_t \tag{18}$$

Equation (18) simply says that if US interest rates (R_t^f) were higher than UK rates (R_t), then the dollar would be at a discount against sterling. The forward rate would give more dollars to the pound than would the spot rate. The rationale behind this is that a relatively higher US interest rate is indicative of relatively greater risk attached to the dollar, and as such it is expected to depreciate against sterling.

Under the arbitrage assumption, the forward rate is presumed to equal the interest parity spot rate of equation (18). That is, the net arbitrage demand for forward currency is assumed to be infinitely elastic so as to eradicate any differential between the actual forward rate and the interest parity spot rate. There are a number of reasons why the arbitrage schedule may not be perfectly elastic, however; transactions costs may prevent small differentials from being eradicated; risks other than pure foreign exchange risk may not be covered by arbitragers (e.g. risk of government intervention) (See Ormerod (1980)). Maintaining the assumptions generating (18), however, the model is closed by

$${}_{t-1}F_t = E_0 + E_1 SS_t \tag{19}$$

where SS_t is the interest parity spot rate, with $E_0 = 0$, $E_1 = 1$; this is examined alongside a more general specification

$${}_{t-1}F_t = E_0 + E_1 SS_t + E_2\,{}_{t-2}F_{t-1} + E_3 SS_{t-1} \tag{20}$$

Before we proceed to an examination of the results of the empirical estimation of the model, we shall discuss some simple forward rate equations as the background to the nature of 'surprises'.

4. THE FORWARD RATE

The standard spot-forward rate regression takes the form:

$$S_t = \alpha + b_{t-1}F_t + \epsilon_t \tag{21}$$

(see, for example, Levich (1978), Frenkel (1977)). There have been more sophisticated econometric studies such as Baillie, Lippens and McMahon (1983), but the underlying test of coefficients has remained essentially the same (see also Foster-Smith (1983) and Murfin and Ormerod (1984)). The Frenkel and Razin (1980) result, that this test of forward market efficiency is only strictly valid when individuals are risk neutral and prices are non-stochastic, is well known, while Wyplosz (1980) has argued that the exclusion of risk leads to a systematic bias in the results.

With regard to the 'surprise' elements in our model this problem may have important implications. Under Fisherian expectations, the forward rate is taken to be the optimum forecast of the spot rate of next period. Thus, 'surprises' in the exchange rate are defined as the difference between the actual spot rate and last period's forward rate. Under the simple market efficiency hypothesis, no variables other than the forward rate should be significant determinants of the spot rate. For equation (16) this implies that *no* coefficients on the right-hand side should be statistically significnant. However, the fact that we do obtain some significant coefficients cannot be taken as a rebuttal of the rational expectations hypothesis, merely of this, the simplest version of the efficient markets hypothesis.

With our data for 1973.06–1982.12, the simple spot on forward rates regression is:

$$\ln S_t = 0.0087 + 0.9858 \ln_{t-1} F_t \qquad (22)$$
$$\qquad (0.0129) \ (0.0179)$$

$$R^2 = 0.9639$$

$$DW = 0.9786$$

$$SSR = 0.06775$$

$$LM(12) = 38.76$$
(Standard errors in parentheses)

There is, perhaps unsurprisingly, considerable evidence of dynamic misspecification, both in terms of first and longer order autocorrelation. The traditional hypotheses (from (21)) of $\alpha = 0$, $b = 1$ are accepted, but the overall fit of the equation is poor. (see Breusch and Pagan (1980) for details of the LM test).

It is apparent from earlier work (see Edison (1981) that the forward premia explain little of the actual movements in spot rates. As such equation (22) differs little from the simple regression of one period's spot rate on that of the previous period:

$$\ln S_t = 0.0060 + 0.9861 \ln S_{t-1} \qquad (23)$$
$$\qquad (0.0122) \ (0.0168)$$

$$R^2 = 0.9683$$

$$DW = 1.0679$$

$$SSR = 0.05956$$

The forward rate is preferred to the lagged spot rate on the grounds of Fisherian expectations. An obvious alternative would be to generate an expected spot rate series to replace the forward rate (see Hartley (1982)), but this is not pursued below. In some ways then, the results for equation (16) below might be interpreted as giving a reduced form proxy for the appropriate risk variables omitted from the simple theory (again, see Wyplosz (1980)). It is possible, for example, for the spot rate to deviate consistently from the forward rate, and for this behaviour still to be consistent with rational expectations. If, for example, risks are not normally distributed, this risk may be reflected in the forward rate even though the 'risky event' may not actually occur. If such a risk were associated with sterling, then the forward rate for the dollar against sterling would always be less than the actual spot rate proved to be. Such underprediction might be quite consistent with a fully specified rational expectations model.

5. RESULTS FOR THE FULL MODEL

The model was first estimated by OLS in single equation form to obtain parsimonious, data-determined specifications. The current account, interest rate and money supply equations have been allowed to be broadly data-determined, using general-to-specific estimation techniques. The ordinary least squares results for 1973.06— 1982.12 were (standard errors in parenthesis):

$$CA_t^f = 9.8157 + 1.0295\ CA_{t-1}^f - 0.1485 CA_{t-2}^f \tag{24}$$
$$(37.75)\quad (0.093)\qquad\qquad (0.093)$$

$$R^2 = 0.8058$$

$$DW = 2.0073$$

$$SSR = 0.1858E + 08$$

$$CA_t = 1276.68 + 0.5865 CA_{t-1} + 0.1780 CA_{t-2} + 241.02\ \ln P_{t-1} \tag{25}$$
$$(596.5)\quad (0.093)\qquad\quad (0.091)\qquad\quad (111.6)$$

$$R^2 = 0.6977$$

$$DW = 1.9812$$

$$SSR = 0.1409E + 08$$

$$(\ln M_t - \ln M_{t-3}) = 0.1147 + 0.3389(\ln M_{t-1} - \ln M_{t-4}) - 6.1159 \ln R_{t-1}$$
$$(0.061) \quad (0.089) \qquad\qquad (1.2691)$$
$$+ 0.0200 \ln M_{t-1} + 0.5029(\ln P_{t-1} - \ln P_{t-4})$$
$$(0.007) \qquad\qquad (0.136)$$
$$+ \text{Seasonal Dummies} \qquad\qquad (26)$$

$R^2 = 0.6976$

$DW = 2.0694$

$SSR = 0.3504$

$$(\ln M_t^f - \ln M_{t-3}^f) = -0.0302 + 0.6932(\ln M_{t-1}^f - \ln M_{t-4}^f) - 1.3025 \ln R_{t-1}^f$$
$$(0.019) \quad (0.068) \qquad\qquad (0.385)$$
$$+ 0.0126 \ln P_{t-4}^f + \text{Seasonal Dummies}$$
$$(0.004)$$

$R^2 = 0.6976$

$DW = 1.2781$

$SSR = 0.005374$

$$\ln R_t = -0.0003 + 0.8909 \ln R_{t-1} + 0.0067 \Delta M_t^* + 0.0009 \ln S_{t-1}$$
$$(0.005) \quad (0.043) \qquad (0.003) \qquad (0.003) \qquad (28)$$
$$+ 0.1031 (\ln R_{t-1} - \ln R_{t-4}) + 0.0653 \ln R_{t-1}^f$$
$$(0.049) \qquad\qquad (0.029)$$

$R^2 = 0.8979$

$DW = 1.9918$

$SSR = 0.000045$

$$\ln R_t^f = -0.0003 + 0.8912 \ln R_{t-1}^f + 0.0078 \Delta M_t^{f*} + 0.0013 \ln S_{t-1}$$
$$(0.0006) \quad (0.042) \qquad (0.005) \qquad (0.0008) \qquad (29)$$

$SSR = 0.00132$

$R^2 = 0.8148$

$DW = 2.5237$

$$\ln S_t - \ln_{t-1} F_t = -0.0242 + 0.8955 \text{ E-07 LQBPD} - 0.9267 \text{ E-05 CA}^{f*}$$
$$(0.1010)(0.23 \text{ E-06}) \qquad\qquad (0.26 \text{ E-4})$$

$$+ 0.3481(\ln S_{t-1} - \ln_{t-2} F_{t-1}) + 5.4720 \ln R_t^*$$
$$(0.082) \qquad\qquad\qquad (1.418)$$

$$- 3.7869 \ln R_t^{*f} - 6.3955(\ln R_t - \ln R_t^*) \qquad\qquad (30)$$
$$(1.367) \qquad\quad (2.920)$$

$R^2 = 0.3996$

$DW = 1.7829$

$SSR = 0.0409$

The estimated versions of equations (10)–(16) show a number of empirically-determined omissions; the UK current account proved insignificant and is omitted from (16) in (30); more surprisingly perhaps the cumulative balance of payments differential (LQBPD) proved insignificant over the whole period, although its coefficient showed some instability, since up to 1982.06 it was strongly positive and significant; the data dictated the inclusion of the lagged dependent variable in (30).

There are a number of interesting points to note:

a)   expected money supply change appears positively related to the expected level of the interest rate;

b)   lagged US interest rates are an important determinant of current UK rates.

c)   UK interest rates operate differently in terms of their actual and expected levels in equation (30). These can be written as $-6.3955 (A-E) + 5.4720 (E)$ which gives $-6.3955A + 11.8675E$, so that expected rates have a net positive impact over actual rates. The 'surprise' in interest rate levels does not counteract expectations in full. Furthermore, the 'forecast error' variable is wrongly signed according to the 'surprises' hypothesis, since if actual rates prove higher than forecast a further *rise* in the strength of sterling would be expected. This is a relatively strong contradiction of the 'surprise' hypothesis in the foreign exchange market;

d)   the coefficients on UK and US interest rates indicate that the higher are expected UK rates the stronger will be sterling, and vice versa. This is the opposite of the effect included within the forward rate equation, but is not a surprising result. Indeed, this is what would be expected in the short run as a response to 'monetary overshooting'. Traditional theories of exchange rate determination indicate that a larger money stock will be associated with a lower level of the exchange rate. However, an overshooting of monetary expansion will tend to be associated with an appreciation of the currency. Currie (1983), for example, suggests that excessive monetary expansion, because it implies 'corrective action in the form of higher interest rates', will cause the exchange rate to appreciate the short term. The implied forward rate effect of, say, a depreciation, in conjunction with an actual short run appreciation, may well be mutually consistent. In fact, any depreciation implicit in the forward rate may reflect the expected reversal of the short run appreciation of the currency. Thus, the result that monetary expansion is associated with a short run appreciation of the currency is neither an unusual, or an unexpected result;

e)   the inclusion of *predicted and actual* levels of intrest rate and current account variables proved to give stronger results than if only the 'error' is included. This is a similar result to that of Backus (1982) as regards *national levels* of variables rather than international differences. Furthermore, the results do not altogether support the straightforward 'surprises' specification. Only the UK interest rate error works in the OLS results as might have been anticipated originally.

Just as we found problems with the simple spot-on-forward rate regression, the forward rate-interest parity spot regression does not correspond to the simple theory.
The forward rate equations obtained were

$$\ln_t F_{t+1} = 0.0015 + 0.9972 \ln SS_t \tag{31}$$
$$\quad\quad\quad\quad (0.003) \quad (0.0036)$$

$$DW = 1.5774$$

$$SSR = 0.00281$$

$$R^2 = 0.9985$$

$$\ln_t F_{t+1} = 0.0004 + 0.9553 \ln SS_t - 0.1551 \ln SS_{t-1} + 0.1945 \ln_{t-1} F_t$$
$$\quad\quad\quad (0.002) \quad (0.019) \quad\quad\quad (0.095) \quad\quad\quad\quad (0.091)$$

$$DW = 2.0067$$

$$R^2 = 0.9986$$

$$SSR = 0.00258$$

which have Lagrange Multiplier (12) test values of 8.14 and 3.85 respectively. These equations are essentially identical since (31) contains a common factor restriction of (32) on the lagged values of F and SS. Little is therefore to be gained from using a specification other than (31) and so in the non-linear full information maximum likelihood estimate, the identity between roward rate and interest parity spot rate is re-imposed.

6. SYSTEMS ESTIMATES

Tables 1 to 6 present the estimates for all seven equations, by OLS, Three Stage Least Squares, Non-linear Three Stage Least Squares and Non-linear FIML. This was carried out using the latest version of TSP on the Henley Centre VAX computer. The latter two have the appropriate cross-equation restrictions imposed from the money supply equations to the interest rate equations, and then from the interest rate and current account equations into the exchange rate equation. Estimates for the UK current account forecasting equation are not presented because the predicted UK current account proved insignificant even in the OLS equation for the exchange rate.

There is obviously room for improvement on certain, if not all, the equations. The results of the model are not uninteresting, however. Various variables are omitted as we proceed through the systems estimates, such as the lagged spot rate from the two interest rate equations, the cumulative balance of payments and expected UK interest rates from the exchange rate equation and the lagged interest parity spot rate from the forward rate equation. In the spot-minus-forward rate equation, a rather peculiar specification emerges: the expected US current account has a negative effect on the $\$:\pounds$ rate, as might be expected; the lagged dependent variable remains strongly significant, the interest rate variables are relatively instable, but an increase in the expected US rate does lead to a *strengthening* of the *dollar* and a positive error in the UK rate forecast (actual-expected) in the previous period leads to a *rise* in *sterling*.

These interest rate effects are, as discussed above, more complicated than those associated with simple Fisherian expectations in which a rise in US interest rates, *ceteris paribus*, would lead to an expected fall in the dollar. The problem with interest rate behaviour in the model perhaps points to a central difficulty with a 'surprises' specification. It is obvious that the authorities of the respective countries may intervene to alter interest rates in response to exchange rate pressures within each period. Such simultaneity would presumably be more worse within a quarterly or annual model but for monthly data it is still a problem. If, for example, the current spot rate is allowed to enter the UK interest rate equation, we find:

$$\ln R_t = -0.002 + 0.9013 \ln R_{t-1} - 0.0064 \ln S_t + 0.0072 \ln S_{t-1} \quad (33)$$
$$ (0.005) \ (0.042) \phantom{+ 0.9013 \ln R_{t-1}} (0.003) (0.003)$$

$$+ 0.1170(\ln R_{t-1} - \ln R_{t-4}) + 0.0061(\ln M_t - \ln M_{t-3})^*$$
$$ (0.048) \phantom{(\ln R_{t-1} - \ln R_{t-4}) +} (0.003)$$

$$+ 0.0513 \ln R_{t-1}^f$$
$$ (0.029)$$

$R^2 = 0.9029$ $SSR = 0.000428$

$DW = 2.0355$ $SE = 0.00629$

$F = 167.54$

Table 1. The change in UK money supply, 1973.06–1982.12 ($\ln M_t - \ln M_{t-3}$).

Variables		Estimates							
		OLSQ		3SLS		NL3SLS		NLF1ML	
$\ln M_{t-1} - \ln M_{t-4}$	α0	−0.1147	(0.060)	−0.1078	(0.055)	−0.0949	(0.056)	−0.06007	(0.068)
	α1	0.3389	(0.089)	0.3626	(0.081)	0.3783	(0.079)	0.4004	(0.086)
$\ln R_{t-1}$	α2	−6.1159	(1.268)	−5.66047	(1.159)	−5.3499	(1.179)	−5.07077	(1.525)
$\ln M_{t-1}$	α3	0.0200	(0.006)	0.0189	(0.006)	0.01718	(0.006)	0.01345	(0.007)
$\ln P_{t-1} - \ln P_{t-4}$	α4	0.5029	(0.136)	0.45698	(0.123)	0.4377	(0.143)	0.3935	(0.161)
SD1	ETA1	−0.0445	(0.009)	−0.04646	(0.008)	−0.04598	(0.008)	−0.04623	(0.012)
SD2	2	−0.0513	(0.009)	−0.05007	(0.008)	−0.04789	(0.008)	−0.04748	(0.012)
	3	−0.0626	(0.009)	−0.06107	(0.008)	−0.05818	(0.008)	−0.05746	(0.018)
	4	0.0034	(0.010)	0.005187	(0.009)	0.00829	(0.009)	0.008792	(0.013)
	5	−0.0163	(0.009)	−0.01408	(0.008)	−0.0113	(0.008)	−0.01084	(0.013)
	6	−0.0276	(0.009)	−0.02637	(0.008)	−0.02468	(0.008)	−0.02412	(0.014)
	7	−0.0374	(0.009)	−0.0342	(0.008)	−0.0319	(0.008)	−0.03012	(0.014)
	8	−0.0276	(0.008)	−0.0285	(0.008)	−0.0288	(0.007)	−0.02865	(0.011)
	9	−0.0237	(0.008)	−0.0228	(0.008)	−0.02151	(0.007)	−0.02049	(0.011)
	10	−0.0333	(0.008)	−0.03117	(0.008)	−0.02894	(0.007)	−0.02808	(0.012)
	11	−0.0193	(0.008)	−0.01581	(0.008)	−0.01342	(0.007)	−0.01173	(0.012)
F		15.2292							
LL		302.356							
DW		2.0694		2.1127		2.1396		2.1701	
SSR		0.03504		0.035309		0.03569		0.03621	
R^2		0.6976							
SE		0.0188		0.01752		0.017617			

Table 2. The change in US money supply, 1973.06—1982.12, $(\ln M_t^f - \ln M_{t-3}^f)$.

		OLSQ		3SLS		NL3SLS		NLF1ML	
	B0	−0.0302	(0.019)	−0.0293	(0.017)	−0.03096	(0.017)	−0.03451	(0.022)
$\ln M_t^f - \ln M_{t-4}^f$	B1	0.6932	(0.068)	0.6945	(0.063)	0.6921	(0.062)	0.6994	(0.088)
$\ln R_{t-1}^f$	B2	−1.3025	(0.385)	−1.2850	(0.357)	−1.31316	(0.356)	−1.3693	(0.493)
$\ln P_{t-4}^f$	B3	0.0126	(0.004)	0.0124	(0.004)	0.01279	(0.004)	0.0135	(0.005)
SD1	ETA12	−0.0246	(0.004)	−0.0244)	(0.003)	−0.02443	(0.003)	−0.0244	(0.004)
SD2	13	−0.0578	(0.003)	−0.05797	(0.003)	−0.05828	(0.003)	−0.0581	(0.006)
SD3	14	−0.0439	(0.005)	−0.04402	(0.004)	−0.04457	(0.004)	−0.0439	(0.006)
SD4	15	0.0017	(0.005)	0.00197	(0.004)	0.001373	(0.005)	0.0022	(0.008)
SD5	16	−0.0122	(0.004)	−0.01229	(0.004)	−0.01275	(0.004)	−0.0123	(0.005)
SD6	17	−0.0072	(0.003)	−0.00711	(0.003)	−0.00745	(0.003)	−0.007179	(0.004)
SD7	18	−0.0327	(0.003)	−0.03315	(0.003)	−0.03344	(0.003)	−0.03339	(0.004)
SD8	19	−0.0070	(0.004)	−0.00649	(0.003)	−0.00655	(0.003)	−0.00637	(0.004)
SD9	20	−0.0266	(0.003)	−0.0265	(0.003)	−0.02678	(0.003)	−0.02664	(0.005)
SD10	21	−0.0203	(0.003)	−0.0207	(0.003)	−0.02104	(0.003)	−0.0208	(0.004)
SD11	22	−0.0015	(0.004)	−0.001387	(0.003)	−0.001915	(0.003)	−0.00187	(0.005)
R^2		0.9036							
DW		1.2781		1.2833		1.2815		1.2873	
F		66.9389							
SE		0.0073		0.00684		0.0068457		0.00539	
SSR		0.005374		0.005382		0.005389			
LL		410.16							

Table 3. The log of UK interest rates, 1973.05–1982.12 (lnRt).

		OLSQ		3SLS		NL3SLS		NLF1ML	
	$\gamma 0$	−0.000317	(0.0005)	−0.00007701	(0.0005)	0.00048989	(0.0004)	0.000259	(0.0005)
$\ln R_{t-1}$	$\gamma 1$	0.8909	(0.043)	0.87885	(0.041)	0.85704	(0.0438)	0.8885	(0.055)
$\ln M^*_t$	$\gamma 2$	0.00670	(0.0026)	0.006407	(0.002)	0.007294	(0.0026)	0.00740	(0.0037)
$\ln S_{t-1}$	$\gamma 3$	0.000916	(0.0005)	0.000699	(0.0005)				
$\ln R_{t-1} - \ln R_{t-4}$	$\gamma 4$	0.1031	(0.495)	0.12543	(0.0447)	0.26127	(0.0621)	0.13359	(0.0623)
$\ln R_{t-1}$	$\gamma 5$	0.0653	(0.029)	0.06966	(0.0283)	0.08375	(0.0296)	0.0769	(0.0362)
R^2		0.8979							
DW		1.9918		2.0199		2.0948		2.0062	
F		191.757							
SE		0.000643		0.000627		0.0006595			
SSR		0.00004504		0.00004523		0.00005002		0.00004554	
LL		685.107							

Table 4. The log of US interest rates, 1973.06–1982.12 (lnR^f_t).

		OLSQ		3SLS		NL3SLS		NLF1ML	
	$\delta 0$	−0.00028	(0.0006)	−0.000205	(0.0006)	0.000539	(0.0003)	0.000529	(0.0004)
$\ln R^f_{t-1}$	$\delta 1$	0.8912	(0.0416)	0.89846	(0.0408)	0.90485	(0.0431)	0.90334	(0.0439)
$\ln M^*_t$	$\delta 2$	0.0078	(0.0049)	0.00854	(0.0048)	0.006905	(0.0050)	0.00817	(0.0087)
$\ln S_{t-1}$	$\delta 3$	0.0013	(0.0008)	0.001064	(0.0008)				
SE		0.000109		0.00107		0.00108			
SSR		0.000132		0.000132		0.0001345		0.0001346	
R^2		0.8148							
F		162.831							
LL		623.386							
DW		2.5237		2.5413		2.5131		2.5078	

Table 5. Exchange rate equation, 1973.06–1982.12 ($\ln S_t - \ln_{t-1} F_t$).

	OLSQ	3SLS	NL3SLS	NLF1ML
	−0.0242 (0.0105)	−0.02238 (0.0102)	−0.0163 (0.0095)	−0.02275 (0.0114)
LQBPD	0.8955 E-07 (0.23E-06)	0.1248 E-06 (0.21E-05)		
CA_t^f	−0.9267 E-05 (0.26E-04)	−0.8554 E-05 (0.27E-05)	−0.0000 5713 (0.27E-05)	−0.8308 E-05 (0.35E-05)
$\ln S_t - l_{t-2} - \ln F_{t-1}$	0.3481 (0.0825)	0.3634 (0.1243)	0.44301 (0.1382)	0.3759 (0.0873)
$\ln R_t^*$	5.4720 (1.4172)	0.5324 (5.6638)		
$\ln R_t^{f*}$	−3.7869 (1.3676)	−3.86605 (1.3680)	−3.96595 (0.7126)	−4.0479 (1.236)
$\ln R_t - \ln R_t^*$	−6.3955 (2.9176)	4.8136 (5.3789)	4.72151 (1.4039)	5.4945 (1.378)
SSR	0.0409	0.0466	0.04705	0.0474389
SE	0.195	0.0201	0.020227	
R^2	0.3996			
F	11.9797			
LL	293.46			
DW	1.7829	1.7736	1.9037	1.7939

Table 6. Log of $: £ forward rate, 1973.06–1982.12 ($\ln_{t-1} F_t$).

		OLSQ		3SLS		NL3SLS		NLF1ML
	EPSO	0.000425	(0.0026)	0.000852	(0.0025)	0.000973	(0.0026)	IDENTITY:
$\ln_{t-2} F_t$	1	0.19453	(0.0912)	0.197321	(0.0895)	0.11001	(0.0312)	EPSO = 0
$\ln SS_t$	2	0.9552	(0.0196)	0.9186	(0.0315)	0.88743	(0.0315)	EPS1 = 0
$\ln SS_{t-1}$	3	−0.15114	(0.0946)	−0.1181	(0.0984)			EPS2 = 1
								EPS3 = 0
R^2		0.998623						
DW		2.0067		1.9774		1.7663		
SE		0.004817		0.00481		0.004989		
SSR		0.002576		0.002657		0.002862		
F		26826.6						
LL		452.453						

Table 7. Dynamic simulations for 1982.01–1982–12 using NL3SLS parameters for 1973.06–1981.12.

| | UK money supply (M1) | | US money supply (M1) | | UK interest rate | |
	Actual	Predicted	Actual	Predicted	Actual	Predicted
1982.01	34089	31927	453.4	447.3	1.0106	1.0114
02	33942	33611	437.2	434.2	1.0105	1.0109
03	33999	33409	440.0	439.2	1.0099	1.0105
04	34637	32883	445.5	451.6	1.0102	1.0102
05	34703	35007	445.1	442.9	1.0099	1.0101
06	35288	34607	450.5	454.2	1.0097	1.0099
07	35781	33705	454.0	459.7	1.0088	1.0099
08	36126	35639	454.0	457.5	1.0079	1.0098
09	36297	35483	460.5	464.4	1.0079	1.0098
10	37585	34173	470.5	468.9	1.0071	1.0097
11	37440	36691	478.5	475.9	1.0079	1.0097
12	38391	37380	490.5	490.8	1.0080	1.0098

| | US interest rate | | Spot rate $:£ | |
	Actual	Predicted	Actual	Predicted
1982.01	1.0105	1.0099	1.886	1.898
02	1.0098	1.0096	1.847	1.886
03	1.0105	1.0092	1.808	1.874
04	1.0098	1.0089	1.772	1.861
05	1.0091	1.008	1.811	1.847
06	1.0104	1.0087	1.758	1.834
07	1.0084	1.0086	1.735	1.820
08	1.0062	1.0085	1.726	1.806
09	1.0063	1.0084	1.712	1.793
10	1.0065	1.0083	1.697	1.779
11	1.0067	1.0083	1.634	1.766
12	1.0064	1.0084	1.618	1.755

Thus, the contemporaneous spot rate is inversely related to the interest rate. This, of course, is inconsistent with our model since the spot rate then depends on the expected interest rate which itself is governed by the expected spote rate. The problem is essentially one of how 'surprises' are defined. For the interest rate, the authorities can obviously react within a month, but within an hour, or a day, the interest rate would be more likely exogenous. 'Surprises' or items of 'news' and their effects are necessarily obscured by monthly data, although clearly the use of quarterly data will greatly intensify this proble.

7. SIMULATION RESULTS

It has been shown that a rational expectations, simultaneous equation surprises model can be estimated with comparative ease although the particular equations are open to respecification. It is of course also important to examine the model's forecasting performance. In Table 8 we show the dynamic forecasts based on the model's estimated parameters for the period 1973.06–1981.12 (see appendix for listing of parameters). Overall the NL3SLS parameters are very similar to those obtained over the full sample, the pattern of the forecasts can perhaps be summarised as one of picking up the general movements but not to the full extent. Most noticeably, while the spot rate falls during 1982, the model does not reproduce all of the fall. In Table 9 the diagnostic statistics show room for improved specification. However, the spot rate forecasts are a distinct improvement on the forward rate predictions of 1981.12.

Table 8. Comparison of actual and predicted series (in logs).

	M	M^f	R	R^f	S
Correlation coefficient	0.7845	0.9738	0.8297	0.7875	0.9707
Regression coefficient (actual on predicted)	0.7509	0.9391	1.973	2.762	1.637
Thiel's inequality coefficient	0.0214	0.0039	0.0007	0.0007	0.0234
Root mean squared error	1506	3.526	0.0014	0.0015	0.839

Table 9. Comparison of forward and forecast rates.

	1981.12 Forward rate	Model prediction	Actual
1982.01	1.901	1.898	1.886
.03	1.895	1.874	1.808
.06	1.893	1.834	1.758
.12	1.891	1.755	1.618

8. CONCLUSIONS

A simultaneous equation 'surprises' model of the exchange rate has been proposed, and estimated subject to the imposition of the implied non-linear (rational expectations) restrictions. The model serves to show the ease with which such a model can be estimated: where the expected value of a variable appears as an explanatory variable, one can substitute directly the appropriate forecasting equation for that variable and estimate subject to non-linear restrictions by 3SLS or FIML. The above framework demonstrates that economic models of national economies can be linked in a coherent way via the exchange rate. Domestic monetary policies will have impacts on the various exchange rates in the domestic models, with consequences for output, employment and inflation.

DATA APPENDIX

Consumer price index (p, p^f)

These are taken from the monthly OECD Main Economic Indicators, various issues, and rebased at $1972 = 100$.

Current account (CA, CA^f)

These are the most recent quarterly current account data series available from the OECD Main Economic Indicators, interpolated to a monthly basis using monthly trade balance data from the same source, as in Murfin and Ormerod (1983). UK data converted to dollars.

Interest rate (R, R^f)

These refer to the Three Month Treasury Bill Rates from the OECD Main Economic Indicators, converted using the formula shown in Murfin and Ormerod (1983).

Money supply (M, M^f)

Sterling M1 UK and dollar M1 USA taken from OECD Main Economic Indicators and Bank of England Quarterly Bulletin. Seasonally unadjusted data (used throughout) was used, following Wallis (1974).

Spot exchange rate (S)

Monthly averages $:£, London closing, taken from Henley Centre computerised databank, 'Centrex'.

Foreward exchange rate (F)

1978–1982: Monthly average, London closing $:£ one month forward rate. Source: Henley Centre databank, 'Centrex'.

1973–1977: Monthly average of spot rate, set against one month discount/premium for the last available working day of each month. Source: back Issues of Financial Times, Henley Centre databank, 'Centrex'.

NOTES

We are grateful to David Currie for valuable comments and suggestions, and to the participants at the LSE Money and Macro-economics workshop.

REFERENCES

Backus, D. (1982), 'Empirical Models of the Exchange Rate: Separating the Wheat from the Chaff', *Queen's University Discussion Paper No. 463*.

Baillie, R.T., R.E. Lippens and P.C. McMahon (1983), 'Testing Rational Expectations and Efficiency in the Foreign Exchange Market', *Econometrica*, 51(3), pp. 553–564.

Bean, C. (1982), *The Estimation of 'Surprise' Models and the 'Surprise' Consumption Function* (HM Treasury Academic Panel).

Breusch, T.S. and A.R. Pagan (1980), 'The LM Test and its Application to Model specification in Econometrics', *The Review of Economic Studies*, 47, pp. 239–257.

Chow, G.C. and A. Lin (1971), 'Best Linear Unbiased Interpolation, Distribution, and Extrapolation of Time Series by Related Series', *Review of Economics & Statistics*, 53 (4).

Currie, D. (1983), 'Monetary Overshooting and the Exchange Rate', *Manchester School* (forthcoming).

Dornbusch, R. (1980), 'Exchange Rate Economics: Where Do We Stand?', *Brookings Paper on Economic Activity*.

Dornbusch, R. and S. Fisher, (1980), 'Exchange Rates and the Current Account', *American Economic Review*.

Driskill, R. (1981), 'Exchange Rate Dynamics: An Empirical Investigation', *Journal of Political Economy*, 89, pp. 359–371.

Edison, H.J. (1981), *The Rise and Fall of Sterling: Testing Alternative Models of Exchange Rate Determination*, Mimeo, LSE, April.

Fair, R.C. and J.B. Taylor (1983), 'Solution and Maximum Likelihood Estimation of Dynamic Non-linear Rational Expectations Models', *Econometrica*, 51 (4), pp. 1169–1186.

102

Foster-Smith, J. (1983), 'Market Efficiency and the Hong Kong Dollar', *Henley Centre for Forecasting Working Paper*.

Frenkel, J.A. (1977), 'The Forward Exchange Rate, Expectations and the Demand for Money: The Germany Hyperinflation', *American Economic Review*, 67, pp. 653–670.

Frenkel, J.A. (1981), 'Flexible Exchange Rates, Prices and the Role of News;: Lessons from the 1970's', *Journal of Political Economy*, 89, pp. 665–705.

Frenkel, J.A. and A. Razin (1980), 'Stochastic Prices and tests of Efficiency of Forecasting Exchange Markets', *Economic Letters*, 6, pp. 165–170.

Fromm, G. (1979), 'Use of Econometric Models for International Economic Policy Formulation', in: P. Ormerod (ed.), *Economic Modelling*, Heinemann, London.

Hahn, F.H. (1980), 'Monetarism and Economic Theory', *Economica*.

Hall, R.E. (1978), 'Stochastic Implications of the Life Cycle Permanent Income Hypothesis: Theory and Evidence', *Journal of Political Economy*, 86, pp. 971–987.

Hartley, P.R. (1982), 'Rational Expectations and the Foreign Exchange Market', *National Bureau of Economic Research Working Paper no. 863, February*.

Levich, R.M. (1978), 'Tests of Forecasting Models and Market Efficiency in the International Money Market', in: J.A. Frenkel and H.G. Johnson (eds), *The Economics of Exchange Rates: Selected Studies*, Addison-Wesley.

Liu, T. (1969), 'A Monthly Recursive Econometric Model of the United States: A test of Feasibility', *Review of Economics and Statistics*, February, pp. 1–13.

Lucas, R.E. and 1.A. Rapping (1969), 'Real Wages, Employment and Inflation', *Journal of Political Economy*, 77, pp. 721–754.

McCallum, B.T. (1970), 'The Effect of Demand on Prices in British Manufacturing: Another View', *Review of Economic Studies*, p. 149.

Muellbauer, J. (1983), 'Surprises in the Consumption Function', *Economic Journal, Conference Papers Supplement*, pp. 34–50.

Murfin, A. and P. Ormerod (1983), 'The Sterling Dollar Exchange Rate 1973–1982: Surprises and Expectations', *Henley Centre Discussion Paper No. 2*.

Murfin, A and P. Ormerod (1984), 'The Forward Rate for the US Dollar and the Efficient Markets Hypothesis 1978–83', *Manchester School* (forthcoming).

Muth, J.F. (1961), 'Rational Expectations and the theory of Price Movements', *Econometrica*, 29, pp. 315–335.

Ormerod, P. (1980), 'The Forward Exchange Rate for Sterling and Efficiency of Expectations', *Weltwirtschaftliches Archiv*, pp. 206–224.

Ormerod, P. and A. Murfin (1983), 'The Forward Rate for the US Dollar and the Efficient Markets Hypothesis', *Henley Centre for Forecasting Working paper*.

Ormerod, P. and G. Walshe (1981), 'Monetary Linkages in the Eurolink System', *Economist Intelligence Unit, Mimeo*.

Shiller, R. (1982), 'Stock Market Prices, Interest Rates and the Business Cycle', *Paper presented to the Colloque International sur Les Developpements Recents de la Modelisation Macroeconomique, CEPREMAP*, September.

Wallis, K.F. (1974), 'Seasonal Adjustment and Relations Between Variables', *Journal of the American Statistical Association*, 69, 345, pp. 18–30.

Wyplosz, C.A. (1980), 'The Expected Future Spot Exchange Rate, The Forward Rate and the Trade Balance', *INSEAD* Working Paper no. 80/06.

PART II

MODELLING AND SIMULATING THE INTERNATIONAL ECONOMY

CHAPTER 5

I. AN AGGREGATE MODEL OF THE WORLD ECONOMY

Patrick Artus
*Ecole Nationale de la Statistique et de l'Administration Economique,
Malakoff-Cedex, France*

1. INTRODUCTION

Most of the existing models of the world economy consist of national models linked together by commercial and financial flows (see for instance Project LINK, INTERLINK (1979), the COMET model (1980), the ATLAS model (1983) . . .). Some papers however (Parkin-Zis (1976), Beenstock-Dicks (1983)) consider the world as a whole to be modelled as a single country. A similar approach has been followed in this paper. Its advantages (commercial and financial flows between countries as well as exchange rate fluctuations disappear) and shortcomings (data is difficult to build on an aggregate basis) are rather straightforward.

The model built is a small-size one, but which for obvious reasons cannot represent the functional complexity of the world economy, resulting from both interactions among individual countries, and agreements and cooperation between some of them. The building of such a model must be considered as an academic research, aiming to analyse whether usual macroeconomic schemes suited for modelling the economics of developed countries can be applied to the world economy as a whole.

The method utilized to construct aggregate data series will first be described. Secondly the choice of the model structure for the world economy, based on an analysis of estimation results of a disequilibrium model with quantity rationing will be discussed.

A complete model including estimation and simulation results will be presented.

2. DATA AGGREGATION

The aggregation of data is a difficult task and results are far from perfect. Annual series, for the period 1960–1981, have been built for the following variables:

Artus, P. and Guvenen, O. (eds.): International Macroeconomic Modelling for Policy Decisions.
© *1986. Martinus Nijhoff Publishers, Dordrecht/Boston/Lancaster.*
ISBN 90-247-3201-8. Printed in The Netherlands.

- the gross domestic product and its various components: private consumption, public expenditures, variation of stocks, investment;
- the capital stock;
- deflators for the gross domestic product and for the various components of demand;
- total employment, employment in the manufacturing sector, hours worked, the rate of unemployment, the labour force;
- the degree of capacity utilisation;
- the hourly wage rates;
- the money stock (M2), short-term and long-term interest rates;
- direct and indirect taxes, social security contributions;
- the price of raw materials (including energy);
- the distribution of national income between wages of employees, indirect taxes, subsidies, depreciation of capital, net property and entrepreneurial income.

All those series exist for the OECD countries which produced in 1975 80.4% of the world GDP. For OECD countries, they have been taken from the *National Accounts of OECD Countries* and from the *Main Economic Indicators*. For the other areas (Africa: 3.8% of world GDP in 1975; Latin America: 6.9%; Middle-East: 4.0%; Asia (Japan excluded): 4.9%) they have been taken from the *Yearbooks of National Accounts Statistics*. The communist countries have not been taken into account. Therefore, there appears in the definition of the world GDP a statistical discrepancy due to foreign trade with communist countries, and also to discrepancies appearing in national accounts.

The series built are moreover heterogenous, since some of them (money stock, interest rates, wage rates, employment, capacity utilisation) only exist for the OECD countries.

The series are primarily compiled in current prices, either in domestic currencies or in US dollars and converted into a Unit of account based on a basket of various currencies[1], using current exchange rates. Volume series have been converted using average 1975 exchange rates and added up for the various countries for which data are available. When only indices are known (weekly hours, wage rates) and in the case of interest rates and of rates of unemployment, the series have been aggregated using the respective weights of the countries in the world GDP.

3. WHICH MODEL TO CHOOSE FOR THE WORLD ECONOMY?

Before building a complete model for the world economy, it is useful to carry out some tests in order to choose the kind of model to be completed: a model with competitive equilibrium in all markets or a model with disequilibrium (keynesian or classical unemployment ...). To help in the choice of a model type, several small models with quantity rationing were constructed to analyse first the goods market, and then both the goods and labour markets.

3.1. A first analysis of the functioning of the goods market[2]

The first small model only relies on the comparison of the demand and supply of commodities. Firms are assumed to be characterized by a single production function of the Cobb-Douglas type:

$$Q = Q_0 e^{\gamma T} K_{-1}^{\alpha} L^{\beta} \tag{1}$$

where Q: GDP

$\quad e^{\gamma T}$: technical progress

$\quad K_{-1}$: capital at the beginning of the period

$\quad$ L: employment

and to maximise their profits:

$$\pi = pQ - wHL(1 + \tau_{cs}) \tag{2}$$

where p: GDP deflator

$\quad$ H: weekly hours

$\quad$ w: hourly wage rate

$\quad \tau_{cs}$: rate of employers' social security contributions.

The supply of goods is therefore defined by:

$$Q^0 = (\beta)^{\frac{\beta}{1-\beta}} \left(\frac{p}{w_1 H}\right)^{\frac{\beta}{1-\beta}} e^{\frac{\gamma}{1-\beta} T} K_{-1}^{\frac{\alpha}{1-\beta}} Q_0^{\frac{1}{1-\beta}} \tag{3}$$

where

$$w_1 = w(1 + \tau_{cs})$$

The demand of goods consists in three endogenous components (private consumption, investment, inventory variations) and one exogenous component (public expenditures).

The consumption equation is very simple:

$$\text{Log } C = c_0 + c_1 \text{ Log } C_{-1} + c_2 \text{ Log } \frac{RD}{P_c} + c_3 \dot{p}_C \tag{4}$$

where RD: disposable income

$\quad P_C$: deflator for private consumption

The disposable income is calculated as:

$$RD = WHL(1 - \tau_{ID}) + ENE(1 - \tau_{ID}) \tag{5}$$

τ_{ID}: ratio of direct taxes to income
ENE: net profits, given by:

$$ENE = pQ(1 - \tau_{II}) - WHL(1 + \tau_{cs}) - Am - Div \tag{6}$$

where τ_{II}: ratio of indirect taxes to production
Am: depreciation of capital $(= k_A K_{-1})$
DIV: various exogenous items

when estimates are made only on the goods market, RD/p_c is considered exogenous.

Apart from income, no variable other than the inflation rate could successfully be introduced in the consumption equation; the unemployment rate, the real monetary balances, the ratio between wage and non-wage income, the nominal or real interest rates showed no significant result.

An attempt to use an error-correction model for consumption also proved unsuccessful.

Investment is considered as a demand component, and a major simplification is introduced since expected possible shifts from one regime to another are ignored; firms are assumed to always invest so as to reach a given target of capacity, equal to the expected demand, itself simply extrapolated from the observed past levels of production. The choice of the optimal capital level then simply stems from the usual program:

$$\text{Min } c_K K + WHL(1 + \tau_{cs}) \tag{7}$$

where c_K: user cost of capital calculated as:

$$c_K = p_D(r_{LT} + \delta - \dot{p}^a) \tag{8}$$

p_D: deflator for the components of demand other than consumption
r_{LT}: long-term interest rate
δ: rate of depreciation of capital
$\dot{p}^a$: expected rate of inflation ($\dot{p}^a = 0.4\dot{p} + 0.3\dot{p}_{-1} + 0.3\dot{p}_{-2}$ which gave the best results)

(7) is minimized under the constraint:

$$Q_0 e^{\gamma T} K^\alpha L^\beta = Q^a$$

where Q^a: desired capacity

Hence the optimal capital stock and employment:

$$K^* = \frac{\alpha}{\beta}^{\frac{\beta}{\alpha+\beta}} \left(\frac{WH(1+\tau_{cs})}{c_K}\right)^{\frac{\beta}{\alpha+\beta}} (Q^a)^{\frac{1}{\alpha+\beta}} e^{-\frac{\gamma}{\alpha+\beta}T} Q_0^{-\frac{1}{\alpha+\beta}} \tag{9}$$

$$L^* = (Q^a)^{1/\beta} e^{-\gamma/\beta T} (Q_0)^{-1/\beta} (K^*)^{-\alpha/\beta} \tag{10}$$

and, differentiating (9), the expression of the optimal investment rate:

$$\left(\frac{I}{K_{-1}}\right)^* = + \frac{1}{\alpha+\beta}(\dot{Q}^a) + \delta - \frac{\gamma}{\alpha+\beta} + \frac{\beta}{\alpha+\beta}\left(\frac{WH(1+\tau_{cs})}{c_K}\right) \tag{11}$$

where, through an iterative procedure, $\dot{Q}^a$ has been specified as:

$$\dot{Q}^a = 0.37\dot{Q} + 0.30\dot{Q}_{-1} + 0.20\dot{Q}_{-2} + 0.13\dot{Q}_{-3}$$

The specification of the inventory investment equation is the following:

$$DS = d_0 + d_1 DS_{-1} + d_2 \Delta D + d_3 \Delta D_{-1} + d_4 \Delta D_{-2} + d_5 p_{\dot{M}} \tag{12}$$

where DS: inventory investment
ΔD: change in demand (change in inventories excluded)
$p_{\dot{M}}$: price of raw materials

Other variables (the rate of profit, interest rates . . .) have been tried but were not significant.

The disequilibrium model on the goods market can finally be written as:

$$Q - \text{Min} (Q^0 + \epsilon_0, Q^d) \qquad (\epsilon_0 \sim \mathcal{N}(0, \sigma_0)) \tag{13}$$

where Q^d is the sum of demand components:

$$Q^d = \exp\left(c_0 + c_1 \text{ Log } C_{-1} + c_2 \text{ Log } \frac{RD}{P_c} + c_3 p_{\dot{c}}\right) + \epsilon_C \tag{14}$$

$$+ K_{-1}\left(\delta - \frac{\gamma}{\alpha+\beta} + \frac{\beta}{\alpha+\beta}\left(\frac{WH(\dot{i}+\tau_{cs})}{c_K}\right) + \frac{1}{\alpha+\beta}\dot{Q}^a\right) + \epsilon_I$$

$$+ d_0 + d_1 DS_{-1} + d_2 \Delta \dot{D} + d_3 \Delta D_{-1} + d_4 \Delta D_{-2} + d_5 p_{\dot{M}} + \epsilon_{DS}$$

$$\epsilon_C \sim \mathcal{N}(0, \sigma_C); \epsilon_I \sim \mathcal{N}(0, \sigma_I); \epsilon_{DS} \sim \mathcal{N}(0, \sigma_{DS})$$

$\epsilon_0, \epsilon_C, \epsilon_I, \epsilon_{DS}$ being independently distributed.

The rationing scheme (the way the total rationing on the goods market is split between the various demand components when $Q^0 + \epsilon_0 < Q^d$) remains to be specified.

However, no reduction in inventory investment has been found. The demand equations can therefore be written as follows when $Q < Q^d$:

$$
\begin{cases}
C = \exp\left(c_0 + c_1 \, \mathrm{Log}\, C_{-1} + c_2 \, \mathrm{Log}\, \dfrac{RD}{P_C} + c_3\, p_{\dot{c}}\right) + \epsilon_c - \rho_c(Q^d - Q) \cdot \\[2em]
I = K_{-1}\left(\delta - \dfrac{\gamma}{\alpha+\beta} + \dfrac{\beta}{\alpha+\beta}\left(\dfrac{WH(1+\tau_{cs})}{c_K}\right) + \dfrac{1}{\alpha+\beta}\,\dot{Q}^a\right) \\[2em]
\qquad + \epsilon_I - (1 - \rho_c)(Q^d - Q) \\[1.5em]
DS = d_0 + d_1 DS_{-1} + d_2\Delta D + d_3\Delta D_{-1} + d_4\Delta D_{-2} + d_5\, p_{\dot{M}} + \epsilon_{DS}
\end{cases}
\tag{15}
$$

rationing being shared between consumption and investment.

Estimation of (13), (14), (15) has been done using a full-information maximum likelihood routine. The results are shown in the left column of Table 1.

The hypothesis of constant returns to scale is accepted, and therefore the parameters of the production function have constrained so as to get $\beta = 1 - \alpha$. The estimated long-term elasticity of consumption with respect to income is 1.15, inflation having apparently a strong negative influence on consumption. Stocks follow demand, the short-run amplification of the movements in demand being corrected afterwards ($d_1 < 0$). Rationing in case of excess demand seems to bear almost entirely on investment and very little on consumption ($\rho_c = 0.11$). That result was however of little significance: observation of the left column of Table 2 shows that the probability of being in the excess supply regime ($Q = Q^d$) is very high for 14 years out of a total of 18. Demand was significantly rationed ($Q = Q^0 + \epsilon_0$) only from 1972 to 1974 and in 1979. The level of demand seems to have determined the level of production in a large majority of periods.

An aggregate modelization (introducing only a single equation for demand) of the goods market of the world economy has been used to test the assumption of competitive equilibrium on that market.

The system (13), (14), (15) has been transformed taking the logarithm of the supply of goods (3) and of the aggregated demand (14), the latter being linearized so as to make linearly appear $\log p^3$; the following price equation is added to the transformed model:

Table 1.

	Estimation on the goods market (12)(13)(15)	Estimation on the goods and labour markets
Production function		
Q_0	0.07	0.10
	(0.04)	(0.05)
γ	$-$ 0.0003	0.009
	(0.004)	(0.002)
α	$1-$ 0.41	$1-$ 0.55
β	0.41	0.55
	(0.11)	(0.13)
σ_0	1.4	1.95
	(0.22)	(0.24)
Consumption		
c_0	$-$ 0.36	$-$ 0.28
	(0.06)	(0.07)
c_1	0.74	0.70
	(0.06)	(0.14)
c_2	0.30	0.36
	(0.06)	(0.05)
c_3	$-$ 0.40	$-$ 0.22
	(0.11)	(0.05)
	0.47	0.26
	(0.10)	(0.05)
Investment		
σ_I	0.54	0.58
	(0.19)	(0.12)
Stock variation		
d_0	$-$ 0.10	$-$ 0.10
	(0.21)	(0.11)
d_1	$-$ 0.48	$-$ 0.52
	(0.21)	(0.21)
d_2	0.09	0.08
	(0.05)	(0.04)
d_3	0.24	0.22
	(0.04)	(0.05)
d_4	0.09	0.08
	(0.05)	(0.05)
d_5	0.81	0.82
	(0.31)	(0.30)
σ_{DS}	0.13	0.13
	(0.06)	(0.06)

Table 1 (*continued*)

	Estimation on the goods market (12)(13)(15)	Estimation on the goods and labour markets
Rationing scheme		
ρ_c	0.11	0.77
	(0.01)	(0.04)

The figures between brackets are the estimated standard errors of the coefficients.

Table 2. Probabilities of the regimes

	Estimation on the goods market		Estimation on two markets		
	Excess supply regime	Excess demand regime	Keynesian unemployment	Classical unemployment	Repressed inflation
64	100	0	100	0	0
65	100	0	99	0	1
66	100	0	96	0	4
67	98	2	0	0	100
68	100	0	4	0	96
69	100	0	4	0	96
70	100	0	1	0	99
71	95	5	0	0	100
72	45	55	24	0	76
73	30	70	12	0	88
74	35	65	0	0	100
75	100	0	100	0	0
76	100	0	100	0	0
77	100	0	100	0	0
78	72	28	100	0	0
79	0	100	100	0	0
80	100	0	100	0	0
81	100	0	100	0	0

$$\Delta \text{Log } p = p_0 + p_1 \Delta \text{Log } p_{-1} + p_2 \Delta \text{Log CSU} + p_3 \Delta \text{Log } p_M$$
$$+ (\Delta \tau_{II} - p_1 \Delta \tau_{II-1}) + p_4^-(\text{Log } Q^0 - \text{Log } Q^d)^- \qquad (16)$$
$$+ p_4^+(\text{Log } Q^0 - \text{Log } Q^d)^+ + \epsilon_p (\epsilon_p \sim N(0, \sigma_p))$$

where CSU: unit labour cost $= \dfrac{WH(1 + \tau_{cs})}{Q}$

$(\text{Log } Q^0 - \text{Log } Q^d)^+$ is the discrepancy between supply and demand of goods when positive, $(\text{Log } Q^0 - \text{Log } Q^d)^-$ when negative. The estimated parameters for the demand and supply equations are very close to those given in Table 1; therefore, only the price equation will be shown here.

p_4^+ has always been non-significant. One gets (the figures between brackets are the standard errors):

$$\Delta \operatorname{Log} p = \underset{(0.006)}{0.004} + \underset{(0.08)}{0.58\Delta \operatorname{Log} p_{-1}} + \underset{(0.09)}{0.29\Delta \operatorname{Log} CSU} + \underset{(0.01)}{0.04\Delta \operatorname{Log} p_M}$$

$$- \underset{(0.17)}{0.29(\operatorname{Log} Q^0 - \operatorname{Log} Q^d)^-} \qquad \sigma_p = \underset{(0.003)}{0.008}$$

An excess of 1% of demand over supply (which rarely appeared) would lead to an increase in prices by 0.3% for the year in which excess demand occurs. According to our estimates this would increase the supply of goods by 0.2% and reduce demand by 0.1%. Over two-thirds of the ex.ante disequilibriums would therefore persist after the increase in prices, which is pleading in favour of eliminating a competitive equilibrium model for the goods market of the world economy. After this first analysis, the estimated probabilities of the two regimes (cf. Table 2) seem to indicate that a keynesian-unemployment type model with partial price flexibility would be best suited.

3.2. Second analysis on both the goods and labour markets

Again for this second analysis, we use the previously described specifications of the production function[4] of the demand equations ((14), (15), (16)), of the rationing scheme (15), but the labour market is now introduced in the model to be estimated. This implies that a labour supply equation is specified; like in Artus-Laroque-Michel (1982), we have chosen to use:

$$L^0 = l_0 + l_1 POP + \epsilon_L \qquad \epsilon_L \sim \mathcal{N}(0, \sigma_L) \tag{17}$$

where POP is the labour force.

In this case three regimes are possible:

— *the keynesian unemployment regime*, defined by:

$$Q = Q^d$$
$$\pi_L' > 0 \ (\Pi: \text{short term profits of firms, see (2))}$$
$$L < L^0$$
$$Q = Q_0 e^{\gamma T} K_{-1}^\alpha L^\beta$$

— *the classical unemployment regime:*

$$\pi'_L = 0$$
$$Q < Q^d$$
$$L < L^0$$
$$Q = Q_0 e^{\gamma T} K^\alpha_{-1} L^\beta$$

– *the repressed inflation regime:*

$$Q < Q^d$$
$$\pi'_L > 0$$
$$L = L^0$$
$$Q = Q_0 e^{\gamma T} K^\alpha_{-1} L^\beta$$

The estimation results for this model are set out in the second column of Table 1, the corresponding conditional probabilities of the regimes in the second column of Table 2.

The classical unemployment regime never appears, and estimation has therefore been limited to the two other regimes: keynesian unemployment and repressed inflation. The estimated coefficients are close to those estimated previously; the hypothesis of constant returns to scale has been accepted. The estimated rationing scheme differs significantly from that estimated for the goods market alone: most of the rationing bears here on consumption, which seems more reasonable. The previous estimation was certainly not very robust, since the excess demand regime only appeared for a very small number of years.

Apparently, the world was in a keynesian unemployment regime for most of the period, with however a long period (1967–1974) of repressed inflation during which firms were unable to get the needed labour.

We have also tried to estimate the model of firms' behaviours proposed by Artus-Laroque-Michel (1983), where the short-term profits of firms include an adjustment cost of employment and a cost of over or under utilisation of capacity:

$$\pi = pQ - WHL(1 + \tau_{CS}) - k_1 WHL_{-1}(L/L_{-1} - 1)^2 - k_2 pQ_0 e^{\gamma T} K^\alpha_{-1} L^\beta \cdot$$

$$\mathrm{Max}\left(\frac{Q}{Q_0 e^{\gamma T} K^\alpha_{-1} L^\beta} - 1, 0\right)^2$$

(21)

A fourth regime (under-consumption) may appear because of the flexibility introduced by the production function.

Unfortunately, it has not been possible to test this more complex model due to the small number of observations (18) in the sample period: in all attempts the estimated values of k_1 and k_2 could not converge towards a stable value.

3.3. Reaction functions of the authorities and price of raw materials

We must now analyse which variables have to be taken as exogenous for the world model. Up to now, the tax rates (τ_{ID}, τ_{II}, τ_{CS}), the public expenditures (G) and the price of raw materials (p_M) have been considered as such, as well as money supply (M), interest rates (r_{LT}) and the labour force (POP).

To decide whether these variables remain exogenous in the final model or if they are to be endogenized using reactions functions of the authorities (for the policy instruments τ_{IS}, τ_{II}, τ_{CS}, M, r_{LT}) or equations explaining the behaviour of private agents (p_M, POP), reaction functions and equations were estimated.

Except in the case of public expenditures, no reasonable result showing a stable behaviour could be found. Neither tax rates nor money supply or the determination of interest rates could be explained in sensible equations by such variables as the inflation rate, unemployment rate, capacity utilisation, growth rate, public deficit . . . .

Some examples of the unsatisfactory results obtained are given below for the cases of interest rates and money supply:[5]

— the long-term interest rate could only be significantly linked to the inflation rate:

$$r_{LT} = \underset{(8.2)}{0.043} + \underset{(7.3)}{0.51\,p_{\dot{c}}} \qquad R^2 = 0.75\, DW = 0.94$$

— the growth rate of money supply with the growth rate of the GDP deflator and with the degree of capacity utilisation:

$$\dot{M} = \underset{(2.5)}{0.30} + \underset{(1.2)}{0.20\dot{p}} - \underset{(1.7)}{0.0025\,TU_{-1}} \qquad R^2 = 0.20\, DW = 1.14$$

It has proved impossible to explain the evolution of the relative price of raw materials (p_M/p), and in particular of its sharp rises in 1973–1974 and in 1979, as was expected.

The only equation which has given rather sensible results has been that estimated for the growth rate of public expenditures, related to the growth rate of potential output (a scale factor), to the inflation rate and to the degree of capacity utilisation lagged one period:

$$\dot{G} = \underset{(2.1)}{0.25} + \underset{(2.0)}{0.32\dot{Q}^0} - \underset{(3.1)}{0.40\dot{p}_{C-1}} - \underset{(1.8)}{0.003\,TU_{-1}}$$

$$R^2 = 0.39$$

$$DW = 1.21$$

Given the lack of precision of the above equation, the policy instruments, the labour force and the price of raw materials have been kept exogenous.

3.4. Conclusion: the structure of the model

The estimates helped us in selecting a structure for the model of the world economy:

- the goods market is not in competitive equilibrium, which was the assumption made by Beenstock-Dicks (1983);
- the estimates made for the goods market and for the goods and labour markets also show that the classical unemployment regime never appears. Firms have apparently always been constrained on the goods market or on the labour market. If the model to be built cannot exhibit a multiplicity of possible regimes, the best choice is certainly a keynesian unemployment model, corresponding to the situation of the economy over the recent period;
- finally, it has proved very difficult to endogenize sensibly the various policy instruments or the price of raw materials.

It seems therefore justified for the world economy to build a model of the neo-keynesian type, which is the usual choice for western industrialized countries. However, one must bear in mind that this kind of model cannot represent the limitations of the production level due to an insufficient labour supply that appeared quite frequently prior to the first oil crisis.

4. THE MODEL

In the model, we incorporate the expectation mechanisms [(31), (32)], the construction of production costs and income distribution [(38), (39), (40), (41), (42), (43)], the equations for demand components (consumption: (19); inventory investment: (22); investment: (20) and (21)), for the optimal production level in the short run [(26) and (27)], and the production function ((25)) that have been previously described. The only change is the introduction of an adjustment lag of employment to its optimal short-term level.

To close the model and in order to calculate prices and nominal values, we have to add a number of equations (see Table 3):

- unemployment is related to the labour force and to employment through equation (28), which allows for short-run fluctuations in the participation rates;

- the deviations of weekly hours from a quadratic time trend depend on the degree of capacity utilisation (29);
- the wage-rate is determined by an equation of the usual 'Phillips type', making it depend on the inflation rate, the unemployment rate and the evolution of labour productivity ((3));
- the producer price (35) results from a mark-up on a geometric average of the unit labour costs and of the price of raw materials. The mark-up rate depends on the rate of investment, but not on the degree of capacity utilisation, which apparently exerts a short-term influence on the consumer price ((36)), but not on the producer price;
- the money demand equation (44) displays the usual specification.

The model of Table 3 has been estimated by a FIML routine. It can be simulated in two different ways depending on the choice of the exogenous monetary policy instrument: money supply (M^0) or interest rates (r_{LT}). The estimation was much easier and gave much better results in the first case (M^0 exogenous). Estimation results are shown in Table 4.

One can observe that:

- consumption is rather sticky (the coefficient of C_{-1} is 0.84); the long-term elasticity of consumption with respect to disposable income is 1.2; an increase by 1 p point per year of the inflation rate would lead to a decrease in consumption by 2%;
- the coefficient of labour in the production function (0.55) seems sensible; technical progress increases production by 1.1% a year.
- as in previous estimates made in this paper, inventory variations display an initial overshooting when demand or the price of raw materials change;
- employment is not very sticky, the mean lag of the adjustment towards the short-term optimal employment level being 1.3 year;
- significant cyclical changes in the participation rate appear: a 100% increase of the labour force would result in an increase of unemployment by 56%; a 100% increase of the employment level would reduce it by only 20%; apparently, the labour supply is strongly stimulated if employment increases;
- an increase by 1 percent point of the degree of capacity utilisation results in an increase by 0.2% of weekly hours worked;
- the degree of indexation of wages to prices is significantly higher than one (1.3); this is certainly a consequence of the large real wage gains observed in several countries (Japan, Asia, . . .). The effect of unemployment on wage income is quite visible: an increase by 1 point in the rate of unemployment would, according to the estimates, induce a reduction by 1.5 points of the annual growth rate of the wage rate. Productivity gains are partly ($w_4 = 0.33$) transferred to employees;

Table 3. The model

Demand	

Demand

$$(19) \quad C = e^{c_0 + c_3 \dot{p}_C} C_{-1}^{c_1} \left(\frac{RD}{P_C}\right)^{c_2} \qquad \text{Consumption}$$

$$(20) \quad K = \left(\frac{1-\beta}{\beta}\right)^{\beta} \left(\frac{WH(1 + \tau_{CS})}{C_K}\right)^{\beta} Q^a e^{-\gamma T} Q_0^{-1} \qquad \text{Capital}$$

$$(21) \quad I = K - K_{-1}(1 - \delta) \qquad \text{Investment}$$

$$(22) \quad DS = d_0 + d_1 DS_{-1} + d_2 \Delta D + d_3 \Delta D_{-1} + d_4 \Delta D_{-2} \qquad \text{Inventory Investment}$$
$$\qquad + d_5 \dot{p}_M$$

$$(23) \quad Q = I + DS + C + G \qquad \text{Equilibrium on the goods market}$$

$$(24) \quad D = I + C + G \qquad \text{Total demand, inventory investment excluded}$$

Employment and supply

$$(25) \quad L = L_{-1}^{\lambda} \left[(Q^a)^{1/\beta} Q_0^{-1/\beta} e^{-\frac{\gamma}{\beta} T} K_{-1}^{-\frac{1-\beta}{\beta}}\right]^{1-\lambda} \qquad \text{Employment}$$

$$(26) \quad Q^0 = \beta^{\frac{\beta}{1-\beta}} \left(\frac{p}{WH(1 + \tau_{CS})}\right)^{\frac{\beta}{1-\beta}} e^{\frac{\gamma}{1-\beta} T} K_{-1} Q_0^{\frac{1}{1-\beta}} \qquad \text{Short-term supply}$$

$$(27) \quad TU = 100(Q/Q^0) \qquad \text{Degree of capacity utilisation}$$

$$(28) \quad u = 100 \left(\frac{u_0 + u_1 POP + u_2 L}{POP}\right) \qquad \text{Unemployment rate}$$

$$(29) \quad H = h_0 + h_1 T + h_2 T^2 + h_3 u \qquad \text{Weekly hours worked}$$

$$(30) \quad PR = Q/(LH) \qquad \text{Productivity}$$

Expectations

$$(31) \quad \dot{p}^a = 0.4\dot{p} + 0.3\dot{p}_{-1} + 0.3\dot{p}_{-2} \qquad \text{Expected inflation rate}$$

$$(32) \quad Q^a = Q^{0.37} Q_{-1}^{0.30} Q_{-2}^{0.20} Q_{-3}^{0.13} \qquad \text{Expected output}$$

Table 3 (*continued*)

Prices and costs

(33) $\quad \dot{W} = w_0 + w_1\dot{p}_C + w_2\dot{p}_{C-1} + w_3u + w_4\dot{PR}$ $\qquad$ Wage rate

(34) $\quad CSU = \dfrac{WLH(1 + \tau_{CS})}{Q}$ $\qquad$ Unit wage cost

(35) $\quad p = p_{-1}^{\theta}(CSU^{\mu}p_M^{1-\mu})^{1-\theta}(1 + \tau_{CS})$
$\qquad\qquad (1 + \tau_{CS-1})^{-\theta}e^{p_0 + p_2(I/K_{-1})}$ $\qquad$ Producer price

(36) $\quad p_C = p_{C-1}^{\eta}(p^{\mu_1}p_M^{1-\mu_1})^{1-\eta}e^{p_1 + p_3 TU}$ $\qquad$ Consumer price

(37) $\quad p_D = (Qp - Cp_c)/(I + D + G + (\text{adjustement}))$ $\qquad$ Demand deflator (excl. consumption)

(38) $\quad C_K = p_D(r_{LT} - \dot{p}^a + \delta)$ $\qquad$ User cost of capital

Income distribution

(39) $\quad ENE = pQ(1 - \tau_{II}) - WHL(1 + \tau_{CS}) - Am - Div$ $\qquad$ Net entrepreneurial income

(40) $\quad Am = k_A K_{-1}$ $\qquad$ Capital depreciation

(41) $\quad RD = WHL(1 - \tau_{ID}) + ENE(1 - \tau_{ID})$ $\qquad$ Disposable income

(42) $\quad IM = \tau_{ID}(WHL + ENE) + \tau_{II}pQ + \tau_{CS}(WHL)$ $\qquad$ Taxes

(43) $\quad DE = Gp_D - IM$ $\qquad$ Public deficit

Money

(44) $\quad M/p = (M/p)_{-1}^{\phi}(e^{m_0 + m_2 r_{LT} Q^{m_1}})^{1-\phi}$ $\qquad$ Money demand

(45) $\quad M = M^0$ $\qquad$ Equilibrium on the money market

— producer prices adjust rather slowly (mean lag: 2 years) towards the unit cost resulting for 90% from the unit wage cost and for 10% of the price of raw materials. An increase by 1 point in the rate of investment (corresponding on average to an increase by 5% in investment) would lead to a long-term increase by 2% in the producer price level. The high sensitivity of the wage rate to unemployment and of prices to the investment rate indicate that world inflation must respond strongly to the cyclical fluctuations in world output;

Table 4. Estimation results

Consumption		Rate of unemployment	
c_0	$-$ 0.18	u_0	$-$ 16.83
	(3.1)		(9.9)
c_1 (C_{-1})	0.84	u_1	0.56
	(14.5)		(8.1)
$c_2(RD/_{PC})$	0.19	u_2	$-$ 0.20
	(3.4)		(1.6)
$c_3(P_{\dot{C}})$	$-$ 0.38	D.W.	2.01
	(3.3)		
		S.E.E. (%)	0.27
D.W.	1.88		
S.E.E (%)	0.73		
Capital		Production capacity	
Q_0	0.65		
	(32.4)		
β(coeff. of L)	0.55		
	(6.8)		
γ(technical progress)	0.011		
	(25.1)		
D.W.	0.66	D.W.	0.024
S.E.E. (%)	1.60	S.E.E. (%)	0.86
Inventory investment		Weekly hours worked	
d_0	$-$ 0.12	h_0	86.7
	(0.6)		(34.0)
$d_1(DC_{-1})$	$-$ 0.5	$h_1(T)$	0.49
	(2.4)		(6.1)
$d_2(\Delta D)$	0.09	$h_2(T^2)$	0.009
	(1.7)		(2.6)
$d_3(\Delta D_{-1})$	0.25	$h_3(TU)$	0.21
	(5.6)		(6.7)
$d_4(\Delta D_{-2})$	0.09	D.W.	1.39
	(1.7)		
$d_5(\dot{p}_M)$	0.82	S.E.E.	0.46
	(2.6)	level	0.46
D.W.	1.68	as a % of H	0.47
S.E.E.			
level	0.16		
as a % of GDP	0.15		
Employment		Wage rate	
		w_0	0.06
$\lambda(L_{-1})$	0.56		(4.1)
	(7.8)		

Table 4 (*continued*)

		$w_1(\dot{p}_c)$	0.97
			(5.9)
		$w_2(\dot{p}c_{-1})$	0.33
			(1.3)
		$w_3(u)$	− 0.015
			(2.5)
		$w_4(\dot{P}R)$	0.33
			(2.3)
D.W.	2.32	D.W.	0.79
S.E.E. (%)	1.86	S.E.E. (%)	1.23

Consumer price		Producer price	
$\eta(P_{c-1})$	0.33	$\theta(P_{-1})$	0.67
	(5.9)		(17.5)
$\mu_1(P)$	0.92	$\mu(CSU)$	0.90
	(67.6)		(19.7)
$1-\mu(p_M)$	0.08	$1-\mu(P_M)$	0.10
	(2.3)		(2.2)
p_1	− 0.04	p_0	0.04
	(1.1)		(0.6)
$p_3(TU)$	0.0006	$p_2(I/K_{-1})$	0.68
	(1.5)		(2.1)
D.W.	1.18	D.W.	1.46
S.E.E. (%)	0.61	S.E.E. (%)	0.80

Money demand	
$\phi((M/p_{-1})$	0.50
	(2.9)
m_0	− 1.58
	(2.7)
$m_2(r_{LT})$	− 0.019
	(3.1)
$m_1(Q)$	1.30
	(3.1)
D.W.	1.36
S.E.E. (%)	2.24

The figures between the brackets are the estimated student t.

- the consumer price adjusts very quickly to the changes in producer prices, the price of raw materials play also a direct role. An increase by 1 percentage point in the degree of capacity utilisation leads to a long-term increase by 0.1% in the consumer price.
- money demand shows large elasticities with respect to production (1.3) and to interest rates (an increase by 1 percentage point of the interest rate reduces

money demand by 3.8% in the long run). This high elasticity of money demand w.r.t. interest rates must imply that monetary policies are relatively inefficient in stabilizing world output since changes in money supply would only imply small variations in interest rates.

The model has been estimated on the basis of the period 1964–1981 and simulated over the sample period. The results obtained seem reasonable; the average absolute simulation errors for the various variables are given in Table 5: it appears that the model is more precise when money supply is exogenous than when interest rates are exogenous.

Table 5. Mean absolute errors (dynamic simulation, 1972 to 1981)

	M^0 exogenous	r_{LT} exogenous
GDP (as a perc. of av. GDP)	0.9	1.3
Consumer price (as a perc. of av. price)	1.5	2.0
Unemployment rate (in per cent)	0.5	0.6
Interest rate (percentage point)	1.5	–
Employment (as a perc. of the av. employment)	0.8	1.1

5. SIMULATIONS

The usual multipliers (increase in public expenditures (Table 6), increase in money supply or interest rates (Table 7)) were calculated with this world model. When money supply is exogenous, the increase in public expenditures has only a transitory effect on production; moreover, the effect is weak because of the instantaneous increase in interest rates. When the interest rate is exogenous, the public expenditures' multiplier is high (2.9 after 10 years), which is normal, the world being a closed economy; large inflationary pressures follow an increase in public expenditures, resulting from the real wage gains due to increased employment.

Increasing money supply does not influence significantly production levels, which was expected because of the high elasticity of money demand with respect to interest rates; it has however an important effect on inflation rates: monetary policies seem, at a world level, more efficient for keeping inflation under control than growth. Raising interest rates cause a significant slowdown in growth and inflation, investment being particularly depressed after the increase in the relative cost of capital. The recent upswing in interest rates would, according to this model, have had strong consequences on world inflation and growth.

Table 6. Increase by 1 (= 1% of the average GDP) in public expenditures

Effects on . . .	After 1 year	After 2 years	After 5 years	After 10 years
GDP (level)				
· M exogenous	+ 1.0	+ 0.9	+ 0.4	− 1.7
· r_{LT} exogenous	+ 1.2	+ 1.5	+ 2.0	+ 2.9
Consumer prices (level)				
· M exogenous	+ 0.1%	+ 0.3%	+ 1.5%	+ 5.7%
· r_{LT} exogenous	+ 0.3%	+ 1.1%	+ 3.7%	+ 13.8%
Interest rates (percentage points)				
· M exogenous	+ 0.6	+ 0.8	+ 1.5	+ 3.0
· r_{LT} exogenous	−	−	−	−
Investment (level)				
· M exogenous	− 0.1	− 0.2	− 0.4	− 1.1
· r_{LT} exogenous	+ 0.1	+ 0.3	+ 1.0	+ 2.4
Wage rate (level)				
· M exogenous	+ 0.3%	+ 0.6%	+ 2.7%	+ 8.6%
· r_{LT} exogenous	+ 0.4%	+ 1.2%	+ 6.1%	+ 22.2%
Employment				
· M exogenous	+ 0.7%	+ 1.0%	+ 1.2%	+ 0.2%
· r_{LT} exogenous	+ 0.8%	+ 1.4%	+ 2.2%	+ 0.6%

Two simulations on the historical period have also been made. The first assumes steadily increasing prices of raw materials (i.e. 1.8% per annum) over the period 1973–1981, which corresponds to its average growth rate between 1960–1972. In that case, according to the model, the consumption growth rate would have been higher by 1.6% a year, and the inflation rate reduced by 2.7% a year (cf. Table 8). Households would have benefited from the improved growth, since real wages would have increased quicker (by 2.6% a year), the savings rate being lower because of the reduction in inflation. The induced reduction in unemployment is spectacular, employment being increased by 23% in 9 years time. This result seems hardly reasonable, and is a consequence of the other policy instruments (money supply, public expenditures) having been left at their reference levels.

In the second simulation, money supply is assumed to have grown between 1972 and 1981 at a constant rate (10% a year), equal to its average growth rate between 1960 and 1971. According to the model, GDP growth would have been reduced by 0.5% a year, and inflation by 1.2% a year, which confirms the efficiency of monetary policies in controlling price movements. If during the seventies both

Table 7. Increase by 1% in money supply (M exogenous)

Effects on ...	After 1 year	After 2 years	After 5 years	After 10 years
GDP (%)	+ 0.3	+ 0.2	+ 0.2	+ 0.2
Consumer price (%)	+ 0.1	+ 0.3	+ 0.5	+ 0.6
Interest rates (percentage points)	− 0.5	− 0.1	− 0.1	− 0.1
Investment (%)	+ 1.5	+ 0.8	+ 0.7	+ 0.6
Wage rate (%)	+ 0.3	+ 0.5	+ 0.8	+ 0.9
Employment (%)	+ 0.2	+ 0.2	0	0
Consumption (%)	0	0	+ 0.1	+ 0.2

Increase by 1 percentage point in the interest rate (r_{LT} exogenous)

Effects on ...	After 1 year	After 2 years	After 5 years	After 10 years
GDP (%)	− 0.4	− 0.4	− 0.8	− 1.3
Consumer price (%)	− 0.3	− 0.5	− 1.5	− 3.3
Investment (%)	− 2.1	− 2.3	− 3.7	− 4.7
Wage rage (%)	− 0.3	− 0.8	− 2.4	− 5.3
Employment (%)	− 0.2	− 0.4	− 0.3	− 0

Table 8. Price of raw materials on its previous trend between 73 and 81 (M exogenous

Effects on ...	73	75	77	79	81
GDP (%)	+ 0.8	+ 7.1	+ 10.7	+ 12.1	+ 14.9
Consumer prices (%)	− 2.2	− 13.9	− 20.5	− 20.9	− 21.9
Investment (%)	+ 0.7	+ 0.5	+ 3.0	+ 5.3	+ 5.0
Consumption (%)	+ 1.3	+ 9.5	+ 15.5	+ 17.9	+ 22.3
Wage rate (%)	− 1.9	− 13.7	− 18.2	− 13.0	− 5.7
Employment (%)	+ 0.6	+ 7.4	+ 14.4	+ 18.9	+ 23.2

Money supply on its previous trend between 73 and 81 (M exogenous)

Effects on ...	73	75	77	79	81
GDP (%)	− 2.6	− 2.4	− 3.5	− 4.0	− 4.8
Consumer prices (%)	− 2.4	− 5.1	− 7.7	− 9.8	− 10.9
Investment (%)	− 11.0	− 12.3	− 15.5	− 14.5	− 15.4
Consumption (%)	− 0.2	− 0.4	− 0.9	− 1.8	− 3.0
Wage rate (%)	− 3.6	− 8.0	− 12.1	− 15.4	− 17.0
Employment (%)	− 2.4	− 1.5	− 1.0	− 0.2	+ 0.3

prices of raw materials and money supply had maintained the same growth rates as during the sixties, inflation would have been lower by 3.4% per year, the average inflation rate over 1972–81 decreasing from 11.8% to 8.4% per year.

6. CONCLUSION

The disequilibrium estimates made lead to the choice of a neo-keynesian model to represent the functioning of the world economy. This model gives significant results inspite of the complexity of the economy to be described. The main conclusions drawn from the simulation results are the following: world inflation is very sensitive to the level of activity and to monetary policies, whereas world output depends more on fiscal policies and on interest rates, the latter being relatively unelastic with respect to world money supply.

APPENDIX

List of variables

Am	=	depreciation of capital
C	=	consumption
C_K	=	user cost of capital
CSU	=	unit wage cost
D	=	demand, inventory investment excluded
DEF	=	public deficit
DS	=	stock variation
DIV	=	miscellaneous exogenous variables in the firms' accounts
δ	=	rate of capital depreciation
ENE	=	net entrepreneurial income
G	=	public expenditures
H	=	weekly hours worked
I	=	investment
IM	=	taxes
K	=	capital stock
K^*	=	optimal capital stock
k_A	=	rate of fiscal capital depreciation
L	=	employment
L^*	=	optimal employment
π	=	short-term firms' profits
M	=	money stock (M2)
M^0	=	money supply
p	=	GDP deflator
p^a	=	expected price level
p_c	=	consumer price
p_M	=	price of raw materials

Q	= GDP
Q^a	= expected GDP
Q^d	= total demand
Q^0	= supply
RD	= disposable income
r_{LT}	= long-term interest rate
T	= time
TU	= degree of capacity utilisation
τ_{CS}	= rate of employers' social security contributions
τ_{ID}	= rate of direct taxes
τ_{II}	= rate of indirect taxes
U	= unemployment
u	= unemployment rate
W	= hourly wage rate

NOTES

1) With the following weight: US Dollar: 43.3%; Canadian Dollar: 4.6%; Yen: 14.1%; Deutsch Mark: 11.8%; French Franc: 9.6%; Sterling: 6.6%; Belgian Franc: 1.8%; Danish Kron: 1.1%; Dutch Guilder: 2.4%; Italian Lira: 4.7%.
2) See the appendix (list of variables).
3) Log p_c replaced by θ Log p + $(1 - \theta)$ Log p_M; the aggregated linearized demand can be written.

$$\text{Log } Q^d = c_0 + c_1 \text{ Log } C_{-1} + c_2 \text{ Log } \frac{RD}{p_c} + c_3(\text{Log } p_c - \text{Log } p_{c_{-1}}) \qquad (14')$$

$$+ \left(\frac{\bar{C}}{K_{-1}}\right)\left(\delta - \frac{\gamma}{\alpha + \beta} + \frac{\beta}{\alpha + \beta}\left(\frac{WH(1 + \tau_{CS})}{K}\right) + \frac{1}{\alpha + \beta}\dot{Q}^a\right)$$

$$+ \left(\frac{\bar{1}}{C}\right)(d_0 + d_1\Delta S_{-1} + d_2\Delta D + d_3\Delta D_{-1} + d_4\Delta D_{-2} + d_5 p_M) + \epsilon_D$$

where $\left(\dfrac{\bar{C}}{K-1}\right)$ is the mean of $\dfrac{C}{K-1}$ and $\left(\dfrac{\bar{1}}{C}\right)$ the mean of $\dfrac{1}{C}$.

4) Adding a trend to (17) does not change the results significantly.
5) The equations here have been estimated by ordinary least squares procedures; when they were integrated in the model and estimated simultaneously with the rest of it, similar results were obtained.

REFERENCES

Atlas (1983), *Le Modèle Atlas*, deuxième version, Mimeo, Direction de la Prévision, Paris.
Beenstock, M. and G.R. Dicks (1983), 'An aggregate monetary model of the World economy', *European Economic Review*, May.

COMET III (1980), *The COMET III Model*, A. Barten, G.D'Alcantara, D. de Crombrugghe, E. Schokkaert, Mimeo, Communion des Communautés Européennes.

INTERLINK (1979), *The OECD international linkage model*, occasional economic studies, January.

Parkin, M. and G. Zis (1976), *Inflation in the world economy*, Manchester University Press and University of Toronto Press.

CHAPTER 6

II. A GLOBUS OECD/COMECON SIMULATION MODEL

Grant Kirkpatrick
Wissenschaftzentrum, Berlin, Federal Republic of Germany

1. INTRODUCTION

Economic crisis, or serious lack of performance relative to an expectation, raises questions relating to causation and to policy in the broadest sense. Given the close interdependence existing between countries, it is usually thought desirable to use international or multi-country models in order to investigate the two questions. However, economic crises are not only interesting in their own right but also because they are usually thought to be associated with political ones. Even if not associated, causation and policy clearly involve political factors. For this broader political economy analysis, international models are also required.

This paper describes a component of the international economic model which has been developed for the GLOBUS global modeling project. GLOBUS seeks to model political economic processes both nationally and internationally with the objective to investigate possible stresses and strains, how they might arise, what their possible consequences are, and how policy might react (Bremer (1982)). The model comprises 25 countries and the time span covers a 25–30 year period which is long enough for major feedbacks to work themselves through, and for mildly unstable processes to manifest themselves. Unlike projects such as LINK which utilizes 'custom built' models for each country, we use a prototype approach: for groups of countries the same model form is used, the differences between countries of a group being parametric. The models themselves are fully dynamic and are written in continuous time i.e., differential equations. Following the ideas of Bergstrom and Wymer (1976) and Gandolfo (1981) they possess analytical longrun solutions (e.g. steady state growth) which require that they be relatively small in size.

In Section 2 we outline our OECD prototype model which is used to represent the USA, Germany, France, Canada, UK, Italy and Japan. As the model has been described in detail elsewhere (Kirkpatrick (1983)) we shall be brief, preferring

Artus, P. and Guvenen, O. (eds.): International Macroeconomic Modelling for Policy Decisions.
© *1986. Martinus Nijhoff Publishers, Dordrecht/Boston/Lancaster.*
ISBN 90-247-3201-8. Printed in The Netherlands.

to focus on potential crisis areas associated with union and government reaction functions. Section 3 discusses bilateral trade, financial and policy relations between OECD countries.

A major concern of our model is the wider set of economic and political relations and how the problems in one country impinge on another. Usually this is thought of as a North/South problem but the East/West relations are surely of equal importance. Section 4 therefore outlines our CPE (Centrally Planned Economy) model which is used to represent the USSR, Poland, CSSR and DDR. Section 5 draws together the models interactions illustrating how they might be used to analyse 'economic' crisis.

It is appropriate at this stage to list what we regard as important problem areas since this extra model perception governs model structure. For OECD economies welfare state problems in the context of economic and demographic change clearly dominate. Unemployment, inflation and union/government relations in the context of a game situation are all clearly important. On an international scale is the importance of imported raw materials, protectionism and the move toward a greater emphasis on bilateral rather than multi-lateral trade relations. Inter-government policy making as an inferior non-cooperative game is also a major factor. For the CPE economies the problems are similar. Living standards, economic growth, debt and bilateral trade and financial relations are clearly important as is the role of planning as an equilibrating mechanism. The two 'blocks' are linked via economic, political and military developments.

Finally, we must stress that although our models are currently being estimated using continuous time econometric estimation techniques (see Gandolfo (1981)) they in no way provide statistical forecasts. They are intended solely as aids for scenario analysis. As such, they serve to provide a method for examining complex dynamic processes for which no analytical solution is possible. The models are used for numerical simulation but unlike statistical forecasts a substantial theoretical and numerical input is necessary from outside the model. In any case it would be hard to take seriously a statistical forecast for such a long period.

2. PROTOTYPE OECD MODEL

(a) The prototype OECD model recognizes four income sectors: household, firm, government and overseas. Such an aggregation allows a wide range of policy instruments such as personal and corporate taxes to be investigated. The aggregation is also required for other political economy aspects, (see Kirkpatrick and Widmaier (1983)).

Given the long-run nature of the model it is necessary to fully incorporate stock and flow effects. This is done through a flow of funds accounting framework, Table 1. The top half of the Table covers the national accounting aspect of the model and illustrates the connection between the four income sectors. For clarity we have included taxation flows under the heading 'Net transfers'. For each income sector the column is termed Financial surplus or deficit and indicates the asset effect of current transactions. The second half of the Table indicates stock composition or portfolio effects. For the simple OECD model we recognize only domestic net financial claims, foreign net financial claims and reserves. Hence the method of financing (i.e., bonds, money, equity) is regarded as of a second order of importance to the size of the portfolio effect. For a long-run model this may not be such a bad assumption and in any case the money/bonds dichotomy is not without theoretical and empirical challenge (e.g. Kohli and McKibbim (1982) and Purvis (1980))[1].

The behavioural equations of the abbreviated model are set out in Table 2 and comprise 20 first order differential equations, 6 of which are identities. For ease of exposition the definitional equations are not substituted thereby giving the

Table 1. OECD prototype model sectoral relationships*

	Household	Firm	Government	Overseas	Total	
Income	Y_1	Y_2	Y_3		=	Y
Net transfers	T_1	T_2	T_3	T_4	=	0
Consumption	$-C_1$		$-C_2$		=	$-C$
Investment	$-I_1$	$-I_2$	$-I_3$		=	$-I$
Bal. of goods & services				$-X+M$	=	$-X+M$
Financial surplus/deficit	F_1	$-F_2$	$-F_3$	F_4	=	0
=						
Financial assets Domestic financial claims	ΔWIF	ΔSIF	ΔSIG	ΔWIO		0
Foreign financial claims	ΔBM			ΔBM		0
Reserves	−		ΔR_3	ΔR_4		0
=	F_1	$-F_2$	$-F_3$	F_4		

Net nominal financial claims held, household $W = \int_{-\alpha}^{t} F_1 dt$

Net nominal financial claims issued $SI = \int_{-\alpha}^{t} F_2 dt + \int_{-\alpha}^{t} F_3 dt$

*For information on the definitions of variables, see Appendix A.

Table 2. OECD prototype model[*]

Aggregate supply

$$D \ln Y = \alpha 1 \ln \frac{YS}{Y} \tag{1}$$

$$YS = \gamma 1 e^{\lambda 1 t} \frac{W}{P}^{-\beta 1} \frac{EWPH}{P}^{-\beta 2} BK \tag{1a}$$

Labour demand

$$D \ln ZLF = \alpha 2 \ln \frac{ZLFS}{ZLF} \tag{2}$$

$$ZLFS = \gamma 2 e^{\lambda 2 t} \frac{W}{P}^{-\beta 4} \frac{EWPH}{P}^{-\beta 5} BK \tag{2a}$$

Raw material/Energy import demand

$$D \ln EN = \alpha 3 \ln \frac{ES}{EN} \tag{3}$$

$$ES = \gamma 3 e^{\lambda 3 t} \frac{W}{P}^{-\beta 7} \frac{EWPH}{P}^{-\beta 8} BK \tag{3a}$$

$$EWPH = EW.DOLR \tag{3b} \text{ identity}$$

Investment demand

$$Dk = \alpha 5 \left\{ \alpha 51 \left(\beta 9 \frac{YS}{BK} - rc \right) + \beta' - k \right\} \tag{4}$$

$$D \ln BK = k \tag{4a} \text{ identity}$$

$$rc = \gamma 5 + \beta 10 (r - D \ln P) \tag{4b}$$

Price equation

$$D \ln P = \alpha 10 \ln \frac{VS}{V} - \alpha 11 D \ln V \tag{5}$$

$$VS = \gamma 15 Y^{\beta 41} e^{rc\beta 42} \tag{5a}$$

$$DV = Y - DBK - \frac{C.PC}{P} - G - TX + \frac{TMY.PM}{P} \tag{5b} \text{ identity}$$

Final good import demand

$$D \ln TMY = \alpha 6 \ln \frac{TMYS}{TMY} \tag{6}$$

Table 2 (*continued*)

$$TMYS = bC \left(\frac{PM}{PC}\right)^{-\beta 11} \qquad (6a)$$

$$PC = \{bPM^{1-\beta 11} + (1-b)P^{1-\beta 11}\}^{1/1-\beta 11} \qquad (6b)$$

$$PM = PF.DOLR \qquad (6c) \text{ identity}$$

Exports

$$D \ln TX = \alpha 7 \ln \frac{TXS}{TX} \qquad (7)$$

$$TXS = \gamma 7YO \left(\frac{P}{PM}\right)^{-\beta 12} \qquad (7a)$$

Linked model

$$TX = \quad TMYi.DOLR \qquad i = 1 \ldots 25 \qquad (7b)$$

Consumption demand

$$D \ln C = \alpha 8 \ln \frac{CS}{C} \qquad (8)$$

$$CS = \gamma 9 e^{-\beta 13.r} e^{-\beta 14.ro} \frac{YH^{\beta 16}}{PC} \frac{WI^{\beta 17}}{PC} \qquad (8a)$$

$$BMS = \gamma 10 e^{\beta 18.ro} e^{-\beta 19.r} YH^{\beta 21} WI^{\beta 22} \qquad (8b)$$

$$YH = (W.ZLF + FACTY + ro.BM).(1 - \gamma 8) \qquad (8c) \text{ identity}$$

$$WI = BM + WIH \qquad (8d) \text{ identity}$$

Wage rate

$$D \ln W = \alpha 9 \ln \frac{WS}{W} \qquad (9)$$

$$WS = \gamma 14 e^{\lambda 4t} PC^{\beta 38} \frac{ZLF^{\beta 39}}{LF} \qquad (9a)$$

$$LF = e^{\lambda 5t} LF(0) \qquad (9b)$$

Total government expenditure

$$D \ln G = \alpha 16 \ln \frac{GS}{G} - \alpha 17 \ln \left(\gamma 12 \frac{ZLF}{LF}\right)$$

$$- \alpha 18(D \ln P - \gamma 13) + \alpha 19 \ln \left\{\frac{\gamma 18 TX.P}{TMY.PM + EWPH.EN}\right\} \quad (10)$$

Table 2 (*continued*)

$$GS = \gamma 17 Y \tag{10a}$$

$$\text{Tax} = \gamma 4 \text{PI}1 + \frac{\gamma 8 \text{YH}}{(1 - \gamma 8)} \tag{10b}$$

Interest rate reaction function

$$\text{Dr} = \alpha 12 (\text{rs} - \text{r}) \tag{11}$$

$$\text{rs} = -\alpha 15 \ln \frac{(\gamma 11.\text{P})}{(\text{PF}.\text{DOLR})} + \beta 40 \ln \left(\gamma 12 \frac{\text{ZLF}}{\text{LF}} \right) \tag{11a}$$

Exchange rate

$$D \ln \text{DOLR} = \alpha 13 \ln \frac{\text{BMS}}{\text{BM}} - \alpha 14 D \ln \text{BM} \tag{12}$$

Exchange market intervention

$$D \ln \text{ZIR} = 0 \tag{13}$$

Alternative

$$D \ln \text{ZIR} = \alpha 20 \ln \frac{(\gamma 11.\text{P})}{(\text{PF}.\text{DOLR})}$$
$$+ \alpha 21 D \ln \text{DOLR} + \text{Dummy} \tag{13a}$$

Balance of payments

$$\text{DBM} = \text{TX}.\text{P} - \text{TMY}.\text{PM} - \text{EN}.\text{EWPH} + \text{ro}.\text{BM} - \text{DZIR}$$
$$- \text{FACTO} \tag{14 identity}$$

Government budget restriction

$$\text{DSIG} = \text{G}.\text{P} - \text{Tax} + \text{DZIR} \tag{15 identity}$$

Corporate taxation and divident payment

$$D \ln \text{ZDIV} = \alpha 4 \ln \frac{\text{ZDIVS}}{\text{ZDIV}} \tag{16}$$

$$\text{ZDIVS} = \gamma 6 (1 - \gamma 4) \text{PI}1 \tag{16a}$$

$$\text{PI}1 = \text{P}.\text{Y} - \text{W}.\text{ZLF} - \text{EWPH}.\text{EN} - \text{DV}.\text{P} \tag{16b identity}$$

Corporate borrowing

$$\text{DSIF} = \text{YH} - \text{PC}.\text{C} - \text{DSIG} - \text{DBM} \tag{17 identity}$$

Table 2 (*continued*)

Domestic holding of domestic securities

$$DWIH = YH - PC.C - DBM \qquad \text{(18) identity}$$

Total securities on issue by country i

$$SI = SIG + SIF \qquad \text{(19) identity}$$

Wealth income

$$YFACT = ZDIV + r.SIG \qquad \text{(20) identity}$$

$$FACTY = \frac{WIH}{SI}.YFACT \qquad \text{(21)}$$

$$FACTO = YFACT - FACTY \qquad \text{(22) identity}$$

---

*For information on the definitions of variables, see Appendix A.

incorrect impression of a relatively large model. The differential equations are generally written in dynamic adjustment form:

$$D \ln X = \alpha \ln \frac{(XS)}{(X)} \qquad (1)$$

where ln is the natural logarithm and XS is the unobserved level toward which X is adjusting at a rate determined by α. A logarithmic transformation is used since we are dealing with growth processes. It is also useful since when we linearize the time varying system around the steady state to examine its local stability, we obtain a remainder which does not involve time explicitly. Where another term is added to the right hand side of (1) i.e.,

$$D \ln X = \alpha \ln \frac{(XS)}{X} + \beta \ln \frac{(Y)}{(Z)} \qquad (2)$$

the interpretation is that the original adjustment speed is influenced by the additional term, (2) being simply a linear approximation (see Wymer 1976). Direct spillover effects associated with disequilibrium may therefore be easily handled. Indirect spillover is handled via buffer stocks, the most important being inventories.

The models supply structure is represented by equations (1)–(7). Following a great deal of recent work (e.g. Findlay and Rodriguez (1977), Bruno and Sachs (1980)) we recognize imports as comprising final goods and raw materials/intermediates. The economy wide production function therefore comprises three factors (capital BK, labour ZLF, raw materials/energy EN) producing a gross output, Y,

$$Y = f(BK, ZLF, EN) \tag{3}$$

The exclusion of domestically produced raw materials/energy requires very strong separability assumptions but is undertaken here in order to keep the model as small as possible. Differences between countries in technology and domestic raw material production manifests itself in different demand elasticities in addition to differing EN/Y ratios.

With three factors of production the specification of the functional form of (3) requires care. For econometric purposes the transcendental logarithmic production function has achieved a great deal of popularity. However, being only a local approximation (i.e., a truncated Taylor series expansion) it is not helpful in simulation outside of sample periods values. The simplest alternative is the two stage CES production function (e.g. Bruno and Sachs (1979)). For simulation studies this is the functional form used.

In line with theoretical models we assume neo-classical profit maximization subject to a given capital stock and derive a set of partial equilibrium targets for output, employment and energy imports (YS, ZLFS, ES). Constant returns to scale are assumed. The underlying production function parameters are reflected in complex within and between equation parameter restrictions on $\beta 1, \beta 2, \beta 4, \beta 5, \beta 7, \beta 8^2$. The dynamics of (1)–(3) are determined by partial adjustment coefficients $\alpha 1 - \alpha 3$. Nadiri and Rosen (1969) have shown that if the production function is to hold at each instant then one has a system of interdependent factor demand equations. The adjustment coefficients would therefore be related to one another. We do not recognize this cross equation restriction since, without factor utilisation, we have excluded factors of production, thereby rendering the restrictions redundant. The production function is not a purely technological relationship so that in the short run it need not hold.

Many recent contributions (e.g. Lipton and Sachs (1983)) have stressed the need to incorporate micro foundations rigorously. By this is meant intertemporal profit or utility maximization subject to costs of adjustment. The problem with such approaches is that analytically tractable solutions are based on such limited functional forms. We therefore prefer a well worked out static solution embedded in a dynamic structure which is to some extent ad hoc[3]. However, it is true that the logic of the model calls for the replacement of real wages and real raw material prices by their expected values. Specification of an error learning process for expectations increases substantially the dimension of the system. For clarity it is therefore excluded.

In more conventional terms equation (1) defines the usual upward sloping aggregate supply curve in P, Y space. Notice that an exchange rate depreciation leads to a leftward shift of the schedule thereby raising the possibility of a virtuous cycle. Wage increase also lead to a leftward shift. Equation (3) meets the criticisms of writers such as Burgess (1974) who claim that aggregate import equations are usually totally misspecified. Finally, equation (2) integrates the large labour market literature which emphasizes slow employment adjustment with macro-economic models, something which is seldom done. For simulation studies one may therefore investigate the effects of policies which change the costs of labour adjustment and therefore the adjustment speed.

As in all macro-economic models two crucial relations are those determining investment and producer prices, equations (4)–(5). Equation (4) follows studies such as Gandolfo (1981) and Bergstrom and Wymer (1978) in specifying investment as governed by a second order differential process (i.e. an Alman lag distribution). The partial equilibrium rate of capital formation is assumed to be a linear function (with constants $\alpha 51$ and β') of the excess of the marginal product of capital, $\beta 9$ YS/BK over the cost of capital, rc. The latter is viewed as a linear function of the real rate of interest. This formulation is convenient in a macro-economic model which is aggregated so as to include only one interest rate. The constant $\alpha 5$ also ensures that the cost of capital may well be positive even though the real rate of interest is negative (Baily, Hall and Phillips (1980)). One should also emphasize that in simulations involving change in the corporate tax rate, $\gamma 4$, the marginal product of capital must be net of tax. Hence, welfare state financing (or the financing of a defense build up) via an increased corporate tax rate would lead to a slower rate of investment, lower tax base etc. The effects may take quite some time to appear, certainly longer than an election cycle.

The producer price equation (5) is crucial for the disequilibrium form of the model. In disequilibrium, information flows on market possibilities occur via inventory movements. Firms have a desired inventory level based on a transactions demand and the cost of capital[4]. When there is disequilibrium, prices will alter and this will bring about an output effect in the same direction. The rate of change of inventories also has a direct flow effect on price determination. The relative contribution of price and output response to goods market disequilibrium will, of course, depend on a number of parameters. Under or overshooting of price and output is likely. Artus and Bismut (1983) have recently observed that many price models ignore completely market clearing tatonnement based on excess demand. Our formulation does not suffer from this criticism and is more in line with the information ideas of Benassy (1976) and Gordon and Hynes (1970).

Many models rely upon the law of one price in specifying domestic price levels. The reason for so doing is mainly for analytical convenience which is not a problem here. However, the assumption of perfect substitutability between home and foreign goods is theoretically weak and empirically dubious. We accordingly assume imperfect substitutability between home and final goods which is why we are able to specify an independent price function. This also leads us to a further discussion of the models demand side.

Equation (6) views final goods imports, TMY, as being used solely in private consumption, C. A convenient way of introducing product differentiation is to follow Armington (1969) in defining an aggregate or composite commodity, in this case C, which is a constant elasticity of substitution (CES) function of imports, TMY, and domestic goods for domestic consumption, CY:

$$C = (bTMY^{-\rho} + (1 - b)CY^{-\rho})^{-1/\rho} \tag{4}$$

where b and ρ are parameters and $\beta 11 = 1/(1 + \rho)$ is the trade substitution elasticity between foreign and domestic goods. Minimizing the cost of acquiring the composite good yields the import function (6a) and the uniquely defined consumer price index (6b). The latter is extremely important for it allows us to define a consumer and a producer real wage. Differentiation of the real wage concept is increasingly seen as important in understanding domestic and international transmission mechanisms (e.g. Corden (1983)).

The other components of aggregate demand are exports, equation (7), aggregate consumption, equation (8), and government expenditure, equation (10). The former is only included for the steady state analysis and will be discussed below in the context of bilateral trade relations. The latter will be discussed presently. For now we must note that the model defines the usual downward sloping aggregate demand function in P, Y space, wages and the exchange rate entering as shift factors. As in Corden (1983), employment and output effects are transmitted between countries via shifts in the bilateral terms of trade.

(b) One of the most important relations determining the transmission of disturbances is the behaviour of the real wage and of government policy. The former is in part dependent on the wage setting mechanism, equation (9). In OECD economies trade unions are an important factor though the importance does vary considerably. Equation (9) can be variously interpreted as the unions controlling a decision variable, the nominal wage W, or that the actual nominal wage increase granted by Employers is positively related to the increase desired by Unions. Either way equation (9) is not more than a reduced form of a rather complex system (see Kirkpatrick and Widmaier (1983)). If Unions are concerned with maximizing real income of all members then it is reasonable to suppose that the consumer price index and the unemployment enter into wage demands. The extent of indexation is the key question, a factor already stressed by Branson (1980) and Modigliani and Schioppa (1978).

The relative importance of the Union structure is, however, such that Union wage setting should be firmly placed in the context of game behaviour (e.g. Gylfason and Lindbeck (1983)). If this is so then equation (9) must be seen as a Nash Cournot solution with government policy variables perhaps also appearing in (9a). However, it is well established that a Nash Cournot solution is inferior to a cooperative one so that the model can be used to highlight the costs of particular institutions. More importantly, and in the context of crisis, is that one may be faced not with a Nash Cournot situation but one of unstable Stackelberg leadership. This is particularly so if Unions and Government do not share a common reduced form model as to how the economy works.

This leads us to the other side of the game situation: government policy, equations (11), (10), (13). To keep this paper brief we shall focus only on government expenditures holding the tax rate constant[5]. In deriving a government reaction function one can either specify a vote maximizing government or goal oriented government subject to an electoral constraint. Either way the government must have a model as to what causes political support and one is faced again with the role of trade unions. An important intermediate role is the relationship between political support and union behaviour. Equation (10) is a best case equation. The government has in mind targets for inflation and unemployment, $\gamma 12$, $\gamma 13$, and deviations about such targets affect the governments budgetary policy. But how do such targets evolve? Does it matter if they are essentially arbitrary? The first question is of immediate relevance for if $\gamma 12$ were 1% in 1970 it is hard to imagine it is the same today[6]. One plausible method is to allow the target to evolve by an error learning process i.e.,

$$D\gamma 12 = \alpha\left(\gamma 12 - \frac{LF}{ZLF}\right) \tag{5}$$

Hence sustained unemployment would lead to an increase in the 'desired' unemployment rate. Clearly one might be dealing with an unstable process even if gaming situations are not incorporated.

Answers to the second question must be handled by both qualitative and numerical analysis and this also brings us to the wider question of crisis. The simplified model has been solved for its steady state growth path and results are reported in Table 3. What concerns us here are very strong restrictions on the wage growth rate, restrictions (a)–(c). What processes ensure such restrictions? When we turn to the question of levels then it seems the target evolution process becomes important. At the time of writing, however, no analytical solution has been found for initial conditions.

Crisis has also another economic aspect: the dynamic stability of the system. The model has been linearized about its steady state and parameter sensitivity analysis conducted (see Kirkpatrick (1983)). Broadly speaking the model is highly sensitive to nine parameters and four equations, two of which are the wage and

Table 3. Steady state growth rates of the endogenous variable

Variable	Real	Steady state growth rate
Y, BK, V, TMY		$\lambda 8$
C, TX, G		$\lambda 8$
EN		$\lambda 8 + \lambda 7 - \lambda 6$
ZLF		$\lambda 5$

	Nominal	
W		$\lambda 10 - \lambda 5 = \lambda 4 + \lambda 10 - \lambda 8$ when $\beta 38 = 1$
DOLR		$-\lambda 7 - \lambda 8 + \lambda 10$
P		$\lambda 10 - \lambda 8$
PC		$\lambda 10 - \lambda 8$
ZDIV, SIF, PI1, Taxf, YH, WI		$\lambda 10$
BM, SI, SIG		$\lambda 10$

Restrictions

(a) $\lambda 4 = \dfrac{1}{\beta 1} \{\lambda 1 - \beta 2(\lambda 6 - \lambda 7)\}$

(b) $\lambda 4 = \dfrac{1}{\beta 4} \lambda 1 - \beta 5 \{\lambda 6 - \lambda 7) + \lambda 8 - \lambda 5\}$

(c) $\lambda 4 = \dfrac{1}{\beta 7} \{\lambda 1 - (\beta 8 - 1).(\lambda 6 - \lambda 7)\}$

(d) $\beta 16 + \beta 17 = 1$

(e) $\beta 21 + \beta 22 = 1$

Where $\rho 20 = \lambda 10$

$\lambda 8 = $ growth rate of world income (YO)

$\lambda 7 = $ growth rate of world prices (PF)

$\lambda 6 = $ growth rate of world raw materials prices (EW)

expenditure functions. Increases in government sensitivity to inflation increased the amplitude of cycles and made a plausible system unstable. When gaming solutions are added not surprisingly the model exhibits classic saddle point stability. The dynamic model therefore seems capable of handling a wide variety of situations involving rather unpleasant results.

3. INTER COUNTRY LINKAGE

3.1. Bilateral trade

In order to link countries via trade one may use either a pool or a bilateral approach. In either case the global adding up restrictions must be ensured. We have chosen to use the bilateral approach so that the export equations for each country are replaced by a summation over all importing countries i.e.,

$$TXj = \sum_{i=1}^{n} TMYij \qquad i = 1 \ldots n-1 \tag{6}$$

The reason for preferring the more computationally complex bilateral system is related to the political economy context of the model. Bilateral trade patterns are seen as having an important political content (Pollins (1982)). One has only to look at the controversy raised by US/Japanese and French/German trade balances to see this is so. The greater importance of East/West trade to West European countries than to the US is another example which also illustrates the important economic information generated by bilateral modeling.

In first modeling the determination of aggregate imports (TMY and EN) we have assumed separability. We must therefore utilize a demand system which has the usual system theoretic properties in modeling bilateral allocation. For this purpose we utilize Armington's (1969) trade system where goods are distinguished by country of origin. Assuming a constant elasticity of substitution between suppliers, the desired demand by country i for the goods from country j is given by

$$TMSij = bij\,TMYi\,\frac{(Pij)^{-\sigma}}{(Pi)} \tag{7}$$

where bij is a constant discussed below. The aggregate price index expressed in domestic currency (thereby including exchange rate and tariff effects) is given by

$$Pi = (bijp^{(1-\sigma)} \ldots + binPn^{(1-\sigma)})^{1/1-\sigma} \tag{8}$$

For estimation it is approximated by a Divisia price index. Armington's system is however static. We have therefore embedded it in a simple partial adjustment mechanism subject to an adding up restriction

$$D \ln TMij = \alpha ij \ln \frac{(TMSij)}{(TMYi)} \tag{9}$$

$$D \ln TMi = W1 D \ln TMi1 \ldots + WjD \ln TMij \tag{10}$$

where the weights are nominal shares. The adjustment mechanism is rather simple there being no disequilibrium spillover effects. For preliminary estimation results see Pòllins and Kirkpatrick (1983). A drawback with the system is the unit income elasticity and one can, of course, criticize the separability assumption (e.g. Winter (1982)). However, for our purposes the system is theoretically pleasing and parsimonious, something to be taken seriously in a model comprising 25 countries.

Bilateral import shares are, of course, influenced by many factors other than relative price. Countries may physically not be able to supply all that is demanded or indeed refuse to supply at all. Credit conditions and political and cultural conditions may all have a role. For example, it may be difficult to explain greater trade with Eastern Europe by West European countries by relative price alone. Moreover, to keep the model computationally tractable, the same equations are used in modeling East/East trade where arguably relative prices have no role at all.

In modeling these 'other' determinants of bilateral trade we utilize the constant coefficient, bij. If we term these collection of economic and political factors environmental (ENV) then we may write bij as

$$ bij \ = \ aij + \sum_{n} cij \ln ENVij $$ (11)

Associated with the system are various restrictions:

$$ \sum aij \ = \ 1.0, \qquad \sum cij \ = \ 0 $$ (12)

These restrictions have the effect of making bilateral relations multilateral in effect. Hence an increase in imports by FRG from Poland reflected in a cij > 0 must result in a decrease in imports from at least one other country. The modeling of ENV factors in the case of Comecon is discussed further below.

3.2. Exchange, interest rates and policy interdependence

In their review of linked econometric models Deardorff and Stern (1979) observed that a better research strategy would be to focus multi-country models upon the complete set of international interactions from the start. Individual country detail would then be added only as it became necessary to provide an adequate representation of country behaviour. This is the approach we have followed particularly with respect to exchange and interest rates. Indeed, the primary reason for forming a subset of OECD economies was that they are characterised by very close financial linkages. These linkages are by and large of a different order of magnitude from those with other countries rendering policy and policy coordination particularly difficult.

The thrust of recent modeling of exchange rates and financial linkages is very much toward the asset determination of the exchange rate with flow factors having a longer run influence (e.g., on the steady state exchange rate). For theoretical models perfect substitutability is often assumed thereby allowing the use of the interest rate parity equilibrium condition. However, usually the models concern only two countries and it is not at all clear how the results extend to a multicountry setting (e.g. J. Bhandari (1981), Canzoneri (1982)). Moreover, while theoretical models may also assume either floating or pure fixed rate system, the experience would indicate that central bank operations are still a significant policy instrument.

The exchange rate system/financial linkage system currently employed by our OECD model assumes financial securities denominated in one currency to be imperfect substitutes for securities denominated in other currencies. Accordingly equation (8b) defines an asset demand for net overseas securities as a function on income, wealth and domestic and foreign interest rates. The adding up restriction makes the equation defining domestic demand for domestic securities redundant. The evolution of the net foreign security stock is described by the differential identity (14). Foreign exchange market intervention by the Central Bank, equation (13), influences the behaviour of the model via this identity. The exchange rate is determined via stock and flow equilibrium conditions, equation (12). Stock excess demand will result in an exchange rate appreciation while an increase in the rate of change in net overseas securities will dampen the depreciation. Stock and flow influences are thus fully treated.

The equilibrium mechanism is however rather unsatisfactory. There are two possibilities which are easily incorporated. On the one hand one may pursue a Tobin Style approach in which foreign securities are valued in foreign currency so that an exchange rate change alters the valuation in domestic currency. This is easily implemented by changing the valuation of identity (14) and incorporating the exchange rate into the household wealth identity, equation (15). On the other hand one may view the exchange rate equilibrating mechanism as entering via relative rates of return in which case the interest rates would have to be redefined and an exchange rate expectation equation added. Both adjustment mechanisms may, of course, be included. Our model does not as yet incorporate either mechanism since there remain other multilateral problems to which we shall now turn.

The exchange rate equation (12) is unsatisfactory since it only reflects own country influences. There is no role for excess demand by other countries, only for the home country. If one were to allow such influences then bilateral financial flows would have to be incorporated and net excess demand modeled in a way similar to the determination of exports. This would increase enormously the complexity of what is already a difficult model. One would also have to specify the elasticity of substitution between each currency pair.

A solution appears to be along the lines of Armington (1969) and more particularly the global exchange rate system of Richard (1980). It is not incorporated in the present model for there are still unresolved problems with respect to non OECD countries and central bank intervention. Broadly speaking one must re-define the unit of foreign exchange, DOLR, as a basket currency, weights being given by relative financial size. This is common to many models (e.g. Knight and Mathieson (1979)) and will then involve us in re-calculating cross rates for bilateral trade calculations. Following Armington, Richard assumes a CES function as between assets of different denominations and incorporates a global flow of funds adding up restriction (i.e., financial securities issued must be equal to those held in the form of net wealth). Incorporating the expected exchange rate change as the equilibrating mechanism Richard derives a complex but parsimonious system of exchange rate equations. The system obviates the need to model bilateral financial flows. The system in a modified form will be incorporated into our model and will result in a dualistic world exchange rate system. For macro-economic estimations purposes another less satisfying system will have to be used.

Specification of imperfect asset substitutability allows us to specify an interest rate equation (11), in which government policy is directed towards internal equilibrium (e.g., unemployment) and 'external' balance indicated by a relative competitiveness term. In the full model inflation is also a factor. An intervention function may also be specified incorporating a 'leaning against the wind' effect and an exchange rate target or competitiveness term. Finally, the government expenditure function may also directly incorporate a balance of payments target. The policy choices as represented by targets and coefficient value may of course be intertemporally and internationally inconsistent. This aspect together with the international game context will be discussed in the last section.

4. A PROTOTYPE CPE MODEL

Despite the increasing number of macro-econometric models of CPE's, progress is still hindered by the lack of an agreed macro-economic theory. In this section we briefly describe the theoretical structure of our CPE model. A detailed description is in Kirkpatrick (1983a) where we also discuss issues such as Net Material Product/Gross National Product, foreign trade accounting and the specification of identities (see Brada *et al.* (1981) and Szakolczia (1982)). Description of the political model is in Widmaier (1983a) while strategic interactions are discussed in Ward (1982) and Ward and Kirkpatrick (1983).

In constructing a theoretical simulation model of a CPE one is immediately confronted with the twin issues of planners preferences and the equilibrating role of planning. One approach is along the lines of optimal control. However, for a number of reasons we use a static approach which is embedded in a dynamic framework. The latter emphasizes information flows. Optimal objectives, plans and plan implementation are conceptually separated. They interact with household, production and international sectors. Real planning is also supported by financial control via a state budgeting model.

A simplified version of the model excluding explicitly modeled raw materials is presented in Table 4. The first component relates to the formation of optimal

Table 4. CPE prototype model – version 1[*]

Optimal state objectives

$$CP = \gamma1.Z.ENV \tag{1}$$

$$MILP = \gamma2.Z.ENV \tag{2}$$

$$GP = \gamma3.Z.ENV \tag{3}$$-

$$DBKP = \gamma4.Z.ENV \tag{4}$$

$$VP = (1 - \gamma1 - \gamma2 - \gamma3 - \gamma4).Z.ENV \tag{5}$$

$$TMP = \gamma5.YP\frac{PXE^{\beta1}}{PME} \tag{6}$$

$$XOSTP = \gamma6.YOSTE \tag{7}$$

$$XWESTP = (DBP - XOSTP.PXIE + TMP.PME + R.BE)/PXE \tag{8}$$

$$YP = \gamma7e^{\lambda1t}(\gamma8ZLE^{-\beta2} + (1 - \gamma8)BKE^{-\beta2})^{-1/\beta2} \tag{9}$$

$$Z = \left(1 + \gamma5\frac{PXE^{\beta1}}{PME} - \gamma5\frac{PXE^{\beta1-1}}{PME}\right)YP + VE - \frac{DPB}{PXE}$$

$$- R.\frac{BE}{PXE} - \frac{(PXE - PXIE)}{PXE} . \gamma6.YOSTE \tag{10}$$

$$WP = \gamma7(CP.PC)^{\beta3}\frac{1}{ZLE} \tag{11}$$

Expectation formation

$$ZLE = \gamma8.POP \tag{12}$$

$$D \ln BKE = \alpha1 \ln\frac{BKE}{BK} \tag{13}$$

$$D \ln YOSTE = \alpha2 \ln\frac{YOSTE}{YOST} \tag{14}$$

$$D \ln PXE = \alpha3 \ln\frac{PXE}{PX} \tag{15}$$

$$D \ln PXIE = \alpha4 \ln\frac{PXIE}{PXI} \tag{16}$$

$$D \ln BE = \alpha5 \ln\frac{BE}{B} \tag{17}$$

Table 4 (*continued*)

$$D \ln PME = \alpha6 \ln \frac{PME}{PM} \tag{18}$$

$$D \ln VE = \alpha7 \ln \frac{VE}{V} \tag{19}$$

$$D \ln ZME = \alpha8 \ln \frac{ZME}{ZM} \tag{20}$$

Announced plan formation

$$D \ln CS = \alpha9 \ln \frac{CP}{CS} \tag{21}$$

$$D \ln GS = \alpha9 \ln \frac{GP}{GS} \tag{22}$$

$$D \ln VS = \alpha9 \ln \frac{VP}{VS} \tag{23}$$

$$D \ln YS = \alpha9 \ln \frac{YP}{YS} \tag{24}$$

$$D \ln TMS = \alpha9 \ln \frac{TMP}{TMS} \tag{25}$$

$$D \ln XOSTS = \alpha9 \ln \frac{XOSTP}{XOSTS} \tag{26}$$

$$D \ln XWESTS = \alpha9 \ln \frac{XWESTS}{XWESTS} \tag{27}$$

$$D \ln WS = \alpha9 \ln \frac{WP}{WS} \tag{28}$$

Household sector

$$D \ln C = \alpha10 \ln \frac{CS}{C} + \alpha11 \ln \frac{VS}{V} \tag{29}$$

$$D \ln W = \alpha12 \ln \frac{WS}{W} - \alpha13(D \ln ZM - \gamma13) \tag{30}$$

$$CSH = \frac{(YH)^{\beta4}}{(PC)} \frac{(ZM)^{\beta5}}{(PC)} \tag{31}$$

$$ZMH = \gamma10 \frac{YH^{\beta6}}{PC} \tag{32}$$

Table 4 (*continued*)

$$YH = W.ZLF - Taxh \qquad (33) \text{ identity}$$

$$DZM = YH - C.PC \qquad (34) \text{ identity}$$

$$D \ln \gamma 11 = -\alpha 14 \ln \frac{CSH}{C} \qquad (35)$$

International sector

$$D \ln XOST = \alpha 15 \ln \frac{XOSTS}{XOST} \qquad (36)$$

$$D \ln TM = \alpha 16 \ln \frac{TMS}{TM} - \alpha 17 \ln \frac{(DBP)}{(DB)} \qquad (37)$$

$$D \ln PX = -\alpha 18 \ln \frac{XWESTS}{XWEST} - \alpha 19 \ln \frac{(DBP)}{(DB)} \qquad (38)$$

$$XWEST = \sum_{i=1}^{k} TMYi \quad \text{kenon CMEA} \qquad (38a)$$

$$DB = XWEST.PX + XOST.PXI - TM.PM - R.B \qquad (39) \text{ identity}$$

Socialized production

$$YC = \gamma 7 e^{\lambda 1 t} (\gamma 8 (\gamma 11.ZLF)^{-\beta 2} + (1 - \gamma 8) BK^{-\beta 2})^{-1/\beta 2} \qquad (40)$$

$$D \ln Y = \alpha 20 \ln \frac{YC}{Y} + \alpha 23 \ln \frac{YS}{Y} \qquad (41)$$

$$Prof = Y.P - W.ZLF \qquad (42)$$

$$DV = Y - C - G - MIL - DBK - XOST$$
$$- XWEST + TM \qquad (43) \text{ identity}$$

State budgetary sector

$$D \ln G = \alpha 24 \ln \frac{GS}{G} \qquad (44)$$

$$PC = (1 + \gamma 12).P \qquad (45) \text{ identity}$$

$$D \gamma 12 = \alpha 26 (D \ln ZM - \gamma 13) \qquad (46)$$

$$D \ln DBK = \alpha 27 \ln \frac{DBKS}{DBK} - \alpha 25 (D \ln ZM - \gamma 13) \qquad (47)$$

*For information on the definitions of variables, see Appendix B.

plan objectives which by their very nature are based on expectations. Expectation formation is described as an adaptive expectations or error learning process by equations (12)–(20). In conceptualising plan objectives we make the usual assumption of a well defined planners preference function. However, the function is defined over such objects of final satisfaction as external security (sec) and internal development/regime support (Dev):

$$W = W(\text{Sec}, \text{Dev}) \tag{13}$$

The 'goods' cannot be regarded as objective measures, but rather as subjective ones based on perceptions such as freedom from attack, stability of party control etc.

The 'goods' are produced in part by expenditures but the ability of such expenditures to produce final output depends upon what we may call environmental factors. Thus a production function for security can be written (see Smith (1980) and Dunne et al. (1983)):

$$\text{Sec} = \text{Sec}(\text{Milp}, \text{ENV}_1) \tag{14}$$

where Milp is the volume of military expenditures and ENV the strategic environment. The latter includes the stock of military capability held by enemies and allies together with the diplomatic environment as represented by threat and conflict/cooperation. The good, Dev, is similarly produced by private consumption expenditures, CP, government non-military expenditures, GP, and investment, DBKP, where the environment now covers factors such as demographic effects.

$$\text{Dev} = \text{Dev}(\text{GP}, \text{CP}, \text{DBKP}, \text{ENV}_2) \tag{15}$$

The instantaneous utility maximizer is, however, subject to a budget constraint

$$Y = P_1.\text{GP} + P_2.\text{Milp} + P_3\text{DBKP} + P4.\text{CP} \tag{16}$$

where Y is real GNP net of exports and imports and P1 . . . P4 are the relative prices of each expenditure relative to total output. Simple maximation yields the desired or optimal expenditure allocation system

$$\text{MilP} = (Y, \text{ENV}_1, \text{ENV}_2, P_1 \ldots P_4) \tag{17}$$

$$\text{GP} = (Y, \text{ENV}_1, \text{ENV}_2, P_1 \ldots P_4) \tag{18}$$

$$\text{CP} = (Y, \text{ENV}_1, \text{ENV}_2, P_1 \ldots P_4) \tag{19}$$

$$\text{DBKP} = (Y, \text{ENV}_1, \text{ENV}_2, P_1 \ldots P_4) \tag{20}$$

In Table 4 we have excluded the relative price effects from equations (1)–(5) and incorporated intertemporal considerations via an inventory demand.

The economy is an open one so consistent plans must be formulated for exports, imports and balance of payments, equations (6)–(8). Imports (TMP) are viewed as having an intermediate input role so demand is related to output (YP) and the terms of trade (PXE/PME). Separability is assumed so that the allocation equations between East and West need not be included. In order to explicitly recognize the widespread supply restrictions on intra Comecon trade (see Vanous (1982)) a separate Comecon export equation is included, equation (7). Given a balance of payments target, DBP, or alternatively, an international debt target, BE, we may define the required exports to non-Comecon countries.

The output objective, YP, assumes fully employed resources and is defined by a CES production function. Given consumption plans and an estimated flow consumption relation a wage objective is also defined. The expected budget constraint is given by equation (10). One immediately notes the important role of the terms of trade including an intra Comecon effect. Given the frictions within Comecon over Terms of trade arrangements, we regarded it as important to incorporate the effect. A willingness to run an increased deficit naturally relaxes the budget constraint leading to increases in CP, GP etc.

The announced plans or the plans that are to be operationalized, due to uncertainty, bureaucratic inertia etc., evolve only slowly from the optimal static plans. This is modeled by equations (21)–(28) where for the sake of simplicity only one adjustment speed is used. To understand the process in terms of observables, one must substitute the previous equations into (21)–(28) to derive a second order differential equation for the evolution of plans. The explanatory variables are output, prices, environment etc. It is useful to compare our form with that of Portes *et al.* (1982). In his form (it is a discrete model) the plan variable is a function of the plan for that period, realized quantities and an excess demand variable. One is clearly derivable from the other once one realizes that the disequilibrium information flows contain the same information as our more structural and direct variables. Clearly Portes' version is more econometrically tractable but the model here is the theoretical or simulation model. As such we make the processes more transparent.

Plan implementation is influenced by disequilibrium measures such as the deviation of inventories from desired levels, equation (29), or the deviation of the balance of payments (e.g., equation (37)). The state budgetary sector is also strongly influenced by the position of the deficit. In order to control the deficit there are two instruments available: the turnover tax, $\gamma 12$, and the wage rate. Prices are at the moment taken to be constant but it is clear that periodic 'price reforms' are strongly associated with the budget deficit and the consequent need to sterilize household money balances.

Finally, we should briefly mention the linkage equations in the international sector, equations (36)–(39). The most important point to note is that while a CPE may wish to export a certain quantity, XWEST, to non CMEA lands, exports are in fact demand determined, equation (38a). As such a CPE must set its export price in order to try to achieve its targets, equation (38). A change in demand for CPE products for whatever reason will thus be accompanied by a price change followed at a later stage by more fundamental plan changes. Intra CMEA trade is modeled in a similar way to that discussed above for the OECD model. Supply side factors, equation (36), are incorporated via changes in the bij coefficient discussed above. Intra CMEA prices are allowed to adjust to world levels with a considerable lag. The valuta currency exchange rates are treated as constant.

5. USE OF MODELS FOR ANALYSIS

Having briefly described two components of a Globus economic model (the rest of the world and energy/raw material markets are here omitted) we must next consider in more detail their use in analyzing system performance or crisis. Policy analysis follows quite naturally. We should however stress at the outset that the research discussed below has not yet been undertaken. Rather, the following perspectives have led to the design of our models which will in the near future be used as research tools.

In analyzing system performance a mixture of qualitative and quantitative techniques must be utilized. The former includes steady state, comparative dynamics and sensitivity techniques (see Gandolfo (1981)) while the latter is primarily simulation (i.e., numerical integration). The models have been constructed so that these techniques are appropriate which is why in part they are fully dynamic. However, analytical tractability has not been the sole criteria since the models are still non-linear.

Our perspective on system performance or crisis is not a static one (i.e., a particular episode of bad performance) but refers to the time series properties of the whole system. Hence over considerable periods performance may be satisfactory, the periods of crisis being rather short. However, the latter cannot properly be considered without reference to the former. The research program is usefully decomposed into questions of stability and then of underlying paths or levels.

Stability has several different meanings. If the models described above are linearized (usually about a steady state growth path) so that

$$DY = AY + BZ \tag{21}$$

then mathematical stability refers to the Eigenvalues associated with the A matrix. Following Wymer (1976) the partial differentials of the vector of Eigenvalues with respect to each parameter can then be calculated thus presenting a full picture of the models dynamics. The relationship of this technique to system performance is clear. System instability is an undesirable property but one which may take some time to emerge. Thus the present historical 'crisis' in OECD economies could indeed have a much longer crisis interpretation in that our systems may well now be unstable. But even if not unstable the approach to such a region is accompanied by longer and deeper cycles so that a recovery may not tell us very much about the system. The question remains as to which parameters and institutions produce such results? In many cases the parameters are not structural in that they are reduced forms of institutional behaviour, rules of conduct etc., so that they evolve. The international monetary system has certainly evolved and for some it is seen as a major source of crisis. On the other hand there are those who see the evolution of the welfare state and union/government relations as substantially altering the character of the system. Such problems must be viewed in a longer term context and systematically approached.

Examples are helpful. Sensitivity analysis of the linearized OECD model (Kirkpatrick (1983)) shows that the time path of the model (i.e., deviations about the steady state) is particularly sensitive to approximately nine parameters these being associated with the price, investment, wage and government expenditure equations. For 'plausible' parameter combinations the model was slowly unstable. Greater sensitivity of government fiscal policy to inflation made the system more unstable in the sense that the cyclical amplitudes increased. A lagged government policy instrument trying to control a dynamic system with differential adjustment speed clearly created system problems. The analysis did not include any complex game situation between actors, either external or internal, so was certainly a best case. The degree of wage indexation also emerged as a key parameter, something important for the international transmission mechanism (e.g. Branson (1980)).

The CPE model appears at first sight to be definitionally stable. However, such systems easily display strong cyclical properties and also instability. This is because knowing what to do is one thing, doing it on time and in the correct amount is quite another. Hence differential speeds of plan formation (i.e., different $\alpha 9$ coefficients) due to political or bureaucratic factors create quite strong cycles. Poland is a quite good example as are the periodic price reforms in response to 'crisis' liquidity situations of governments and consumers.

The last example does, however, draw attention to the fact that mathematical stability is not necessarily the most useful concept. Thus Eliasson (1983) used the concept of a bounded domain, called the stability domain. 'It is bad for the system ... to be outside that domain. It represents danger unpleasant social conditions etc. As soon as the system gets outside that stability domain, time becomes important, namely the time needed to get back.' p. 277. This definition is clearly more compatible with the Globus interest in stress and strain and again requires the system properties as a whole to be investigated. For example, OECD economies might well be experiencing unemployment purely as part of a cyclical adjustment to the oil price shock. Eventually they will return to equilibrium so they are stable about a 'full' employment path. But how long will the process take, how far will the deviation be, what factors determine the path and, is the growth path solution unique? Clearly, many of the techniques described above are still useful but the models must now make greater use of simulation. This is so since the non-linear features of the model must be more fully utilized.

Related to the question of path in non-linear models is the reaction of the model to 'shocks' in 'exogenous' variables such as population, technology, and raw material prices. In linear models the matrix B of (21) can be neglected but in non-linear models this is not so. For this analysis the model must be used in simulation mode.

In addition to stability one may also enquire as to the comparative dynamics of the model. There are two aspects. On the one hand is the question of the determinants of the underlying growth path even though the model may hardly ever approach this path in an acceptable period. In a single country OECD model we may refer to Table 3. There it is clear that the growth path of the wage rate, for example, has a steady state path determined in part by the terms of trade. On the other hand, and perhaps of more importance, is the question of steady state levels. The growth rate may remain constant but the whole path may shift towards or downwards. In principle our models have an analytical solution for initial conditions (or steady state levels) but in practice it is not feasible. Numerical solutions seem to be the only technique available.

The importance of such questions is highlighted in the multi-national and national contexts by a number of writers. Thus Corden (1983a) and Johansen (1982) call attention to the possibility of low level equilibrium traps resulting from a non-cooperative game solution between policy making countries. On the national level, Gylfason and Lindbeck (1983) and Calmfors (1982) draw the same conclusions from Union/Government non-cooperative game models. Thus many of the key problems must be approached from a stability and level perspective using a wide range of tools.

We must finally turn to the question of policy in a more traditional meaning. In his conference review Calmfors (1982) discussed a number of analytical issues associated with the long run effects of short run stabilization policy. He drew attention to the need for a careful distinction between various types of shocks since the effects on the economy differed greatly. Intertemporal resource allocation effects were stressed as was the need for adequately modeling government and union behaviour. Our model seeks to address many of the questions raised by Calmfors and the Conference participants. Thus, for example, increased corporate taxation may be an adequate short run policy but in our model would have the effect, *ceterus paribus*, of lowering investment and the rate of growth. Whether *ceterus* is indeed *paribus* is however the whole point of simulation models.

We do not wish to exaggerate the uses of our models. They may indeed prove to be inadequate. But models should be used to highlight what is included and how and what is excluded and why and therefore all conclusions must be accordingly framed. Nozick's observations on philosophy are also appropriate to modelers: 'One form of philosophical activity feels like pushing and shoving things to fit into the same fixed perimeter of specified shape. All those things are lying out there, and they must be fit in. You push and shove the material into the rigid area getting it into the boundary of one side and it bulges out on another. You run around and press in the protruding bulge, producing yet another in another place. So you push and shove and clip off corners from the things so they'll fit and you press in until finally almost everything sits unstably more or less in there: what doesn't get heaved far away so that it won't be noticed. (Of course, it's not all that crude. There's also the coaxing and cajoling. And the body English.) Quickly, you find an angle from which it looks like an exact fit and take a snapshot; at a fast shutter speed before something else bulges out too noticeably. Then, back to the darkroom to touch up the rents, rips, and tears in the fabric of the perimeter. All that remains is to publish the photograph as a representation of exactly how things are, and to note how nothing fits properly into any other shape.' R. Nizock (1968), Anarchy, State and Utopia, Blackwell, p. 8.

APPENDIX A

OECD prototype model

Endogenous variables

Real:

Y	=	real gross product (i.e., GDP + imported raw materials
BK	=	real capital stock
ZLF	=	total employment
EN	=	real imported raw material input in raw material prices
V	=	real inventory stock
k	=	growth rate of capital stock
TMY	=	real imports of final goods in own price
C	=	real consumption in consumer prices
TX	=	real exports in Y deflator prices

DBK   = real investment − capital stock increment
G   = real government total current expenditure in Y prices

Nominal:
W   = direct wage payments per man year
P   = Y deflator
EWPH = imported raw material price index in domestic currency
DOLR = exchange rate in domestic currency per $
PI1   = nominal operating surplus of producers
Taxf = nominal tax payments by producers
ZDIV = dividends and profit distributions by producers
SIF   = net financial claims by firms of country (i) on issue
PM   = domestic price of imported final goods
PC   = composite price index, Y deflator and PM, here used as consumer price index
ZIR   = overseas reserves held by government in domestic currency
YH   = nominal household after tax disposable income
SIG   = net financial claims issued by government
r   = domestic nominal interest rate
WI   = total net nominal wealth of households
SI   = net financial claims issued by country (i)

Exogenous variables

EW   = world foreign currency raw material price index
PF   = world foreign currency final goods price index
YO   = real world income
ro   = world nominal interest rate
LF   = domestic labour supply
t   = time

APPENDIX B

CPE prototype model − version 1

An S after a variable denotes a final planned variable and a P an intermediate planned variable. This is a clearer way of expressing planned variables as complex lags of forcing variables. $D = d/dt$, ln = natural logs, α = adjustment coefficients, β = elasticities, γ = proportions or marginal propensities.

Endogenous variables

ZM = stock of currency and state bank deposits held by households — current roubles

B = net debtor or creditor position of CPE

Tax = tax receipts valued in current terms

Prof = current surplus of state owned enterprises in roubles

Output and Expenditure Variables:

Y = real GNP

C = real household consumption expenditure

G = real total government expenditure

BK = stock of fixed capital

V = inventories of goods and work in progress

ZLF = employment

$\gamma 5$ = efficiency units of employment

TM = real imports of goods and services

Mil = real defence expenditures

Xwest = real exports of goods and services to non-Comecon

Xost = real exports of goods and services to Comecon

W = wage rate, roubles per man year

P = price level of composite good

PC = price level of consumer goods gross of turnover tax

Exogenous variables

t = time

R = world interest rate

Px = world export price of CPE exports

Px1 = intra-Comecon export price

Pm = world import price of CPE imports

Yost = other Comecon production levels

DBP = target on current account balance

Pop = population

DOLR = accounting exchange rate roubles/foreign currency

NOTES

1) An equally challengeable assumption is, of course, the equity/bond aggregation (see Leijonhufvud (1968)).

2) For example, with a Cobb Douglas production function

$$Y = \gamma e^{\lambda t} LF^{\beta_3} EN^{\beta_6} RK^{\beta_9}$$

we have

$$\lambda 1 = \lambda 2 = \lambda 3 = \frac{(\beta 3 + \beta 6)}{(9)} \lambda$$

$$\beta 1 = -\frac{\beta 3}{\beta 9}, \beta 2 = -\frac{\beta 6}{\beta 9}, \beta 4 = \left(-\frac{\beta 3}{\beta 9} - 1.0\right)$$

$$\beta 5 = -\frac{\beta 6}{\beta 9}, \beta 7 = -\frac{\beta 3}{\beta 9}, \beta 8 = \left(-\frac{\beta 6}{\beta 9} - 1.0\right)$$

Where a unit elasticity of substitution is not assumed the restrictions are highly non-linear functions so that equations (1)–(3) in this paper must be regarded as quasi-linearizations.

3) It is, however, true that the partial adjustment model is compatible with intertemporal maximization subject to adjustment costs (see Sargent (1979)).

4) Interest rate effects on inventory demand have been notoriously difficult to detect. For recent empirical evidence see Akhtar (1983).

5) In the larger version tax receipts adjust with a lag to the desired tax rate. The latter is influenced by the level of the budget deficit, unemployment and inflation.

6) Political support is also modeled in a similar manner which explains why governments are re-elected with unemployment levels previously regarded as conducive to turmoil (see Widmaier (1983)).

REFERENCES

Akhtar, M. (1983), 'Effects of Interest Rates and Inflation on Aggregate Inventory Investment in the US', *American Economic Review*, 73, pp. 319–328.

Allen, M. (1982), 'Adjustment in Planned Economies', *IMF Staff Papers*, Vol. 29, pp. 398–421.

Armington, P. (1969), 'A Theory of Demand for Products Distinguished by Place of Production', *IMF Staff Papers*, Vol. 16, pp. 159–178.

Artus, P. and C. Bismut (1983), *Exchange Rate and Wage Price Dynamics*, Institut National de la Statistique et des Etudes Economiques, Document de Travail No. 8308.

Bailey, R.W., V.B. Hall and P.C.B. Phillips, 'A Model of Output Employment, Capital Formation and Inflation', *Cowles Foundation Discussion Paper No. 552*.

Benassy, J.P. (1981), 'The Disequilibrium Approach to Monopolistic Price Setting and General Monopolistic Equilibrium', *Review of Economic Studies*, 43.

Bergstrom, A.R. and C.R. Wymer (1976), 'A Model of Disequilibrium Neo Classical Growth and its Application to the United Kingdom', in: A.R. Bergstrom.

Bergstrom, A.R. (1976), *Statistical Inference in Continuous Time Economic Models*, North-Holland Publishing Company, Amsterdam.

Bhandari, J. (1981), 'Toward a Multi-Country Model of Exchange Determination', *Journal of Macroeconomics*, Vol. 3, pp. 501–516.

Brada, J.C. *et al.* (1981), 'The Optimality of Socialist Development Strategies', *Journal of Economic Dynamics and Control*, Vol. 3, pp. 1–27.

Branson, W. and J. Rotemberg (1980), 'International Adjustments with Wage Rigidity', *European Economic Review*, Vol. 13, pp. 309–332.

Bremer, S. (1982), 'The GLOBUS Model – A Guide to its Theoretical Structure', *IIVG Discussion Paper 82–105.*

Bruno, M. and J. Sachs (1979), 'Supply Versus Demand Approaches to the Problem of Stagflation', *Maurice Falk Institute, Discussion Paper 786.*

Burgess, D. (1974), 'Production Theory and the Derived Demand for Imports', *Journal of International Economics,* 4, pp. 103–117.

Calmfors, L., 'Long Run Effects of Short Run Stabilization Policy', The

Canzoneri, M. (1982), 'Exchange Intervention Policy in a multi Country World', *Journal of International Economics,* Vol. 13, pp. 267–290.

Corden, W.M. (1983), 'Macroeconomic Policy Interaction under Flexible Exchange Rates: A Two Country Model', *Institute for International Economic Studies, Seminar Paper 264.*

Deardorff, A. and R.M. Stern (1979), 'What Have We Learned from Linked Exonometric Models?', *Banca Nazional del Lavoro Quarterly Review,* pp. 415–532.

Dunne, J.P., F. Pashardes and R.P. Smith (1983), 'Needs, Costs and Bureaucracy: The Allocation of Public Consumption in the UK', *Paper Presented to the European Econometric Society Conference,* Pisa.

Eliasson, G. (1983), 'On the Optimal Rate of Structural Adjustment', in: Eliasson *et al., Policy Making in a Disorderly World Economy,* Almquist, Stockholm.

Findlay, R. and C. Rodriguez (1977), 'Intermediate Imports and Macroeconomic Policy under Flexible Exchange Rates', *Canadian Journal of Economics.*

Gandolfo, G. (1981), *Qualitative Analysis and Econometric Estimation of Continuous Time Dynamic Models,* North-Holland.

Gordon, R. and A. Haynes (1970), 'On the Theory of Price Dynamics', in: E. Phelps, *Macroeconomic Foundations of Employment and Inflation Theory,* New York.

Gylfason, T. and A. Lindbeck (1983), 'The Macroeconomic Consequences of Endogenous Government and Labor Unions', *Institute for International Economic Studies, Seminar Paper 232,* Stockholm.

Johansen, L. (1982), 'A Note on the Possibility of an International Equilibrium with Low Levels of Activity', *Journal of International Economics,* 13, pp. 257–266.

Kirkpatrick, G. (1983), 'A Prototype National Economy for a Multi Country OECD Model', *IIVG Discussion Paper 83–105.*

Kirkpatrick, G. (1983a), *A Prototype Model of a CPE Economy,* Berlin, Mimeo.

Kirkpatrick, G. and U. Widmaier (1983), 'Political/Economic Relations between and within OECD Countries', *Paper delivered to the ECPR Workshop,* February.

Kohli, V. and McKibbin (1982), 'Are Government Deficits the Prime Cause of Inflation?', *Journal of Policy Modeling,* 4 (3), November, pp. 279–310.

Lipton, D. and J. Sachs (1983), 'Accumulation and Growth in a Two Country Model: A Simulation Approach', *Journal of International Economics,* 15, pp. 125–160.

Nadiri, M.I. and S. Rosen (1969), 'Interrelated Factor Demand Functions', *American Economic Review,* 59, September, pp. 457–471.

Pollins, B. (1982), 'The Political and Economic Determinants of International Trade Flows in Globus', *IIVG Discussion Paper 82–110.*

Pollins, B. and G. Kirkpatrick (1983), 'Specification and Estimation of an International Trade System with Political and Economic Determinants', *Paper presented to the International Political Science Association Roundtable at Urbana-Champaign,* Illinois.

Portes, R. *et al.* (1982), 'Macroeconomic Planning and Disequilibrium', *Birkbeck College Discussion Paper No. 126.*

Purvis, D. (1980), 'Monetarism: A Review', *Canadian Journal of Economics,* 13 (1), pp. 96–122.

Richard, D. (1983), 'A Global Adjustment Model of Exchange and Interest Rates: Empirical Analysis', in: D. Bigman and T. Taya (eds), *The Functioning of Floating Exchange Rates,* Ballinger.

158

Richard, D. (1983), 'International Adjustment, Exchange Rates and Growth', *Paper presented at World Congress of the Econometric Society*, Aix-en-Provence.

Smith, R.P. (1980), 'The Demand for Military Expenditure', *The Economic Journal*, 90, pp. 811–820.

Szakolczai, G. (1982), 'Comments on the Optimality of Socialist Development Strategies', *Journal of Economic Dynamics and Control*, 4 (1).

Vanous, J. (1982), 'Disequilibrium Economic Trade Model for Socialist Economies', *Paper prepared for VIth International Conference on the Econometric Modeling of the Socialist Economies*, Budapest.

Ward, M.D. (1982), *Differential Paths to Parity: A Study of the Contemporary Arms Race*, Mimeo, Berlin.

Ward, M.D. and G. Kirkpatrick (1983), 'International Stability and Arms Competition between the Superpowers', *Paper presented to Workshop on Supplemental Ways for Improving International Stability*, Laxenburg.

Widmaier, U. (1982), 'Political Performance, Political Support and Political Stability: The Globus Framework', *IIVG Discussion Paper*, pp. 82–108.

Widmaier, U. (1983), *A Model of Domestic Political Developments for Socialist Economies*, Mimeo, Berlin.

Winters, A.L., 'Separability and the Specification of Foreign Trade Functions', *University of Bristol, Discussion paper 82/126*.

Wymer, C.R. (1978), *The Use of Continuous Time Models in Economics*, Mimeo, Washington.

Wymer, C.R. (1978), 'Continuous Models in Macroeconomics: Specification and Estimation', 7th Conference of Economists, Sydney Macquarie University, August 28–September 1, 1978. Paper prepared for the SSRC-Ford Foundation Conference on *Macroeconomic Policy and Adjustment in Open Economies*, at Fenhams Hall, Ware, England, April, 28– May 1, 1976.

CHAPTER 7

III. COMPETITIVENESS AND EMPLOYMENT IN THE LARGE INDUSTRIALIZED COUNTRIES

E. Kremp and J. Le Dem[*]
*CEPII, Paris, France

1. INTRODUCTION

The relationship between employment and labor-productivity is a key factor on the analysis of the economic crisis. It has also an important impact on medium term forecasts and economic policy debates.

An analysis of the decline of productivity growth since the mid-60s, especially since 1973, raises, despite the amount of research done in the matter, more questions than certainties[1]. These questions cover both the evolution of productivity in each country (oddly in the United States, where from an already slow trend one could observe an early slowing down), and the international differences. By setting apart the manufacturing sector, which constitutes the bulk of the sector exposed to international competition, from the rest of the economy where services and trade predominate, this appears even more clearly. A range of very different developments occurs in the medium term between countries, even if one looks only at the main industrialized economies (Table 1). In Japan, for example, most of the slow-down in productivity growth appears to have been concentrated in the non-manufacturing sector, which continued to create jobs while, after the recession of 1974–1975, manufacturing regained its previous rate. In West Germany nothing of the sort can be observed. The slowdown only affects the manufacturing sector. Apart from the examination of the causes of these movements another question arises concerning the macro-economic conditions in which they occur: in what way, notably, has the seemingly beneficial complementarity observed in Japan affected prices, profits and investment?

It is no longer the slow-down in productivity growth that is questioned, but its possible acceleration due to the introduction into the productive processes of a new technology symbolized by micro-electronics.

Finally, the debates on economic policy are taking place, in the quasi-general

Artus, P. and Guvenen, O. (eds.): International Macroeconomic Modelling for Policy Decisions.
© 1986. Martinus Nijhoff Publishers, Dordrecht/Boston/Lancaster.
ISBN 90-247-3201-8. Printed in The Netherlands.

Table 1. Labour productivity and employment in the private sector

	1960–1973	1973–1979	1975–1980	1980–1981
1) *Labor productivity**				
United States				
• manufacturing	3.6	− 1.0	1.7	2.5
• non-manufacturing	2.1	− 0.1	0.2	0.9
France				
• manufacturing	6.2	2.0	4.8	2.0
• non-manufacturing	4.8	2.3	2.3	0.7
Germany				
• manufacturing	5.0	1.4	3.6	1.1
• non-manufacturing	4.5	2.3	4.0	0.9
Japan				
• manufacturing	9.7	0.3	9.2	5.3
• non-manufacturing	9.1	0.5	2.6	1.0
2) *Persons engaged in production*				
United States				
• manufacturing	1.4	− 4.7	2.2	− 0.2
• non-manufacturing	1.9	0.5	3.7	1.8
France				
• manufacturing	1.0	− 0.8	− 1.3	− 3.5
• non-manufacturing	0.4	− 0.3	0.9	0.1
Germany				
• manufacturing	0.2	− 3.9	− 0.2	− 2.5
• non-manufacturing	− 0.4	− 2.3	0.3	− 0.2
Japan				
• manufacturing	3.3	− 3.3	0.4	1.2
• non-manufacturing	0.6	0.5	1.5	0.4

*Output per person engaged in production.
Source: National accounts.

context of massive unemployment. Productivity and employment are not tools which are at the disposal of the official decision makers. Nevertheless governments are being involved either directly (labour policy or reduction of excess labor in the public sector) or indirectly (work legislation, incentives for a reduction of working hours) in the management of labor in the trade sector. Moreover, they dispose of certain structural actions usually known as supply policies, enabling them to stimulate or reduce new productivity increases. In order to improve the competitiveness of the domestic economy, should they aim at a general progression of productivity, and what would be the consequences on employment? Or should they, as suggest here and there the advocates of dualist policies, shift the effort to some sectors, and by so doing leave to others the role of maintaining or creating employment?

This paper obviously does not aim at answering these questions but at clarifying them by a macroeconomic reflection based on the use of small country-models elaborated at CEPII in the Sachem-Ouest project. More precisely, we will analyse the effects in four countries (i.e. USA, France, West Germany and Japan) of: a) an increase in the rate of manufacturing productivity growth and b) job creation in the non-manufacturing sector; finally we will examine to what extent the two can be combined in order to stabilize the unemployment rate in the medium term.

This paper consists of two parts. The first is a rapid representation of the country models used, on which one will find an annex with a more technical description. In the second part, the results of simulations will be analyzed.

2. PRESENTATION OF THE PROJECT

The CEPII studies of the Western Economies have always placed an emphasis on the importance of the linkages of medium to long-term, and on the other hand the linkages between exchange rates and trade specialization, external constraints and internal adjustments[2]. A continuation of this tradition, the Sachem-Ouest project tries to formalize this approach through a multi-national model.

The project aims at characterizing each domestic economy by bringing forth specific macro-economic frameworks. Since the structure of the models is the same for all the countries, these frameworks differ only in the estimate of a few structural parameters the number of which is voluntarily limited. This structure is based on a splitting of the economy into two sectors (the manufacturing industry and the rest of the economy) which seeks to take into account a triple dualism in the western economies:

− dualism in manufacturers' production which distinguishes itself from the rest of the economy by the size and the sources of productivity gains;
− dualism in the pricing of the product: drawing on the theories of the Scandinavian school (Lindbeck (1979)) and on the works of R. Courbis (1975), it entails, opposing a sector which produces traded goods and thus, is constrained in its price formation by international competition, to a non-traded sector, better able to control its profits;
− finally a dualism in the determination of labor costs; in a number of countries the manufacturing industry has crystalized the monopolistic forms of wage regulation established since the Second World War. One finds indications of this at two levels. First, the wage negotiations in industry have an important effect on the fluctuations in the labor market. The clearest case is doubtlessly that

of the United States, where this dualism reveals itself through the arrival of marginal social groups in a non-manufacturing sector and the creation of jobs with an uncertain future in services, trade etc. . . . Therefore the idea that distortion of wage determination between sectors takes place in these economies.

The construction of five country models (USA, France, West Germany and Japan) allowed a multi-national comparative study to be realised. The construction of the international linkage should soon permit the formation of a truly multinational model. The general structure of the country models and the main differences between countries, are summarized as follows (cf. Table 2).

2 1. The country models

In order to highlight the specificities of the countries, similar structures of national models are used. In this manner, the differences in the behaviors of the models are due mostly to the accounting structures and the results of econometric estimations. Obviously, a logical result of this choice is: the estimated equations are simple and do not incorporate the institutional subtleties of each nation.

The structure of the models is essentially neo-keynesian and is composed of three traditional blocks:

— a relatively simple block determining the main components of demand from which is drawn the value added produced by each sector thanks to an input-output table;
— a more developed price-wage block leading to the determination of income distribution;
— an employment-unemployment block.

A number of simplifying hypotheses have been adopted: the different elements of transfers and of taxation, notably those of households, evolve as factor incomes; there is neither a monetary sector nor interest rate etc. . . .

In the demand block, an equation to determine the rate of household consumption is used; the accelerator and profit effects explain the investment rate of the two sectors. In the manufacturing industry, net investment increases capital stock which permits the determination of potential output. The foreign trade of manufactures, in this initial version, is derived from estimates included in Deppler and Rippley (1978). Some very simple hypotheses are made for the other entries.

Wage and price determination are more detailed and constitute to a certain extent the core of the model. Instead of following the tradition, where the demand prices are formed directly from the costs, production prices for industry and output

Table 2. Summary of the main behavioral parameters

	USA	Japan	Germany	France	UK
Investment in manufacturing					
Lagged dependent variable	+++	+	+	+	+
Rate of return	0	++	+++	+	++
Demand	++	+++	++	++	+
*Trade in manufacturing**					
Imports ● Income elasticity	1.3	2.0	1.9	1.4	1.3
● Price elasticity	1.9	1.5	0.9	0.8	0.4
Exports ● Income elasticity	1.3	1.4	1.1	0.7	0.9
● Price elasticity	1.5	1.7	0.7	2.0	0.5
Export prices					
● Competitors effect	0	+	++	+	+
Price of production in manufacturing					
Unit total cost	0.5	0.6	0.8	0.6	0.5
Effect of capacity utilization rate	0	+	+	0	0
Competitors price	+	0	0	+	++
Profits effect	+	0	0	+	0
Price of output in non-manufacturing					
Unit labour cost	0.6	0.6	0.6	0.7	0.6
Profits effect	+	0	+	+	++
Compensation in manufacturing					
Lagged dependant variable	+	0	0	0	0
Price responsiveness	0.5	1	1	1	1
Unemployment rate effect	0	I I	I	+	0
Labor productivity responsiveness	0	0.2	0.7	0	0
Compensation in non-manufacturing					
Unemployment rate effect	+	0	+	0	0
Employment					
Speed ● manufacturing	+++	+	++	++	++
of adjustment ● non-manufacturing	+++	0	+	+	++
Long run relations					
Productivity	growth	growth	accumulation	growth	growth

prices for the rest of the economy are determined, in accordance with the accounting structure. In this manner, the channels through which the effects of external and internal changes (relative prices of the two sectors) are transmitted, are clearly shown. The effects of the competitiveness are limited to industry and influence both the price of domestic production and export prices.

Only the manufacturing wages are directly determined by the usual determinants which are the prices of private consumption, the productivity and unemployment. Those of the rest of the economy are derived directly, except in some countries where the presence of an unemployment variable permits to take into account wage distortions between sectors.

On the labor market, employment in the two sectors is obtained through an equation derived from the Brechling's model. The expansion or contraction of the labor force, according to employment tendencies or demography are also explained.

Finally, longterm effects in the country models have been introduced. Past rates of growth or capital accumulation periodically affect the trend of manufacturing productivity[3].

Table 2 permits a general description of the main characteristics of the models country by country. Hardly exposed to international competition and not really responsive to the fluctuations in its competitive position, at least in the short run, the United States sees the shift in total demand amplified by the effects of the accelerator, especially for non-manufacturing investment. The adjustments in employment are quick and the labor supply rigid, which induces large fluctuations in employment. This is why the wage distortion can have its full effect and produces important differences in the evolution of labor costs between the two sectors. The internal factors are therefore very important in the evolution of prices. These combine systematically with significant effects on relative prices and thus on the profitability of the manufacturing industry. But they also result in a shift in the share of profits in the value added caused by the effects of wage rigidity.

West Germany is, with the United States, the only country where a wage distortion is observed. Another similarity, the labor market is equally, though to a lesser extent, dominated by a rapid adjustment in employment. On the other hand, the supply of labor is much more flexible, which lets unemployment play a less important role in the price dynamic and the relative price distortions which accompany it. In the German model, industry plays a much more active role than in other countries; that is due first of all to a mass effect; the relative importance of industry in the economy is large. Two types of sequences place, moreover, industry in a dynamic role, which is different from other countries, and find their origin precisely in the dualism manufacturing/non-manufacturing: it is composed, on the one hand, of a Scandinavian effect with the diffusion of wage increases in this sector spreading to the whole of the economy by the strong response of wage to productivity, and on the other hand, of a creation of these productivity gains through a profit-accumulation logic, which permits itself longer term productivity gains.

The main difference between the model of the Japanese economy and those of West Germany and the United States concerns the labor market. The inertia of employment, reflection of the well-known system of the large enterprise and lifetime employment, is clear in the two sectors, but takes on particular proportions in the non-manufacturing sector where labor demand is hardly unaffected by the business cycle. Since labor supply has revealed itself otherwise very flexible, the shifts in unemployment are but very limited[4]. But they have a great deal of influence on wage formation and through that on household incomes. The remarkable insertion of Japan into the world market could constitute an important factor of instability for the model to the extent that fluctuations in foreign demand would be amplified in total demand. This potential instability is powerfully reduced by the precautionary behavior of the households' savings rate, which is decreasing as inflation develops. Consequently internal demand adapts in the short-to-medium run to the fluctuations of international demand.

France appears to be of a less distinct type than these three countries. The evolution of wages is homogeneous and shows a more moderate 'Phillips' effect than in Japan but larger than in West Germany. The determination of manufactured prices of production, in comparison with the latter country, appears to be more responsive to international competitiveness but also quicker to reestablish the price-cost margins to the required levels. Very open to the exterior, the strength of French industry depends on the competitiveness of its prices[5].

3. RESULTS OF THE SIMULATIONS

In order to shed some light on the differences in the importance of industry's competitiveness, we first present a simulation in which the rate of growth of manufacturing productivity is increased by one point[6]. A comparison could have been made with variations on non-manufacturing productivity, but the interpretation would have been blurred by differences arising from the extremely varied employment's speeds of adjustment in this sector. However one is less able to interpret this simulation than in the case of the manufacturing sector because of the numerous problems in measuring this productivity. The problems are linked to the difficulties in distinguishing between the nominal evolutions in volume effects and price effects in such branches as trade and services. We have therefore preferred to directly simulate the increase of one point in the rate of employment creation in the non-manufacturing sector. The divergent effects of these two simulations on employment suggests a third one, in which we study the results of the combination of the first two, permitting to stabilize unemployment in the medium term.

The impact of an increase in the rate of growth of manufacturing labor productivity

The results of the variations of productivity carried out with standard keynesian one-sector-models are well-known[7]: an increase of productivity reduces employment and increases unemployment thus reducing real compensations. The negative impact of this on internal demand causes a drop in growth. At the same time, the decrease in labor costs (direct and indirect) causes disinflation.

Nevertheless many mechanisms can forestall this process of disinflation-recession:

— investments, if they are sensitive to the improvement of profitability, exert a stimulating effect;
— a low price responsiveness of wages limits the decrease in real income;
— a redistribution of productivity gains to workers through disinflation and recession;
— an economy open to international trade is sensitive to gains in competitiveness; these permit to limit the consequences of a decreasing internal demand on total growth.

The total effect is theoretically indeterminate. In reality, it is generally more likely to be negative.

The bisectorial model, such as those considered here, permits to test the impact of an increase in the rate of growth of productivity in the sole manufacturing sector. Taking into account the sectoral differences, other links are brought to light, without challenging the overall logic of the outline presented here.

Thus an increase in manufacturing productivity causes a two-step change in the relative internal prices: the fall in labor costs in the manufacturing sector exerts first a dominant effect; then intervene both the possible responsiveness of wage to gains in manufacturing productivity ('Scandinavian' explanation of inflation through productivity) and the eventual divergences of wages between the two sectors because of the unemployment effect; this can lead to a reversal of the relative decrease of prices in the manufacturing sector.

Table 3 presents the results of these simulations for four countries and reveals important differences in this disinflationary scenario.

The United States is characterized by a strong disinflation, a significant development in unemployment and an improvement in industrial profits. The quick adjustment of employment, in the manufacturing sector, causing a drop in labor

Table 3. Simulations made with country models (differences from the standard solution).

Country	Variants	Period	Average annual rates of change over five years																	Average levels over five years					
			Real output (constant)		Real private consumption	Real investment		Real trade in manufacturing		Labor productivity		Real wage		Deflator for consumption	Output price		Trade balance/GDP		Unemployment rate	Capacity utilization rate	Wage shares		Rate of return
			Sector 1	Sector 2		Sector 1	Sector 2	Exp.	Imp.	Sector 1	Sector 2	Sector 1	Sector 2		Sector 1	Sector 2	constant	current		Sector 1	Sector 1	Sector 2	Sector 1
USA (1)		0–5	−0.3	−0.4	−0.4	−0.5	−1.2	0.3	−0.8	0.8	0.0	0.2	−0.2	−0.5	−0.6	−0.5	0.1	0.1	0.8	−0.8	−1.2	−0.2	0.7
		5–10	0.3	−0.1	−0.3	0.5	0.1	1.8	2.1	0.8	0.0	0.4	−0.5	−1.8	−1.3	−2.0	0.7	0.4	1.7	−0.3	−4.2	−1.1	3.2
(2)		0–5	0.9	0.9	1.0	1.2	3.0	−0.5	1.8	0.1	−0.9	−0.6	0.5	2.0	0.2	2.6	−0.3	−0.2	−2.0	2.1	2.0	1.2	−1.7
		5–10	0.2	0.9	1.3	0.0	1.8	−3.9	5.5	0.2	−0.9	−1.5	1.4	6.3	1.7	7.6	−1.5	−0.8	−5.6	3.0	10.2	4.1	−9.0
Japan (1)		0–5	+0.0	−0.0	−0.1	0.5	−0.0	0.2	−0.2	0.7	−0.0	−0.1	−0.1	−0.2	−0.3	−0.1	0.1	+0.0	0.04	−0.1	−1.0	−0.1	0.4
		5–10	0.1	−0.1	−0.4	1.6	−0.1	0.7	−1.1	1.0	−0.0	−0.6	−0.6	−0.8	−0.7	−0.7	0.5	0.2	0.14	−0.7	−4.5	−0.9	1.6
(2)		0–5	0.1	0.3	0.8	−2.2	0.3	−0.8	1.4	−0.0	−0.7	1.0	1.0	1.3	0.4	1.8	−0.4	−0.1	−0.2	0.5	3.1	1.7	−1.6
		5–10	−0.1	0.7	2.0	−7.1	0.7	−2.7	5.0	−0.0	−0.5	2.8	2.8	3.0	2.0	3.9	−2.5	−0.9	−0.6	4.3	14.4	7.3	−6.4
Germany (1)		0–5	+0.1	+0.0	−0.1	+0.8	−0.0	+0.0	−0.1	+0.8	+0.0	+0.3	+0.2	−0.1	−0.3	+0.0	+0.1	+0.0	+0.4	−0.0	−0.7	+0.0	+0.3
		5–10	0.1	+0.1	+0.1	+0.6	+0.3	+0.1	+0.1	+1.0	+0.0	+0.5	+0.1	−0.1	−0.3	+0.1	+0.1	−0.1	+0.9	−0.4	−1.5	+0.1	+0.4
(2)		0–5	+0.0	+0.0	+0.7	−2.2	+0.7	+0.1	+0.8	−0.0	−1.0	+1.0	+0.4	+1.1	+0.4	2.0	−0.6	−0.1	−0.7	−0.4	+1.5	+0.8	−0.8
		5–10	−0.6	0.0	+0.8	−10.0	+0.1	−0.5	1.1	−0.2	+1.0	+0.1	+0.9	+2.4	+0.9	+4.0	−2.0	−0.2	−1.7	+2.3	8.9	+1.9	−3.6
France (1)		0–5	+0.1	−0.1	−0.3	+0.6	−0.1	+0.4	−0.4	0.8	−0.0	−0.1	−0.1	−0.3	−0.5	−0.3	+0.3	+0.2	+0.3	+0.1	−1.3	−0.1	+0.6
		5–10	+0.6	+0.1	−0.2	1.4	+0.1	1.2	−0.6	1.1	+0.0	−0.3	−0.3	−0.7	−1.0	−0.8	1.4	0.7	+0.7	+0.4	−4.6	−0.5	+2.2
(2)		0–5	+0.1	+0.5	+0.9	−0.7	+0.5	−0.6	1.1	−0.0	−0.8	+0.4	+0.4	+1.0	−0.8	1.7	−0.8	−0.4	−1.0	+0.4	1.9	+0.8	−1.0
		5–10	−0.7	+0.6	1.4	−2.9	+0.6	−2.4	2.1	−0.1	−0.9	−1.0	+1.0	+2.5	+1.3	3.7	−3.6	−1.6	−2.6	+0.4	9.1	+2.7	−4.7

Sector 1: manufacturing
Sector 2: non-manufacturing

(1): The rate of growth of manufacturing productivity is increased by one point.
(2): The rate of employment creation in the non-manufacturing sector is increased by one point.

costs explains this disinflation. But, more significantly, it affects the rest of the economy after a few years, because the progression of unemployment particularly slows down the wage growth in the non-manufacturing sector. Moreover, the consequences of the evolution of unemployment on growth are here greater than elsewhere, because the demand depends above all on the domestic market. Finally, the manufacturing sector profits grow with the productivity gains and are then reinforced by the movement of relative prices. A virtuous circle does not develop in manufacturing, because here investment is not sensitive to an improvement in profitability (Table 2).

The most different case is that of West Germany, where disinflation is almost nil, total demand stays up and the relative position of industry changes little, mainly because of the large increase in manufacturing wages. This is due to a partial redistribution of productivity gains, which is transmitted to the rest of the economy. This increase limits, therefore, the disinflationary impact of the slow-down in the creation of jobs and mitigates the decline in disposable incomes of households. Moreover, manufacturing investment progresses significantly because it is more sensitive than the other sectors to higher profits. Thus the effects of an increase in unemployment and of wage distortion are not enough to create a recessionary movement. In return, the medium-term effects are weak because the competitiveness is hardly modified and the change is hardly beneficial for industry.

In France, on the other hand, total growth improves because of a very favorable evolution in industry. The growth in the manufacturing sector is essentially due to the improvement in external trade, related to the price effect. Along with an improvement in profits, this growth in turn exerts a positive influence on industrial investment.

Finally, in Japan, the fluctuation in growth is small, but is accompanied by a shift from domestic to foreign demand. The slow adjustment of employment to the new productivity trend does not cause a significant drop in prices. Disinflation is, therefore, limited from the start and accelerates only when the increase of unemployment, although weak, affects strongly the wage earners. Moreover, household consumption, which regained momentum after a certain amount of time in the order countries, is contracting more and more. Even though exports take up the slack left by internal demand, it is not enough to restimulate total growth in a significant manner.

The importance of the creation of jobs in the non-manufacturing sector

To simulate an ex-ante increase of one point in the rate of employment creation in the non-manufacturing sector presents, as one might expect, a certain symmetry with the preceding study. To create jobs in the non-manufacturing sector is of course costly in terms of inflation and is accompanied by a decrease in relative industrial prices. However, the shift of demand towards its internal component gives a boost, at least in the short run, to the economy, at the expense of exports. These tendencies are more significant in countries where the impact of an increase in productivity permits a more clear-cut improvement in manufacturing position (USA, France). Nevertheless the differences between these two simulations, arising from the different ways in which the sectors insert themselves into the economy, subsist.

The United States has a large increase in inflation in the non-manufacturing sector because the decrease in the unemployment rate induced by employment creation permits an increase in non-manufacturing wages. Since the manufacturing sector is more limited in the way it fixes its prices (inflation stemming from non-manufacturing inputs is slower to spread), the price gap between the two sectors is more significant than in the preceding simulation and amplifies the weakening of profitability in the manufacturing sector.

In West Germany the asymmetry of the role of sectoral productivity in wage determination is the crucial element. A decrease in the growth rate of non-manufacturing productivity has no impact on wages. Therefore the inflationary effect has its full impact, with its negative consequences on the balance of trade. As in the United States, the deformation of relative prices is significant: it leads first to a drop in profitability, then to a drop in manufacturing investment. This sector, which in the first simulation does not benefit much from its own productivity gains, largely supports here the consequences of the creation of supplementary jobs in the rest of the economy.

In France, the deterioration of the balance of trade, accompanied by a decrease in profitability and in investment, places the manufacturing sector in a difficult position. Nevertheless, the progression in private consumption is strong and the non-manufacturing sector experiences during the first years a sustained growth. This improvement in the components of internal demand capable of boosting the economy characterizes this simulation.

In Japan real wages are very responsive to a change in unemployment. The creation of jobs thus works in two ways causing both an increase in the standard of living and giving a boost to the economy through private consumption. Industry is, in the meantime, affected by the drop in exports and by the distortion of its relative prices.

The national trade-off

In order to compare the macroeconomic trade-off between the different nations, a linear combination of these two simulations has been computed in such a way that the ex-ante annual growth in the creation of jobs in the non-manufacturing sector nullifies the effects on unemployment of an increase in manufacturing productivity of one percent (more precisely, unemployment is stabilized on the average for the first 5 years).

The asymmetry of the mechanisms that work in the two sectors has been underlined many times. It is reinforced by the relative importance of industry in the economy as a whole. Thus in West Germany, where the share of manufacturing employment in total employment is larger than elsewhere, an increase in manufacturing productivity has automatically more influence on the number of jobs suppressed.

Moreover, depending on the employment's speed of adjustment, the number of supplementary jobs created in the non-manufacturing sector in order to stabilize unemployment differs from one country to the other. The negative consequences of the creation of jobs brought out below thus intervene to varying degrees. In Japan, a country where the manufacturing employment flexibility is very low, an increase of 0.2% in the labor force of the non-competing sector is sufficient to stabilize unemployment. France finds itself in a similar situation since the model indicates that 0.3% supplementary jobs are needed. The cases of the United States and, more notably, West Germany are different. In these two countries, an increase of one percent in the growth rate of manufacturing productivity requires the creation of 0.4% of new jobs in the rest of the economy.

As shown in Table 4, the results of the simulation permit to distinguish the same two categories of countries as before.

In France, the complementarity between the two sectors, as far as the creation of jobs is concerned, appears to be absolutely beneficial. This country draws an important competitive advantage from a decrease in manufactures' prices. Thus disinflation does not impede an improvement in the manufacturing profitability and compensates, on the other hand, an increase in prices in the non-competing sector leading to a stabilization of consumer prices.

In Japan, the effects of productivity gains on the one hand, and the creation of jobs on the other, compensate each other. Growth and inflation remain practically stable and only a slight drop in relative prices of the manufacturing output occurs while the industrial profit rate improves.

Apart from the effects on relative prices the simulation seems to have no impact in the United States. Not a single improvement in the short to medium term of the external balance is observable, but there is just a slight increase of inflation by which manufacturing profitability is unaffected.

For West Germany, the simulation turns out to be negative. If there is a positive effect on the growth of the economy, it is accompanied by a deterioration of manufacturing profits, and accelerating inflation. The predominant increase of costs in the non-manufacturing sector is accentuated by the consequences of

Table 4. A dualist scenario (differences from standard solution)*

	USA		Japan		Germany		France	
	0–5 years	5–10	0–5 years	5–10	0–5 years	5–10	0–5 years	5–10
Average annual rate of growth								
Output • manufacturing	−0.0	0.1	0.0	0.1	0.1	−0.1	0.1	0.4
• non-manufacturing	−0.1	0.0	0.0	0.1	0.1	0.1	0.0	0.2
• GDP	0.0	0.0	0.0	0.1	0.1	0.1	0.0	0.2
Deflator for consumption	−0.2	0.3	0.1	−0.0	0.4	0.9	0.0	−0.1
Relative price of manufacturing	−1.0	−1.3	−0.5	−0.5	−1.0	−1.7	−0.6	−0.8
Real private consumption	−0.1	−0.1	0.0	0.0	0.2	0.4	0.0	0.1
Manufacturing								
• Exports	0.1	0.4	0.0	0.2	0.2	0.6	0.0	−0.2
• Real wages	−0.1	−0.1	0.1	0.0	0.4	0.6	0.0	0.0
• Output price	−0.5	−0.7	−0.2	−0.4	−0.2	0.1	−0.4	−0.7
Average levels								
Manufacturing rate of return	0.1	−0.1	0.0	0.5	−0.1	−1.1	0.3	0.9
Unemployment rate	0.0	0.0	0.0	0.0	0.0	0.1	0.0	0.0
Trade balance/GDP in current prices	0.0	0.1	0.0	0.0	−0.0	−0.1	0.1	0.3

*We have simulated the impact of an increase of 1% of the manufacturing productivity growth rate combined with an increase in the number of jobs created in the non-manufacturing sector which stabilizes unemployment in the middle run (0–5 years). This employment creation is 0.325% in the USA, 0.2% in Japan, 0.26% in France, and 0.43% in West Germany.

the redistribution of the productivity gains on prices in the manufacturing sector, leading only to an accentuation of the phenomenon.

What lessons can be drawn from such a simulation

A first overall conclusion can be proposed: the combination which realized can be interpreted as a sectoral reallocation of the productivity gains. The results in Table 4, which summarize the reactions of the economies to this particular type of supply shock, do not indicate a homogeneous reaction. The overall impact is sometimes inflationary, sometimes neutral or deflationary, the balance of trade varies positively or negatively, manufacturing profitability improves or deteriorates. These results arise from the different ways in which industry inserts itself into each economy and returns to the previously discussed sequences. Apparently, research into the concentration of productivity gains in the sector exposed to international competition cannot be justified in general. Competitiveness depends on the overall macroeconomic performance. For at least two countries, the results of this simulation directly clarify the recent evolution. In Japan, at first, the path outlined by the simulation was closely followed after the first oil shock. This country was able to maintain productivity growth comparable to those of before 1973, while the growth of the value added slowed down permanently. The non-manufacturing sector absorbed most of the labor force freed by industry, thus permitting a stabilization of domestic demand. The beneficial complementarity observed in the model should be reexplored keeping in mind the observed inflexions between 1960–1973 and 1975–1980: the growth of manufacturing productivity returning to 9% on the one hand, and the increase of 1% in the rate of employment creation in the non-manufacturing sector on the other.

The size of these adjustments shows to what extent Japan was able to profit from this trade-off:

— on the one hand, it favored a dynamism in the exports of manufacturers which was a major reason for putting into use new technologies and new products;
— on the other hand, it permitted to partially check the fall of manufacturing profitability, due to the slowdown of growth which threatened precisely this industrial dynamism.

In West Germany, a contrario, the negative character of the simulation appears coherent with the observed evolutions. This country has maintained and maintains its non-manufacturing productivity rate. A development of inflation due to a deterioration of profits resulting in a decline of investment, does not compensate for the positive effects on private consumption of an increase in the standard of living. The mechanism of wage formation, in West Germany is such, that industry does not benefit directly from an increase of productivity, although indirectly it largely supports a decline in productivity in the rest of the economy.

The results of the simulation give few insights into the interpretation of the evolution of sectoral employment in the United States, because a certain neutrality emerges in the macroeconomic effects of such an arbitrage. In fact, this arbitrage does not really take place. Since 1973, the drop in productivity in the two sectors is comparable. And it is not clear how a further slowdown in non-manufacturing productivity could have taken place, since it had stagnated during the whole period 1975–1980. In these circumstances, the problem is more interesting in a prospective view. If manufacturing productivity will be regaining a rapid rate of growth soon, the creation of employment in the rest of the economy is likely to be massive to compensate for the unemployment effect. This supposes however a phase a sustained growth which arbitrage cannot in itself realize. The possibility of a retake-off of the American economy is rather to be sought in the development of the internal demand, and notably private consumption, than in a dualist management of employment.

On the other hand, in France, it is questionable if the very strong potential complementarity brought to light by the model is really possible. More than the possibility of creating supplementary jobs in the non-manufacturing sector, the freedom to change manufacturing productivity is limited. Unlike Japan, the growth of the manufacturing sector has greatly deteriorated these last years to become negative in 1981. In this context of slow growth, the favorable development of industrial productivity supposes structural changes and a radical change in the mechanisms of internal regulations which are at present difficult to foresee.

APPENDIX – THE COUNTRY MODELS OF SACHEM-OUEST

Sachem-Ouest is a multinational annual model which includes country models for the five main western economies (United States, France, West Germany, United Kingdom, Japan), an international exchange block, and simplified models for the other countries which are divided into four zones (OPEC, Socialist countries, LDC's outside of OPEC, other industrialized nations). The five country models which are used here were developed in a first stage. Each one of them can be viewed as a semi-theoretical simulation model.

1) They are semi-theoretical models because they integrate a large number of empirical parameters, which can be divided into structural parameters and behavioral parameters estimated by simple econometric methods.

The structural parameters include the date of a given base year (1975). The need to have for all countries a bisectorial input-output table for the private sector, on which all the accounting of the model is based, explains the use of this early date. As a matter of fact, the privileged role played in the determination of different prices and notably the prices of production of each sector, required a fairly precise calculation of the intermediate consumptions for both sectors; except for France, the national accounts of the selected countries, publish irregularly and with considerable delay in the input-output tables. The coefficients of the important relations of the models were figured out thanks to some econometric estimates.

2) They are simulation models because they distinguish themselves from other macroeconomic forecasting models by the way they are used. The script of the relations is such that the spontaneous behavior of the model places itself directly on a trajectory where all the volumes on the one hand and all the price on the other grow simultaneously. In fact three rates of growth characterize this path; the rate of growth of GNP, that of employment and finally that of the GNP deflator. These rates of growth correspond to the evolutions observed during the period 1975 to 1980.

The model is therefore used to compare the standard growth paths to those of various simulations. Because of its yearly steps and thus because of the rough nature of the short-term dynamic relations which the model transcribes, simulations are mainly centered on the medium term. Consequently, this permits above all to take into account the tendencial inflections in wage formation, prices, investment etc. . . caused by shocks on certain variables (exogenous or endogenous). Therefore maintained shocks, notably ruptures in the rate of growth of variables such as exchange rates, manufacturing productivity or wages are preferably studied.

In these conditions, it is possible to summarize the results on sub-periods whose length chosen for us in the tables is of five years, corresponding is roughly to the length of an economic cycle.

We have brought together in this appendix:

a) a simplified presentation of the country models;
b) an alphabetic list of the notations used in the equations of the models;
c) a list of the main structural coefficients

The lack of space does not permit us to insert estimation results but they are available from the authors by request.

A) Simplified presentation of country models*

Capital stock growth and potential output in manufacturing

$$K1 = (1 - d_k)K1(-1) + I1(-1)$$

$$YP1 = (1/k)K1$$

*The letters μ, β, γ, δ represent estimated parameters. For simplicity aims, the same letters figure in the different equations. In the same way, ϵ is a constant computed in relationship with the standard solution.

$$I1/K1 = (I1/K1)(-1) + \beta(\bar{\beta}\dot{Y}1 + (1-\bar{\beta})\dot{Y}1(-1) + \beta\left(\frac{UC1 - \overline{UC1}}{UC1}\right)$$

$$+ \gamma(\bar{\gamma}TPRO1 + (1-\bar{\gamma})TPRO1(-1) - \overline{TPRO1}) + \epsilon$$

$$UC1 = Y1/YP1$$

Employment and unemployment

$$N1 = \alpha\dot{N}1(-1) + (1-\alpha)(\dot{Y}1 - \widetilde{\dot{PROD1}})$$

$$N2 = \alpha\dot{N}2(-1) + (1-\alpha)(\dot{Y}2 - \widetilde{\dot{PROD2}})$$

$$N = N1 + N2 + N3$$

$$\Delta NCHO = \alpha\Delta N + \beta\Delta\bar{N} \qquad (\alpha = \beta \text{ in this preliminary version})$$

$$CHO = NCHO/N + NCHO)$$

Wages, prices

$$\dot{W}1 = \alpha\dot{PC} + \beta\left(\sum_{k=0}^{2}\beta_k PR\dot{O}D1(-k)\right) + \gamma CHO + \delta\dot{W}1(-1) + \epsilon$$

$$\dot{W}2 = \dot{W}1 - \alpha CHO + \epsilon$$

$$\dot{W}3 = \dot{W}1$$

$$CU1 = W1.N1/Y1 + a_{11}PU1 + a_{21}PU2$$

$$P\dot{D}1 = \alpha C\dot{U}1 + \beta\left(\frac{PD1}{PM1}(-1) - 1\right) + \gamma\Delta UC1 + \delta(PS1(-1) - \overline{PS1}) + \epsilon$$

$$P\dot{M}1 = \alpha P\dot{X}S1 + (1-\alpha)P\dot{D}1 \qquad (\alpha = 1 \text{ in this preliminary version})$$

$$P\dot{X}1 = \alpha P\dot{X}C1 + (1-\alpha)P\dot{D}1$$

$$PY1 = \frac{PD1(Q1-X1) + PX1.X1 - (a_{11}PU1 + a_{21}PU2)Y1}{Y1}$$

$$PU1 = (PD1(Q1-X1) + PM1.M1)/(Q1-X1+M1)$$

$$CUT2 = W2.N2/Y2$$

$$PY2 = \alpha C\dot{U}T2 + \beta P\dot{E} + \gamma(PS2(-1) - \overline{PS2}) + \epsilon$$

$$CU2 = CUT2 + a_{12}PU1 + a_{22}PU2$$

$$PX2 = \lambda_{XE}PE + (1 - \lambda_{XE})CU2/CU2_{(t=0)}$$

$$PM2 = \lambda_{ME}PE + (1 - \lambda_{ME})PXS2$$

$$PC = (C1.PU1 + C2.PU2)/(C1 + C2)$$

$$PI = \lambda_{IT_1}PU1 + (1 - \lambda_{IT_1})PU2$$

$$P\dot{X}S1 = P\dot{X}S2 = P\dot{X}C1 + \dot{P} \cdot + \dot{E}R$$

Demand and output

$$C/R = \alpha(C/R)(-1) + \beta\dot{R} + \gamma\Delta CHO + \delta\dot{P}C + \epsilon$$

$$C1 \doteq \lambda_{C_1}C$$

$$C2 = (1 - \lambda_{C_1})C$$

$$I2/Y2 = \alpha(I2/Y2)(-1) + \beta(\bar{\beta}\dot{Y}2 + (1 - \bar{\beta})\dot{Y}2(-1)) + \gamma(\bar{\gamma}XPRO2$$
$$+ \gamma(\bar{\gamma}XPRO2 + (1 - \bar{\gamma})XPRO2(-1) - \overline{XPRO2}) + \epsilon$$

$$DI1 = C1 + \lambda_{IT_1}(I1 + I2) + G1 + a_{11}Y1 + a_{21}Y2$$

$$DI2 = C2 + (1 - \lambda_{IT_1})(I1 + I2) + G2 + a_{21}Y1 + a_{22}Y2$$

$$\dot{M}1 = \alpha\dot{D}I1 + \beta \sum_{k=0}^{3} \beta_k \left(\frac{P\dot{D}1}{PM1}\right)(-k) + \gamma Y\dot{P}1 + \epsilon$$

$$\dot{X}1 = \alpha D\dot{M}1 + \beta \sum_{l=0}^{3} \beta_k \left(\frac{P\dot{X}C1}{PX1}\right)(-k) + \epsilon$$

$$M2 = \lambda_{M2} DI2$$

$$\dot{X}2 = D\dot{M}2$$

$$DF1 = DI1 + X1 - M1 - a_{11}Y1 - a_{12}Y2$$

$$DF2 = DI2 + X2 - M2 - a_{21}Y1 - a_{22}Y2$$

$$Y1 = b_{11}DF1 + b_{12}DF2$$

$$Y2 = b_{21}DF1 + b_{22}DF2$$

Incomes and profits

$$RDM = (1 + \tau_M)$$

$$(W1.N1 + W2.N2 + W3.N3) + \lambda_{RP1} PY1.Y1 + \lambda_{RP2} PY2 + Y2)$$

$$R = RDM/PC$$

$$PRO1 = (1 - \tau_{e1})(PY1.Y1 - W1.N1)$$

$$PRO2 = (1 - \tau_{e2})(PY2.Y2 - W2.N2)$$

$$TPRO1 = PRO1/(PI.K1)$$

$$XPRO2 = PRO2/(PI.Y2)$$

Manufacturing productivity in long run

$$\overset{\displaystyle\frown}{\dot{PROD1}} = \alpha [(Y1/Y1(-5))^{1/5} - 1] + \beta \left[\sum_{k=1}^{5} (11/K1)(-k) - \overline{TAC1} \right]$$

$$+ \epsilon - TLY1$$

For periods where $t = 5, 10, 15, 20$.

B) Alphabetic list of the notations used

1: manufacturing sector
2: non-manufacturing sector
3: public sector
no number: whole economy

CHO	= Unemployment rate
CU1	= Total unit costs
CUT1, CUT2	= Unit labor costs
DF1, DF2	= Final demand in constant prices
DI1, DI2	= Total domestic demand in constant prices
DM1, DM2	= Foreign demand in constant prices (exogenous)
ER	= Exchange rate (exogenous)
G1, G2	= Public expenditure in constant prices (exogenous)
I1, I2, I	= Investment
K	= Fixed capital stock
M1, M2, M	= Volume of imports
MG1, MG2	= Mark up

N, N1, N2, N3	= Employment (N3 exogenous)
$\bar{N}$	= Potential labor force (exogenous)
NCHO	= Number of unemployed
P^*	= Foreign price in foreign currency (exogenous)
PC	= Consumption deflator
PD1, PD2	= Price of production
PE	= Price of energy (exogenous)
PI	= Investment deflator
PM1, PM2	= Price of imports (exogenous)
PRO1, PRO2	= Operating surplus
$\widetilde{PROD1}, \widetilde{PROD2}$	= Tendential productivity of labor
PS1, PS2	= Wages' share in the value-added at factor costs
PU1, PU2	= Price of domestic demand in the two sectors
PX1, PX2	= Export prices (PX2 exogenous)
PXS1, PXS2	= Foreign competitors' prices weighted by the structure of imports (exogenous)
PY1, PY2	= Output price
Q1, Q2	= Production in constant prices
R	= Real household income
RDM	= Real disposable income of households
TPRO1	= Rate of return (TPRO1 = PRO1/PI.K1)
UC1	= Capacity production utilization rate
W1, W2, W3	= Total annual compensation
X1, X2	= Volume of exports (X2 exogenous)
XPRO2	= Real profits related to value-added (XPRO2 = PRO2/PI.Y2)
Y1, Y2	= Output in constant prices
YP1	= Potential output

C) List of the main structural coefficients

k	= Capital coefficient (sector one)
d_k	= Depreciation rate of fixed capital (sector one)
(a_{ij})	= Matrix of the coefficients of the Input Output Table Intermediate consumption of good i, of branch j related to the output of sector j
(bij)	= Matrix of the coefficients resulting from the reversal of the I.O table, permits to calculate the output from the final demands
$\lambda_{XE}, \lambda_{ME}$	= Share of energy in exports (respectively the imports) of non-manufacturing goods

λ_{IT1} = Share of machinery and equipment (manufactures) in total productive investment

λ_{C1} = Share of manufactures in private consumption

τ_M = Ratio of the transfers to the state (Social Payments less Taxes and Social Contributions)

RP1, RP2 = Ratio of household non wage incomes (capital and self-employed income) to the value-added of the two sectors

τ_{E_1}, τ_{E_2} = Ratio of the direct taxes of firms of each sector to their net surplus of operations costs

$\overline{\text{TPRO1}}$ = Manufactures' rate of return from the standard solution

$\overline{\text{TAC1}}$ = Manufactures' accumulation rate of the standard solution

$\overline{\text{XPRO2}}$ = Real profits related to the value-added of non-manufacturing sector of the standard solution

$\overline{\text{PS1}}$, $\overline{\text{PS2}}$ = Share of wages in the value-added of the two sectors (corrected increase in employees) of the standard solution

NOTES

This paper owes a lot to the work done in the Sachem-Ouest Project headed by Gilles Oudiz. More information can be had in the CEPII review under the title: 'Dualité, Change et Contraintes Extérieures dans Cinq Economies Dominantes' (EPI, no 13–14 ler et 2éme trismestres 1983). We would also like to thank here Jean Pisani-Ferry who was willing to give us many suggestions and comments.

1) See for example A. Lindbeck (1983) or C.F. Denison (1983) for some of the most recent publications about this subject.

2) These ideas were developed in many studies, of which can be quoted: those of G. Lafay, M. Fouquin and L. de Mautort (1980) and M. Aglietta, A. Orlean and G. Oudiz (1981).

3) A five-years period roughly corresponding with the length of business cycle was chosen.

4) Thus is expressed a specificity of the Japanese economy which seems to go beyond the basic statistical problems linked to measuring unemployment.

5) The United Kingdom model is still in an exploratory phase therefore its simulations are not presented here. Besides the energy problem there are two important points to be resolved concerning the price-wage block: the importance of the Philips effect and the weight of foreign competition in the determination of domestic prices.

6) Ex-post the evolution of productivity differs since the first year because of the employment cycle. In the middle-long term, one also has to take into account the productivity-growth or productivity-accumulation relations. These latter effects remain nevertheless small in the simulations.

7) See for example R. Boyer and P. Petit (1983).

REFERENCES

Aglietta, M. (1976), *Régulation et crise du capitalisme*, Calmann-Levy.

Aglietta, M., A. Orlean and G. Oudiz (1981), 'Des Adaptations différenciées face à la crise', *Revue Economique*, Juillet.

Bailly, M. (1982), 'The productivity slowdown by industry', *Brookings Papers on Economic Activity*, no 2.

Berger, S. and M. Piore (1980), *Dualism and discontinuity in industrial societies*, Cambridge University Press.

Boyer, R. and P. Petit (1983), 'Favoriser la productivité pour accroître l'emploi? A propos de quelques idées reçues', *CEPREMAP*, no 8309.

Brender, A., A. Chevallier and J. Pisani-Ferry, 'Etats-Unis, Croissance, crise et changement technique dans une économie tertiaire', *Economie Prospective Internationale*, no 2.

CEPII (1983), 'Economie Mondiale: la montée des tensions', *Economica*.

Cornwall, J. (1977), *Modern capitalism*, Roberston.

Courbis, R. (1975), *Compétitivité et croissance en économie concurrencée*, Dunod.

Denison, E. (1983), 'The interruption of productivity growth in the United States', *The Economic Journal*, March.

Deppler, C. Michael and Duncan M. Rippley (1978), 'The World Trade Model: Merchandise Trade', *IMF Staff Papers*, 25 (1)(March), pp. 147–206.

Giersch, H. and F. Wolter (1983), 'Towards an explanation of the productivity slowdown: an acceleration-deceleration hypothesis', *The Economic Journal*, March.

Kremp, E., J. Le Dem and G. Oudiz (1983), chapitres II à VI dans: 'Dualité, change et contraintes extérieures dans cinq économies dominantes: le projet Sachem-Ouest', *Economie Prospective Internationale*, no 13–14.

Lafay, G., M. Fouquin and L. de Mautort (1980), 'Spécialisation et adaptation face á la crise', *Economie Prospective Internationale*, no 1, Janvier.

Lewis, W.A. (1984), *Economic development with unlimited supplies of labor*, The Manchester School, May.

Lindbeck, A. (1979), *Inflation and employment in open economies*, North Holland.

Lindbeck, A. (1983), 'The recent slowdown of productivity growth', *The Economic Journal*, March.

CHAPTER 8

THE CURRENT ACCOUNT OF THE UNITED STATES, JAPAN, AND GERMANY: A CYCLICAL ANALYSIS

Peter Hooper and Ralph Tryon
Federal Reserve Board

1. INTRODUCTION AND SUMMARY

The current account positions of the major industrial countries have undergone very large swings in the past three years. Most observers now expect the U.S. current account, which was in surplus in 1981, to show a record deficit in 1983, and an even larger deficit in 1984. Swings in the Japanese and German current accounts have been equally dramatic in the opposite direction, moving from deficit to surplus. The possible continuation of these deficits is a source of concern to policy-makers to the extent, for example, that they and the factors underlying them give rise to protectionist pressures or involve significant adjustment costs in tradable goods sectors.

Several factors have been cited for the projected increase in the U.S. current account deficit on one side and the surpluses of Japan and Germany on the other. One involves exchange-rate developments: the appreciation of the dollar in real terms against the yen and the mark since 1980 has led to a substantial loss in U.S. price competitiveness. A second involves cyclical developments: the U.S. recovery from the 1982 recession has been and is expected to continue to be significantly stronger than the recovery elsewhere, leading to a relative boom in U.S. import demand. A third concerns the effects of the sharp drop in the imports of debt-burdened developing countries.

The present paper focuses on the cyclical factor, and attempts to gauge the quantitative importance of the cyclical components of the recent and expected current account positions in the three countries. It also considers, briefly, the relative importance of the drop in exports to developing countries.

Our method of analysis, outlined in Section 2, is to estimate how the current accounts of the three countries would differ from baseline paths if output in the three countries (and the rest of the world) reached 'cyclically neutral' paths over

Artus, P. and Guvenen, O. (eds.). International Macroeconomic Modelling for Policy Decisions.
© *1986. Martinus Nijhoff Publishers, Dordrecht/Boston/Lancaster.*
ISBN 90-247-3201-8. Printed in The Netherlands.

the next 3 years. The estimates are made using two versions of the Federal Reserve Board Staff's Multicountry Model (MCM). The results obtained depend importantly upon the structure and parameters of the model employed, as well as on the projected baseline and cyclically neutral paths for output we have chosen. One version of the model treats GNP and all other determinants of each country's balance of payments as exogenous variables. The other treats non-GNP determinants of the balance of payment accounts endogenously. In this case the desired GNP paths are reached through the application of monetary and fiscal policy measures: other factors that affect the current account, including prices, interest rates and exchange rates, are allowed to fluctuate endogenously.

The baseline path, described in Section 3, is for the most part taken from available published forecasts. The cyclically neutral output paths are described in Section 4. In view of the inherent difficulties involved in measuring cyclically-neutral or potential output paths, we have chosen two measures. These include a 'peak-to-peak' trend and a 'normal' trend, both calculated from historical data over the past 10 years. Our intention here was not to derive precise measures of potential output, but rather to define paths that appeared to be both free of cyclical fluctuations and realistically attainable over the next 3 years.

The results, presented in Section 5, suggest that the cyclical component of the U.S. current account is surprisingly small, and that the cyclical components of both the U.S. and Japanese current accounts could be in the 'wrong' direction. That is, if output were adjusted to the cyclically neutral paths we have defined, both the U.S. deficit and the Japanese surplus would be *larger* than currently expected.

This result is obtained for two reasons. First, despite its strong recovery in 1983, U.S. output still has further to go to reach its cyclically neutral path than does output in other major countries on average, and in Japan in particular. This is partly because the recent recession was relatively deeper in the United States. Also, Japan's output gap is small, based on our definition of cyclically neutral growth in terms of the trend observed during the 1970's. This trend yielded a cyclically adjusted growth rate of about 4% for Japan, somewhat below the average observed during the 1960's. In our judgment the more recent experience provided the more realistic basis for defining an attainable growth path for Japan in the near term. Even so, we did make an effort to maximize Japan's output gap by assuming a relatively low baseline growth rate of $3\frac{1}{2}$%.

The second reason for our estimate of a small cyclical component in the U.S. case, is that the MCM's estimated income elasticities of import demand are somewhat larger for the United States than for other countries, on average.

Our simulation results also suggest that the estimated cyclical component of current accounts can differ significantly if allowance is made for cyclical movements in other variables besides GNP, depending upon the mix of policies employed to achieve the cyclically neutral GNP. If, for example, fiscal stimulus is used in the United States and monetary stimulus abroad, U.S. real interest rates rise relative to foreign rates, the dollar appreciates, and the cyclically adjusted U.S. current account becomes more negative, while those of other countries become more positive.

We found in analysing recent trends in exports to developing countries, that U.S. exports to these countries fell about $5 billion more than German and Japanese exports between 1981 and the first half of 1983. This accounts for only a small part of the total swing in the relative current account positions of these countries over this period.

We conclude that the relative movements in the U.S. and Japanese current accounts over the period 1982–83 and beyond are likely to have been predominantly the result of movements in real exchange rates. Cyclical factors do appear to have played a role in increasing the German current account surplus, although exchange rate changes also appear to have contributed significantly. The implication of this conclusion is that even if major industrial countries succeed in attaining cyclically normal output paths in the next few years, relative current account positions, particularly those of the United States and Japan, could remain roughly unchanged for some time. Significant readjustment in current account positions probably would require a significant reversal of the real exchange rate movements that have taken place in recent years.

Such a change in exchange rates could be brought about by any number of possible events. Our simulation results suggest that a shift in policy mixes toward fiscal restraint in the United States and fiscal easing in other industrial countries would tend to reduce U.S. real interest rates relative to foreign rates, and put downward pressure on the dollar. Shifts in market expectations about the long-run sustainability of large current account imbalances, or in preferences for dollar-denominated assets could also bring about a substantial depreciation of the dollar.

2. DESIGN OF EXPERIMENT AND DESCRIPTION OF MODEL

The concept of cyclical adjustment of current account positions is by no means new, although the published literature on this subject is scant. During the Bretton Woods era of pegged exchange rates, analysts in national governments and international organizations made such computations for policy makers for the purpose of assessing the appropriateness of underlying demand management policies. Since the move to more flexible exchange rates in the early 1970's, the analysis has been used instead as an indicator of movements in real exchange rates needed to achieve 'sustainable' long-run current account positions.

To date, attempts to quantify the cyclical components of current account balances have focused on the effects of cyclical swings in real activity on trade flows (see, for example, Artus (1978) and Williamson (1983)). The methodology typically involves relating the components of trade or current account balances to income or activity at home and abroad, relative prices, exchange rates and other factors in a model framework. Cyclically-adjusted balances are then computed by substituting cyclically-adjusted paths of home and foreign income or activity for the actual cyclical paths of these variables, and deriving the model's prediction under the alternative paths[1]. Henceforth, we shall refer to this methodology as the 'partial-equilibrium approach', since it treats the various determinants of external balances as exogenous variables in partial-equilibrium models of those balances.

In the present paper we also introduce a more general methodology that treats all of the major determinants of the current account endogenously and takes into account the effects of cyclical fluctuations in prices, interest rates and exchange rates, as well as real activity. This methodology, which we label the 'full-model approach', involves solving the model for policy paths across countries that achieve predetermined levels of cyclically-adjusted output in those countries. The policy shifts also affect the other variables in the model. An important implication of this approach is that the estimated cyclical component of the current account can vary depending upon which policies are used to achieve the given cyclically-adjusted income paths[2]. This is because the effects of non-income determinants of the current account (prices, interest rates and exchange rates, etc.) will vary under different policy settings.

The model employed in our analysis is the Federal Reserve Board staff's Multi-country Model (MCM). The MCM consists of a system of fully developed macro models of five countries — the United States, Japan, Germany, Canada and the United Kingdom — as well as an abbreviated rest-of-world sector. The major determinants of current accounts (GNP, capacity utilization, prices, interest rates, exchange rates and stocks of real and financial foreign claims and liabilities) are treated endogenously. The rest-of-world sector includes the determination of income and prices (which are linked to income and prices in the five MCM countries), trade flows and some (OPEC) financial flows[3].

One significant adjustment was made to the basic structure of the MCM for purposes of the full-model exercise. The exchange rate determination sector was replaced with a set of simplified equations in which bilateral rates of the dollar against the currencies of the other four countries were constrained to move proportionally with each country's prices relative to U.S. prices and with real interest differentials[4]. This adjustment was made in order to simplify the analysis. In the original version of the model exchange rates also respond to shifts in current accounts in an equilibrating direction (i.e, a deficit causes a depreciation, which reduces the deficit). Since part of the reason for undertaking this exercise was to draw implications about the exchange rate, we decided to abstract from the response that was built into the model.

In Section 5 we present estimates of cyclically-adjusted current accounts based on both the partial-equilibrium and full model approaches described above. For purposes of the partial-equilibrium estimates, most of the determinants of the current account were treated exogenously (i.e. equations for incomes, prices, interest rates, etc., were dropped from the model). However, we did allow for changes in net foreign asset stocks resulting from shifts in current account positions. (These asset stocks enter directly into the determination of net investment income).

The partial-equilibrium approach was used to calculate both historical and forward-looking estimates of cyclically-adjusted deficits. The historical analysis involved setting output in the five MCM countries plus the rest-of-world sector to cyclically-adjusted paths (defined in Section 4 below) during 1982–83 to determine the cyclical components of current accounts over that period. This exercise has the advantage of working from a baseline of actual data, though the results may be of limited value to the formulation of economic policy currently, that will have an impact over the next few years.

The forward-looking estimates involve comparing a baseline projection through 1986 with a projection in which incomes grow cyclically-adjusted or potential levels by the end of 1986. (The baseline projection is described in the next section.) This exercise has the disadvantage of working from a projected or hypothetical baseline path, but the advantage of being of greater relevance to current policy decisions.

The full model approach was employed only in forward-looking simulations. In this case several different policy paths were chosen to achieve potential or cyclically-neutral output levels by 1986. These included, a mix of monetary and fiscal stimulus and a pure fiscal stimulus (with no monetary accommodation).

3. BASELINE PROJECTIONS

In order to run forward-looking partial-equilibrium and full model simulations out to 1986, baseline paths for the current accounts and their key determinants had to be constructed. We chose not to use the model itself to produce paths for the key variables (current accounts, trade flows, GNP, prices, and exchange rates). Rather, paths for these variables were for the most part assumed *a priori* and imposed on the model.

Table 1. Baseline assumptions for GNP, prices exchange rates and
current accounts

	GNP growth rates (%)		
	U.S.	Japan	Germany
1983	$3\frac{1}{4}$	3	$1\frac{1}{4}$
1984	5	$3\frac{1}{2}$	3
1985	4	$3\frac{1}{2}$	3
1986	$3\frac{1}{2}$	$3\frac{1}{2}$	3

	CPI inflation rates (%)		
	U.S.	Japan	Germany
1983	4	2	3
1984	5	2	3
1985	5	$2\frac{1}{2}$	3
1986	5	$2\frac{1}{2}$	3

	Exchange rate changes (%)	
	$/Yen	$/DM
1983	3	-3
1984	10	10
1985	5	5
1986	0	0

	Current account balances (billions of dollars)		
	U.S.	Japan	Germany
1983	-40	20	5
1984	-70	20	8
1985	-70	20	8
1986	-70	20	8

The assumed paths, presented in Table 1, were based largely on actual values and linear extrapolations of forecasts published by *Blue Chip Worldscan*, which surveys the regular forecasts of some forty private economic forecasting concerns[5]. These paths were imposed on the model by adjusting residuals in the model's behavioral equations. The numbers given in Table 1 deviate somewhat from the published forecasts inasmuch we tried to make the assumed paths for GNP, prices and exchange rates at least roughly consistent with those for current accounts, given the model's structure. We emphasize that our intention here was not to make point forecasts but to derive plausible paths for key variables as a baseline for the simulations presented.

The baseline can be described as follows. The strong recovery of U.S. GNP in the second half of 1983 continues into early 1984 and then begins to taper off. By 1986 the growth rate has fallen almost to the rate of growth of potential output (as defined in the next section). GNP growth rates in Japan and Germany pick up somewhat in 1984 (in line with recent growth), but remain the neighborhood of those countries' potential growth rates through 1986.

Our assumption for U.S. GNP growth in 1985–86 is about 1 percentage point above the Blue Chip panel's average, while that for Japan is $\frac{1}{2}$ percentage point below the average. These paths were selected to be consistent with unchanged current accounts through 1986 and to emphasize the cyclical differences among countries.

CPI inflation rates are for the most part extrapolated at recently reported rates. The U.S. inflation rate rises in 1984, reflecting the effects of an assumed depreciation of the dollar. The inflation assumptions are well within the range of the Blue Chip forecasts but are about $\frac{1}{2}$–1 percentage point below the average of the forecasts for each country. The published forecasts predict a moderate decline (of about 10%) in the dollar against the mark and yen next year; we have assumed a slight additional depreciation of the dollar in 1985 in light of current account considerations.

Recent historical and baseline current account paths are illustrated in Figure 1. The U.S. current account deficit increases to about $70 billion in 1984. This is somewhat above the Blue Chip range (several forecasters had $60 billion). We have made this adjustment in view of the sharp increase in the U.S. trade deficit in recent months, and the likelihood that continued rapid U.S. growth will widen the deficit further in the near term. The U.S. deficit remains unchanged at $70 billion through 1986, as the effects of higher growth in the United States (as well as higher import elasticities there than in the other countries) are offset by the effects of the depreciation of the dollar in real terms. Likewise, Japan's surplus remains at about $20 billion and Germany's at $8 billion, both slightly ($1–2 billion) above the Blue Chip average for 1984.

Since the focus of our analysis is on the current account position of the United States, Japan and Germany, it is useful briefly to review the recent movements in those series and their underlying factors. As indicated in Table 2, the U.S. current account fell by $30 billion at an annual rate from its peak in 1981 to the first half of 1983. Of this decline roughly two-thirds was in terms of merchandise trade, and one-third in terms of net services and transfers. By the third-quarter of 1983, the trade balance had fallen another $25 billion, to a deficit of more than $70 billion. Given early indications of continued robust U.S. recovery in the fourth quarter, the deficit seemed likely to widen further.

The increase in the U.S. deficit has been attributed to three factors: the

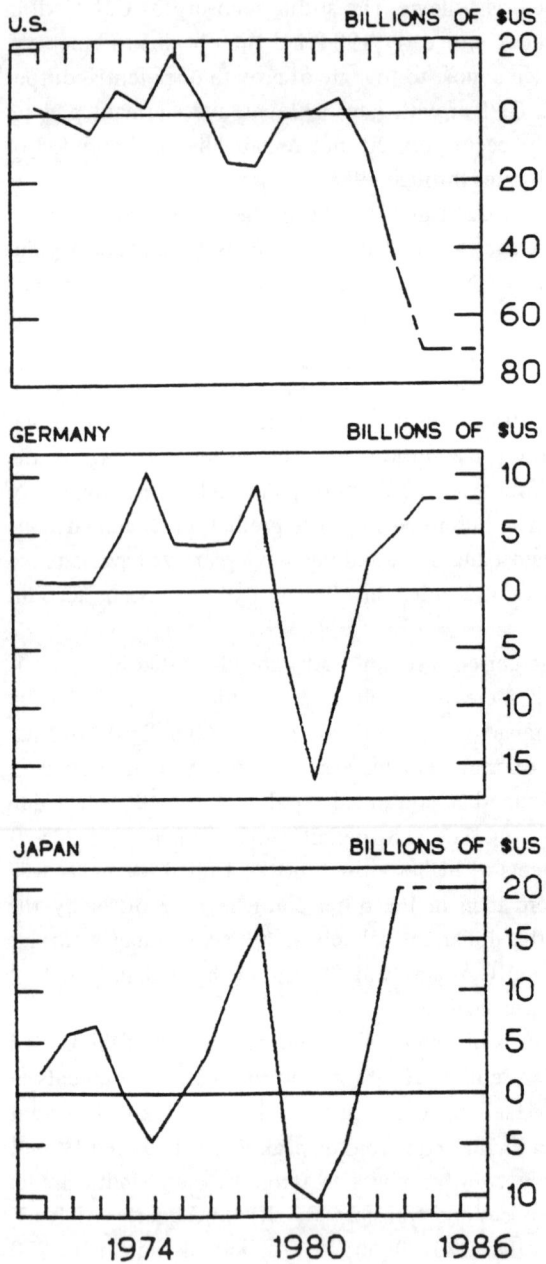

Figure 1. Current account balance. ———— = historical current account; —·——·— = baseline projection.

Table 2. Trade and current account balances U.S., Japan and Germany (billions of U.S. dollars, seasonally adjusted annual rates).

	1980	1981	1982	1983 H1	1983 Q1	Q2	Q3
United States							
Trade Balance	25.5	− 28.1	− 36.4	− 46.9	− 35.2	− 58.6	− 71.6
Net Services and Transfers	26.0	32.7	− 25.2	20.4	20.9	19.8	
Current Account	0.4	4.6	− 11.2	− 26.5	− 14.3	− 38.8	
Japan							
Trade Balance		20.1	18.8	29.2	26.0	32.4	35.2
Net Services and Transfers		− 15.3	− 11.9	− 10.2	− 12.0		
Current Account	− 10.7	4.8	6.9	19.0	14.0	24.0	24.4
Germany							
Trade Balance		11.9	20.6	19.2	22.4	16.0	
Net Services and Transfers		− 4.6	− 17.0	− 14.2	− 15.6	− 12.8	
Current Account	− 16.5	− 7.3	3.6	5.0	6.8	3.2	

appreciation of the dollar in real terms since 1980, a sharp decline in the imports of developing countries (particularly those burdened with large debt service payments), and the relative strength of the U.S. recovery (that is, cyclical factors).

Table 3. Nominal exchange rates, relative CPI's and real exchange rates.

	Nominal exchange rates		Relative CPI's (1978Q4 = 1.0)		Real exchange rates (Col. 1 × Col. 2, indexed in 1978Q4 = 1.0)	
	Yen/$	DM/$	US/Jap	US/Ger	Yen/$	DM/$
1978Q4	190	1.87	1.00	1.00	1.00	1.00
1979Q4	238	1.76	1.07	1.07	1.35	1.65
1980Q4	210	1.91	1.12	1.15	1.25	1.17
1981Q4	224	2.25	1.18	1.18	1.39	1.42
1982Q4	259	2.50	1.20	1.18	1.64	1.57
1983Q3	249	2.61	1.23	1.18	1.61	1.65
		Percentage Changes				
1979Q4/78Q4	24.9	− 5.8	7.5	6.7	34.3	0.5
1980Q4/79Q4	− 11.6	8.2	4.3	7.5	− 7.8	16.3
1981Q4/80Q4	6.6	17.7	5.3	2.9	12.3	21.1
1982Q4/81Q4	15.3	11.3	2.1	− 0.2	17.7	11.0
1983Q3/82Q4	− 3.6	4.2	1.6	0.0	− 1.9	4.2
1983Q3/80Q4	18.6	36.6	9.3	2.6	29.6	40.2
1983Q3/78Q4	31.1	39.6	22.6	18.0	60.7	64.7

As indicated in Table 3, in the past 5 years the dollar has appreciated by 61% in real terms against the yen and 65% against the mark. Although these movements followed a general decline in the dollar during the mid-1970's, they substantially altered U.S. price competitiveness relative to that of Japan and Germany in the past few years. This shift in price competitiveness not only reduces the U.S. trade position, but also contributed to the increase in the Japanese and German surpluses. The effects on Japan and Germany have been less pronounced because their currencies fell considerably less in real terms (and in some cases rose) against non-dollar currencies.

Table 4. U.S., Japanese and German exports to developing countries (billions of dollars, annual rates).

	1978	1979	1980	1981	1982		1985
					H1	H2	H1
U.S. exports							
Total	143.8	182.0	220.8	233.8	224.6	200.0	222.4
To developing countries	55.0	66.1	87.0	95.0	92.0	81.8	83.2
To major debtor countries*	19.7	26.5	35.9	39.1	28.4	34.0	30.6
Japanese exports							
Total	98.4	102.3	130.4	151.5	140.8	136	138.5
To developing countries	59.8	46.9	60.9	70.0	63.6	62.2	61.7
To major debtor countries*	12.5	11.4	12.1	13.4	11.6	9.8	9.7
German exports							
Total	142.5	171.8	192.8	176.1	182.6	170.2	173.1
To developing countries	33.5	36.4	40.6	42.5	41.6	38.8	36.9
To major debtor countries*	4.1	5.1	5.9	5.5	4.8	3.8	4.0

* Argentine, Brazil, Chile, Korea, Mexico, Peru, Philippines, Venezuela.
Source: IMF *Direction of Trade Statistics*, (various issues).

The effects of the second factor, the debt problem and the contraction of demand in developing countries, are illustrated in Table 4. The table lists U.S., Japanese, and German exports to all countries, to all developing countries, (including OPEC) and to eight major debtor countries. Between 1981 and the first half of 1983, U.S. exports fell by almost $12 billion. All of this was accounted for by a drop in exports to developing countries, of which $8.5 billion was to major debtor countries. Part of the decline could have reflected the decline in U.S. price competitiveness, but it is noteworthy that over the same period Japanese and German exports to developing countries and major debtor countries fell (proportionally) at about the same rate as U.S. exports to these areas. Nevertheless, U.S. exports were affected more than either German or Japanese exports in absolute terms, because debtor countries account for a higher portion of U.S. exports.

The third factor, cyclical swings in income and other variables is the focus of the remainder of this paper. It should be noted that service flows can be significantly affected by cyclical factors, just as trade flows are. Most of the decline in U.S. net services between 1981 and the first half of 1983 was accounted for by a drop in direct investment income receipts, reflecting the decline in economic activity and profits in other countries during that period.

Finally, before turning to the cyclical analysis, we should caution that analysis of current account positions is subject to potentially severe statistical constraints. Most notable is the existence of a very large discrepancy in the aggregation of global current accounts. That is, the total of all countries' current account positions, which in principle should sum to zero, summed to −$56 billion in 1981, −$100 billion in 1982 and possibly an even greater magnitude in 1983[6]. Analyses by the OECD and IMF suggest that a substantial part of this discrepancy involves the underreporting of service account receipts in the currrent accounts of industrial countries and OPEC. Based on a purely mechanical allocation of the discrepancy by shares in the trade of industrial countries, the U.S. current account deficit in 1983 could be overstated by as much as $20 billion, while the surpluses of Japan and Germany could be understated by roughly $10 billion and $15 billion, respectively.

4. CALCULATION OF CYCLICALLY NEUTRAL GNP PATHS

In defining our measures of cyclically neutral output we begin with the concept of potential GNP. That is, at any one time there exists a *sustainable* level of real output at which resources in the economy are 'fully' employed. We further assume that the level of potential GNP grows at a rate that is roughly constant over the period we are investigating. Full employment growth is defined not in any absolute sense, but rather using recent experience as a standard.

An implication of this approach is that there is no inherent business cycle. Deviations of output from its potential path can, in principle, be eliminated by selecting an appropriate policy mix. However, the policies needed to maintain this level of output in the face of various exogenous shocks might require unacceptably large deficits or increases in the money supply; we do not argue that it is necessarily desirable to achieve potential GNP. Furthermore, in an uncertain world it is difficult for policy makers either to specify or to implement the 'appropriate policy mix'.

One measure we use, as an approximation of potential output, is a peak-to-peak trend. This is a simple linear interpolation between the two highest peaks in actual output over the period 1972–1982. The series is extended through 1986 using the same growth rate. Although the details differ across countries, the two peaks roughly precede the two OPEC oil price shocks of 1974 and 1979. (Our interpretation is thus that while potential growth may have been altered by the earlier price shock, it was not substantially affected by the more recent one.) We have chosen to abstract from the levels of capacity utilization and unemployment prevailing at the two peaks, because of the statistical problems associated with measuring capacity utilization, and because of the considerable variance over time in measured natural (noninflationary) rates of unemployment. While the peak-to-peak trend may lie below the *maximum* possible level of output at any given point in time, our intention is to define a feasible and sustainable path for the near future, based on recent historical experience.

A second measure we employ, termed 'normal output', uses the rate of growth of potential output implied by the peak-to-peak measure, but reduces the calculated level of that path by a constant percentage. The reduction is such that the means of the actual and cyclically adjusted output paths are equal over the period 1973–1982. This adjustment is made since it seems conceivable, and perhaps even probable, that peak levels of output could not be sustained over time under reasonable policy regimes.

Table 5. Potential output measures for the MCM countries.

| | Current output gap (%) | | Annual growth rate of potential GNP (%) | Average annual growth needed to reach potential by 1986 | |
	peak to peak	normal growth		peak to peak	normal growth
Canada	10.1	6.2	2.9	6.4	5.1
Germany	10.7	5.8	2.7	6.3	4.7
Japan	2.7	−0.1	3.9	4.8	3.9
U.K.	7.2	2.7	1.3	3.6	2.1
U.S.	8.4	3.5	2.9	6.0	4.3

Table 5 shows the current (1983Q3) output gaps, measured as a percentage of current real output, for each country using the two alternative measures of cyclically neutral output. The table also shows the estimated annual growth rate of potential output, and the rate of growth that would be needed to reach potential by the end of 1986.

Japan stands out with by far the smallest output gap among the five countries. Japanese output is currently running very slightly above its 'normal' path, and is only 2.7% below projected peak-to-peak potential. The other countries range from 2.7 to 6.2% below normal output, and 7.2 to 10.7% below peak-to-peak potential.

The United States is in the middle of the group; it is 'ahead' of Canada and Germany in the business cycle, but the difference is not striking, compared with the relative position of Japan.

Japan also has the fastest growth rate of peak-to-peak growth at 3.9%. It is a full percentage point higher than the values for the United States, Germany, and Canada, which are grouped at around 2.8%. The figure for the United Kingdom is 1.3%. The growth rates needed to reach potential are in the range of $4-6\frac{1}{2}$% per year, except for the United Kingdom; this would require a strong recovery, but not one that is outside the bounds of historical experience.

Figures 2 and 3 illustrate the alternative potential output paths as well as our baseline paths for real GNP. In all countries but Germany the baseline case is for output to come near to its 'normal' path by 1986; in Germany the output gap remains roughly constant.

The definition and measurement of potential output raises difficult conceptual problems, and the measurements proposed here are to some extent arbitrary. We also ran the simulations reported in this paper using measures of potential output reported by the OECD[7]. The results did not differ significantly from those reported here, which gives us some confidence that our measures of potential output are at least plausible. Again, they attempt merely to define a reasonable path for the economy at high employment, not necessarily to measure the ultimate capacity of the economy.

5. SIMULATION RESULTS

This section describes the results of the model simulations outlined in Section 2. The simulations involve moving real output from historical or projected baseline paths to cyclically-adjusted (potential and normal) paths as defined in the preceding section. For this exercise we assumed that real activity in the rest-of-world sector (including developing countries) would move in proportion to activity in the five MCM countries[8]. The results, for the most part, are reported in terms of deviations from the historical and projected baseline. We first employ the international accounts sectors of the U.S., German, and Japanese models in the MCM for partial-equilibrium analysis. In these simulations only the variables determined in the balance of payments accounts are endogenous. Real incomes change exogenously but prices, interest rates, exchange rates, and all other variables not determined directly in the balance of payments accounts are fixed. In Figure 4 we show the results of two 'historical' simulations in which real output is assumed to follow potential and normal output paths starting in 1982. The figure shows the results for the current account, compared with the historical baseline, for the

194

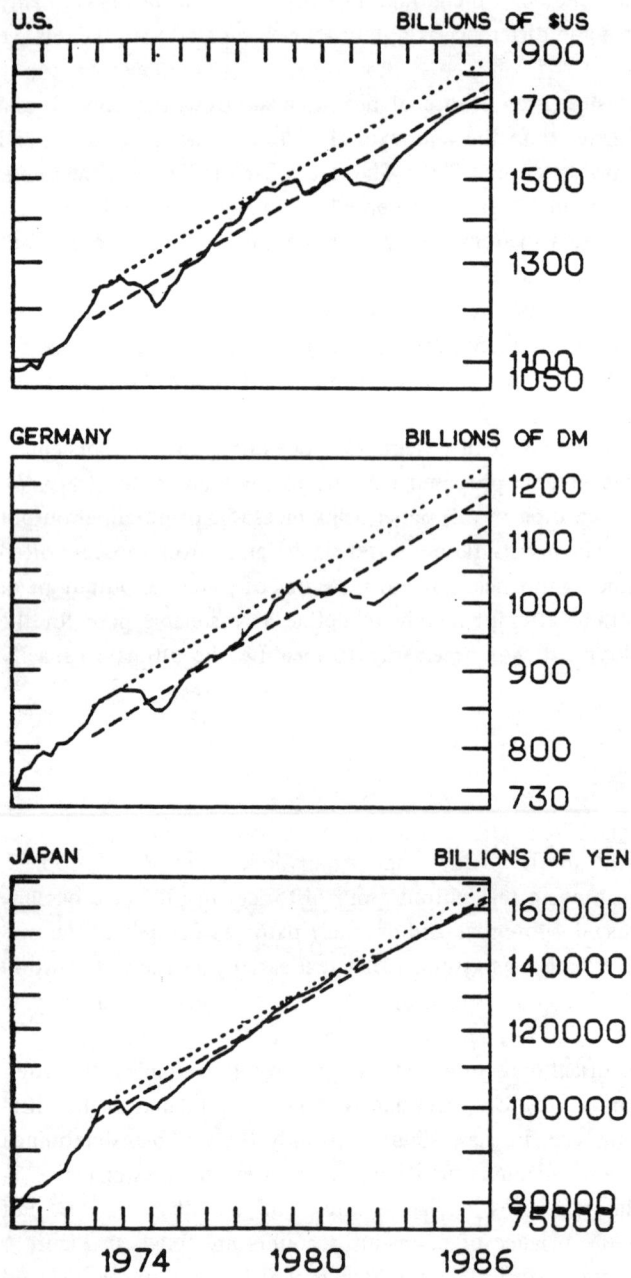

Figure 2. Potential GNP. ———— = historical GNP; —·—·— = baseline forecast; ·········· = peak-to-peak potential GNP; ———— = normal GNP.

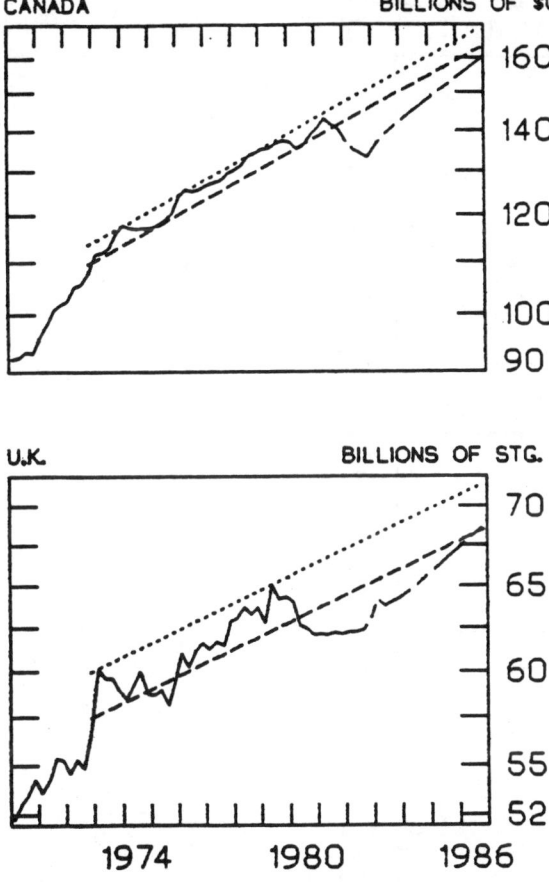

Figure 3. Potential GNP. ———— = historical GNP; —·—·— = baseline forecast; ·········· = peak-to-peak potential GNP; ———— = normal GNP.

three countries (All current accounts are measured in billions of U.S. dollars, at annual rates.)

The top planel of Figure 4 shows the paths for the U.S. current account. In the potential output simulation the U.S. deficit is substantially larger than in the baseline case. This is chiefly because in 1982 the U.S. had a larger output gap than its trading partners, particularly Japan. Raising all countries to potential in 1982 raises U.S. income by more than the increase in the average of its trading partner's income, and U.S. imports increase more than do U.S. exports. Another factor that contributes to the initial widening of the U.S. deficit is that the MCM's U.S. income elasticity of import demand is somewhat higher than the import

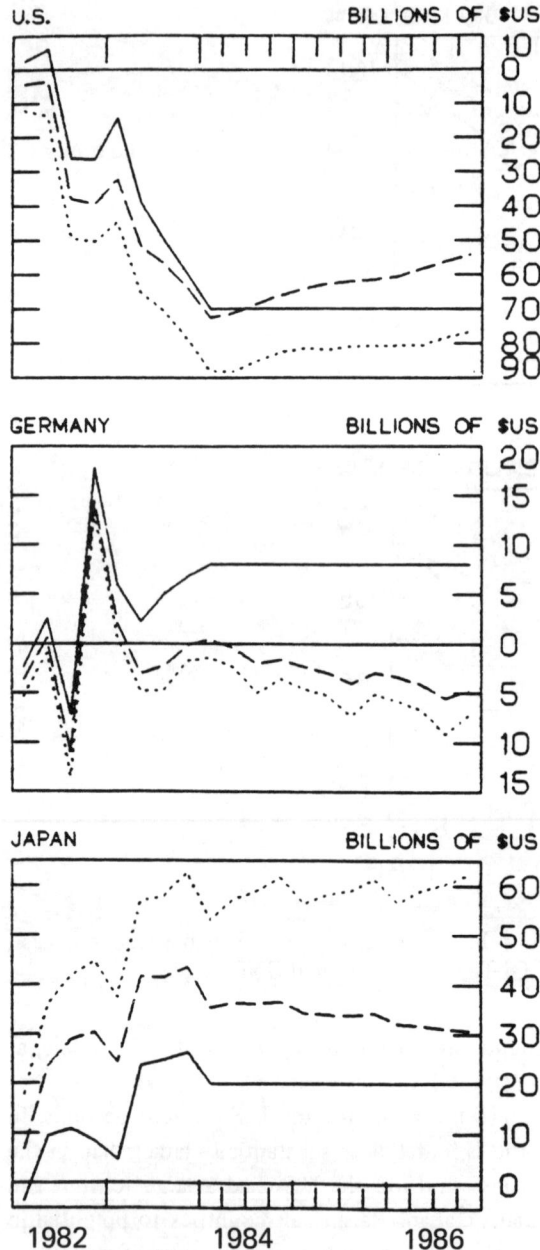

Figure 4. Current accounts: alternative output paths (partial equilibrium analysis). ———— = baseline path; ·········· = at potential output from 82Q1 on; ————— = at normal output from 82Q1 on.

elasticities in other countries[9]. Thus, even if all countries grew at the same rate, the U.S. deficit tends to widen. By the end of the simulation period the output gaps for all countries are smaller and thus the differential impact on the U.S. current account is much smaller than in 1982.

The second simulation shown on this figure is the case where real output is assumed to follow the normal growth path, starting in 1982, for all countries. The U.S. current account initially goes further into deficit, as compared with the baseline case, but in 1984 the trend is reversed and the deficit is gradually reduced through 1986. Again, this is because the United States has a relatively large output gap in 1982. However, the baseline output path for the United States reaches the normal growth path by 1986, while Germany and Japan remain somewhat below their normal paths. Thus in the normal growth simulation foreign output eventually increases more than U.S. output, and U.S. exports rise more than U.S. imports.

The implication of this exercise is that the relative cyclical position of the United States has made the U.S. current account deficit over the past 2 years smaller than it would have been if full output at home and abroad had been maintained at peak-to-peak (or even normal) trend levels during this period, ceteris paribus. The outlook for the U.S. current account in 1986 would be somewhat stronger if the world followed a normal growth path over 1982–86, but a large deficit would nonetheless exist. If output remained at peak-to-peak levels throughout this period the U.S. deficit would exceed its baseline value even in 1986.

The second panel of Figure 4 shows the results for Germany. As for the United States the peak-to-peak output scenario raises German output relative to the average, raising imports more than exports and causing the current account balance to deteriorate. In the German case the deterioration is enough to send the current account into deficit after a few quarters. German output in both high-output cases is well above the baseline through 1986; this means that the deterioration in the current account continues throughout the simulation.

The Japanese results, shown in the third panel, complement those for the United States and Germany. Because Japanese output remains very close to both the normal and peak-to-peak paths in the baseline case, both simulations increase foreign output much more than Japanese output, leading to a large and continuing surplus on current account[10].

Figure 5 shows the results of two forward-looking simulations run with the partial-equilibrium model. In these simulations output in each MCM country is assumed to grow steadily from the current (1983Q3) value to the potential, or normal, level in 1986Q4. The results follow the general pattern of the first exercise: growth along the higher output paths leads to a continued deficit for the United States. On the potential growth path the U.S. deficit is increased; on the normal

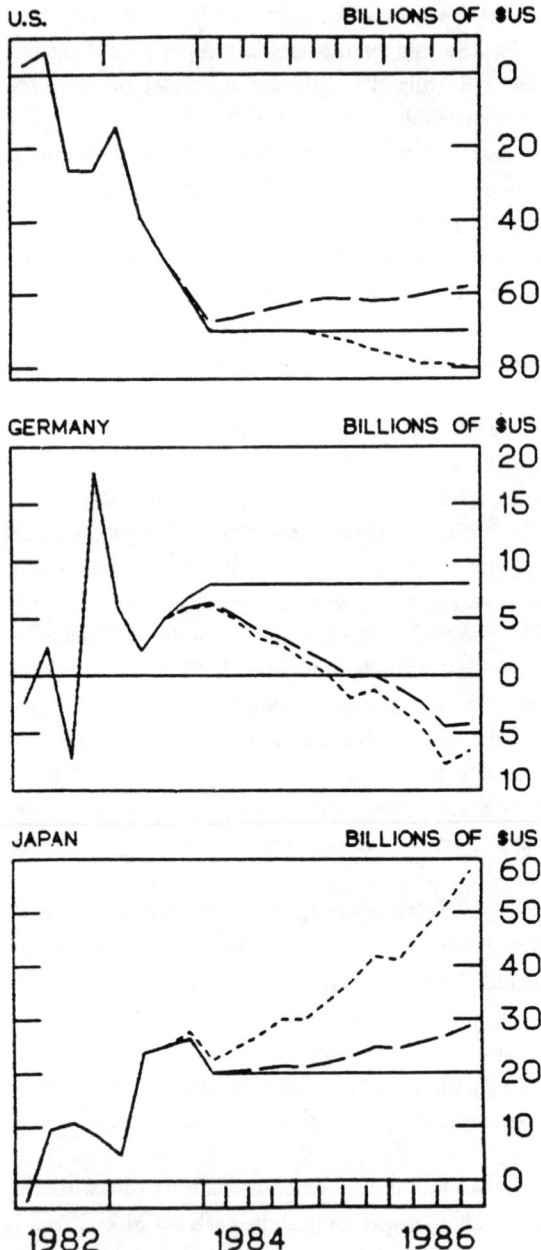

Figure 5. Current accounts: alternative output paths (partial equilbrium analysis). ——— = baseline path; -------- = reach potential output in 86Q4; ———— = reach normal output in 86Q4.

path it is reduced. In Germany the current account balance deteriorates and eventually goes into deficit on both paths, while in Japan the surplus increases steadily. By 1986 the two sets of simulations reach roughly the same points for all countries; in the second set the adjustment toward that point is more gradual, because the change in output paths is more gradual.

The next set of simulations was run using the fully linked MCM. In these exercises each country was assumed to follow a growth path in which real output reached its cyclically neutral (potential or normal) path by the end of 1986. Fiscal policy (government spending) was made endogenous in order to meet the target path for output. Monetary policy was assumed to be at least partially accommodating in Germany and Japan and less so in the United States.

Figure 6 shows the results for the current account balances for the three countries in the two full MCM simulations. The results are broadly similar to those for the partial-equilibrium simulation (compare Figures 5 and 6), but there are some interesting differences. In the potential output simulation, the U.S. balance deteriorates much more sharply in the full model simulation, reaching $100 billion by the end of the exercise, as compared with $80 billion in the partial-equilibrium case. This difference can be traced to the behavior of U.S. interest rates − which rise substantially compared to foreign rates − and their impact on the exchange rate. As indicated in Tables 6−8, the impact on U.S. interest rates exceeds that on Japanese and German rates by over 100 basis points in 1985 and nearly 300 basis points in 1986[11]. This interest differential leads to a real appreciation of the dollar vis-a-vis the yen and the DM, and U.S. goods imports rise relatively more than exports (Net investment income receipts are also up substantially with the rise in U.S. interest rates.) The relative depreciation of the yen and the DM improves the current account in both Japan and Germany, so that Japan runs a larger surplus, and Germany a smaller deficit, than in the partial equilbrium results.

In the simulation involving growth to the normal path U.S. output stays fairly close to its baseline, and no interest differential develops. There is very little change in exchange rates, and the results for all three countries are very similar in the partial-equilibrium and full MCM simulations. It is noteworthy that in this case the U.S. current account increases substantially more than the U.S. trade balance. This is because the Canadian output gap is relatively larger than those of other countries in the normal case and Canadian activity has a disproportionately large impact on U.S. direct investment income receipts[12].

We also ran a simulation with the full MCM in which monetary policy was assumed not to be accommodating − we exogenized M2 in Japan and central bank money in Germany. In this case Japanese real interest rates rise somewhat more than U.S. rates and german rates almost as much as U.S. rates. As a result,

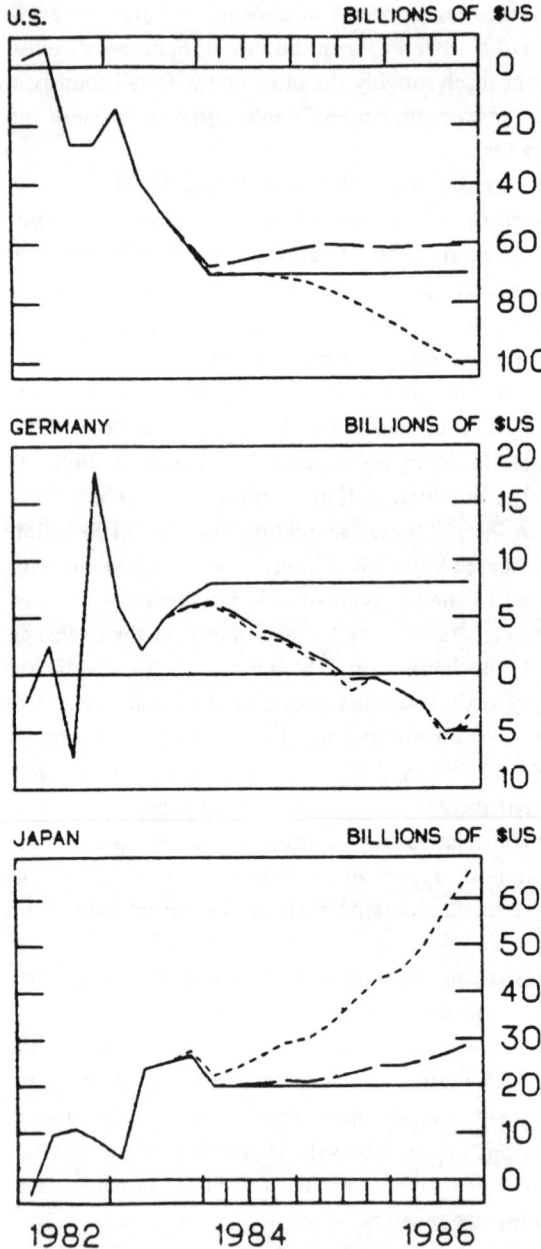

Figure 6. Current accounts: alternative output paths (full MCM analysis). ——— = baseline path; ········· = reach potential output in 86Q4; ——— — = reach normal output in 86Q4.

Table 6. High employment growth — United States (amounts shown are deviations from the baseline path, annual averages, in percentage terms unless noted).

Growth to potential output in 1986	1983	1984	1985	1986
Real GNP	0.1	1.3	3.3	5.6
Real government spending	0.2	2.9	8.3	17.0
Government deficit ($b)	1.0	7.6	23.7	59.7
Price level	− 0.0	− 0.0	0.1	0.8
Interest rate (100 basis points)	0.0	0.4	1.5	3.5
Money supply − M1	0.0	0.2	0.8	1.9
Exchange rate − foreign currency/$	0.0	0.5	1.6	3.0
Real imports	0.1	2.1	6.5	12.4
Real exports	0.1	2.0	4.3	6.3
Trade balance ($b)	− 0.1	− 2.5	− 11.1	− 26.7
Current account balance ($b)	0.1	− 0.1	− 7.3	− 25.0
Growth to normal output in 1986	1983	1984	1985	1986
Real GNP	− 0.0	− 0.1	0.2	0.8
Real government spending	− 0.2	− 0.9	− 0.8	0.4
Government deficit ($b)	− 0.9	− 0.6	− 8.2	− 8.0
Price level	0.0	0.0	0.0	0.0
Interest rate (100 basis points)	− 0.0	− 0.0	− 0.0	0.3
Money supply − M1	− 0.0	− 0.0	− 0.0	0.1
Exchange rate − foreign currency/$	− 0.0	− 0.0	0.1	0.7
Real imports	− 0.1	− 0.7	− 0.6	0.8
Real exports	0.0	0.6	1.5	2.3
Trade balance	0.3	3.1	5.0	2.9
Current account balance	0.4	4.9	9.3	9.0

the dollar depreciates slightly against the yen and appreciates only slightly against the mark. By 1986 the Japanese current account is about $3 billion lower, the German current account about $2 billion lower and the U.S. current account about $4 billion higher than in the accommodating case.

It is also of some interest to consider the simulations as policy packages. The exercises presented in Tables 6—8 can be viewed as a coordinated use of fiscal policy to achieve potential output by 1986. It should be stressed that the MCM in general and these simulations in particular, were designed with most attention given to the international linkages among the countries in the model. The domestic sectors of the country models in the MCM are highly aggregated, and embody a fairly conventional neo-Keynesian, IS-LM model of the macro economy. Moreover, inflation expectations are specified only very crudely (generally as a function of a distributed lag of past inflation). As with any econometric model, the interpretation of the simulation results is conditional on the theoretical and empirical structure of the model.

Table 7. High employment growth – Germany (amounts shown are deviations from the baseline path, annual averages, in percentage terms unless noted).

Growth to potential output in 1986	1983	1984	1985	1986
Real GNP	0.2	2.8	6.1	9.6
Real government spending	0.8	7.7	12.7	16.8
Government deficit ($b)	− 0.6	− 2.7	4.5	15.3
Price level	0.0	0.2	0.9	2.2
Interest rate (100 basis points)	0.0	0.1	0.2	0.3
Central bank money	0.0	0.5	1.5	2.9
Exchange rate – $/DM (%)	− 0.0	− 0.6	− 1.8	− 3.6
Real imports	0.2	2.9	6.3	9.8
Real exports	0.1	1.6	4.0	6.6
Trade balance ($b)	− 0.2	− 2.6	− 5.5	− 8.0
Current account balance ($b)	− 0.2	− 3.7	− 7.9	− 11.4

Growth to normal output in 1986	1983	1984	1985	1986
Real GNP	0.1	1.4	3.1	4.9
Real government spending	0.4	4.9	8.6	11.7
Government deficit ($b)	− 0.4	− 2.8	− 1.3	1.8
Price level	0.0	0.1	0.4	1.0
Interest rate (100 basis points)	0.0	0.0	0.1	0.2
Central bank money	0.0	0.2	0.7	1.4
Exchange rate – $/DM (%)	0.0	0.0	− 0.3	− 1.1
Real imports	0.1	1.6	3.5	5.4
Real exports	0.0	0.2	0.7	1.5
Trade balance ($b)	− 0.2	− 2.4	− 5.3	− 8.1
Current account balance ($b)	− 0.2	− 3.2	− 7.4	− 11.5

The top half of Table 6 shows that in the United States, government spending (at all levels) rises steadily, to a level 17% above the baseline in 1986. This raises the aggregate government deficit by $60 billion and raises real output by 5%. The increase in inflation which results is relatively small, 8% by the end of 1986; the price impact is moderated somewhat by the appreciation of the dollar. The (nominal) short-term interest rate rises by 3.5 percentage points by the end of the simulation: this which gives some measure of the 'crowding out' of private investment that would occur. The increase in the real interest rate is 2.8 percentage points. The money supply increases by only 1.9% over the baseline path in 1986; this is consistent with the slight increase in prices. As noted above, the current account deficit increases by $25 billion in 1986.

Tables 7 and 8 show similar results for Germany and Japan: in both countries fiscal expansion brings output to its potential level with relatively small increases in inflation and interest rates. In 1986, interest rates rise by 0.3 and 0.1 percentage

Table 8. High employment growth — Japan (amounts shown are deviations from the baseline path, annual averages, in percentage terms unless noted).

Growth to potential output in 1986	1983	1984	1985	1986
Real GNP	0.1	1.1	2.3	3.6
Real government spending	0.5	2.4	− 1.2	− 11.7
Government deficit ($b)	0.2	− 1.1	− 10.2	− 30.2
Price level	0.0	0.1	0.4	0.8
Interest rate (100 basis points)	0.0	0.0	0.1	0.1
Money supply — M2	0.0	0.5	1.0	1.6
Exchange rate — $/Yen (%)	− 0.0	− 0.5	− 1.4	− 2.4
Real imports	0.1	1.2	2.4	3.6
Real exports	0.2	3.8	8.8	14.6
Trade balance ($b)	0.2	4.4	11.3	21.3
Current account balance ($b)	0.3	5.5	16.0	34.7

Growth to normal output in 1986	1983	1984	1985	1986
Real GNP	0.0	0.3	0.7	1.1
Real government spending	0.3	2.0	2.0	0.2
Government deficit ($b)	0.2	1.0	− 0.1	− 3.9
Price level	0.0	0.0	0.1	0.2
Interest rate (100 basis points)	0.0	0.0	0.0	0.0
Money supply — M2	0.0	0.2	0.3	0.5
Exchange rate — $/Yen (%)	0.0	0.0	− 0.1	− 0.4
Real imports	0.0	0.4	0.8	1.2
Real exports	0.0	0.5	1.7	3.3
Trade balance ($b)	− 0.0	0.4	1.8	4.3
Current account balance ($b)	− 0.0	0.5	2.4	6.4

points in Germany and Japan, respectively, and the price level rises by 2.2 and 0.8%. Again, these changes are with respect to the baseline path.

The results for the normal growth case are essentially a scaled down version of the peak-to-peak case, although in this scenario most of the expansion occurs in Germany since the baseline case for the U.S. and Japan is fairly close to the normal growth path.

These simulations suggest that there is some scope for coordinated expansion among these three countries. However, it should be understood that behind this relatively optimistic result lies a relatively optimistic set of assumptions. In the MCM, the level of real output is essentially determined by aggregate demand, along the usual Keynesian lines with adaptive expectations. In these exercises we have assumed part of the answer by specifying that some higher path for output is within the productive capacity of the economy and that factor markets are flexible enough that output could be expanded to meet demand at this level without generating excessive inflation. The model does not provide a framework for evaluating these assumptions, but some judgement must be made about them in evaluating the policy package as a whole.

NOTES

This paper initially was prepared for presentation at the Fourth International Workshop of the Applied Econometric Society, Brussels, Belgium, December 8–9, 1983. The views presented here are the authors' and do not necessarily represent the views of the Board of Governors of the Federal Reserve System or anyone else on its staff. We have benefited from discussions with William L. Helkie, Karen Johnson, Ray Lubitz and Jaime Marquez, and especially Dale W. Henderson and Steven Symansky. We also thank Edwin M. Truman for his comments on an earlier draft, and we are grateful to Caryl McNeilly, Sarah Lee and John E, Keniley for their able research assistance.

1) An analogous methodology is used in the computation of cyclically-adjusted budget deficits. See, for example, deLeeuw and Holloway (1983).
2) Klein (1983) makes a similar point with respect to the calculation of full-employment or structure budget deficits.
3) The MCM is described in detail in Stevens *et al.* (1983) and Federal Reserve Board (1983).
4) The prototype exchange rate equation employed in this paper is written:

$$\log(iER) = \log(iP/UP) + \log[(1 + URS)/(1 + iRS)]$$
$$+ \log[(1 + i\pi)/(1 + U\pi)] + Resid$$

where:

iER = Exchange rate (country i's currency/dollar).
iP = Country i's consumer price index.
iRS = Country i's short-term (3-month) interest rate.
iπ = Country i's CPI annual inflation rate over the past six quarters.
Resid = residual
where i = Japan, Germany, Canada and the U.K.: variables preceded by 'U' denote variables.

Note that the second and third right-hand-side terms combined represent an estimate of the short-term real interest differential.

5) *Blue Chip Economic Worldscan*, P.J. Eggert, ed. Capitol Publication Inc., Arlington VA, October 15 and November 15, 1983.
6) *OECD Economic Outlook*, July 1983, p. 60.
7) Analytical Appendix to *Structural Budget Deficits and Fiscal Policy Responses to the Recession, OECD Secretariat, CPE/WP1 (83)2.*
8) This treatment of developing countries, and debtor countries in particular, implicitly assumes that adjustments to lower import levels necessitated by debt servicing are fully accounted for in the baseline, and that these countries' imports would expand in line with their export revenues if industrial countries grew faster.
9) The income elasticities of U.S. imports from other regions in the MCM range between 1.5 and 2.0, while the elasticities of other countries' demand for U.S. goods range between 1.0 and 1.5. These elasticities generally were estimated over the period 1967–1980.
10) The longer-run impact on the Japanese current account is probably overstated by $10 billion in this simulation (and by 1986 in all of the forward-looking peak-to-peak simulations discussed below) because of an implausibly high parameter that leads to a longer-run instability in the Japanese service account sector.

11) Japanese interest rates rise little because they are essentially pegged to the official discount rate. German rates rise much less than U.S. rates because the interest elasticity of money demand is substantially higher in the German model than the U.S. model. A recently updated version of the U.S. monetary sector, which was not completed in time for these simulations, would have yielded a noticeably smaller impact on U.S. interest rates.

12) In the simulations, Canada and the U.K., as well as the rest-of-world sector, were assumed to be expanding towards potential or normal output.

REFERENCES

Artus, J.R. (1978), 'Methods of Assessing the Long-Run Equilibrium Value of an Exchange Rate', *Journal of International Economics*, pp. 227–299.

deLeeuw, F. and Thomas M. Holloway (1983), *Measuring and Analyzing the Cyclically Adjusted Budget*, Federal Reserve Bank of Boston Conference on the Trend and Measurement of the Structural Deficit, October 1983.

Federal Reserve Board (1983), *FRB Multicountry Model*, Quantitative Studies Section, Division of International Finance, Federal Reserve Board, Washington, DC, August 1983.

Klein, L.R. (1983), *The Deficit and the Fiscal and Monetary Policy Mix,* Federal Reserve Bank of Boston, Conference on the Trend and Measurement of the Structural Deficit, October 1983.

Stevens, Guy V.G., *et al.* (1983), *The U.S. Economy in an Interdependent World: A Multicountry Model*, Federal Reserve Board, Washington, DC.

Williamson, John (1983), *The Exchange Rate System*, Institute for International Economics, Washington, DC.

PART III
INTERNATIONAL POLICY COORDINATION

CHAPTER 9

THE COORDINATION APPROACH TO POLICYMAKING IN INTERDEPENDENT ECONOMIES

A.S. Brandsma and A.J. Hughes Hallet
Erasmus University, Rotterdam, The Netherlands

1. INTRODUCTION

Rational policymakers in one country must be expected to try and condition their policies on the anticipated actions pursued in other countries, and vice versa. The recent recession has certainly made industrialised countries more conscious of the interdependence between their economies and of the need for coordinated policies. This mutual dependence of trading economies implies that the policy choices facing each economy are also interdependent. In this respect policies may be called cooperative if they aim to achieve some common goal; but they are noncooperative if each economy pursues its private objectives while accounting fully for the expected actions of others in doing so.

In the cooperative case, the main issue is to design a policy combination which makes all cooperating economies better off in terms of their private objectives. The problem is to convince them to implement the allocated policies. This requires that the distribution of the benefits of cooperation should at least be found equitable in some sense. It is well known that the outcomes of noncooperative games are generally socially inefficient in that other policies could make all participants better off. But Pareto optimality, once aimed for, leaves each player with an incentive to default at the expense of those others who abide by the Pareto solution. Politically sovereign policymakers therefore often have difficulty in agreeing to surrender part of their privately optimal solution for a socially optimal one. On the other hand, the essential problem in a noncooperative approach is one of information; this includes information on the actions of other economies or, alternatively, on how their policies are derived. The more general information problem arises through uncertainty over those variables which are completely beyond the policymaker's control (nature) and those which they can influence only indirectly through the actions of others. The latter is handled in this paper by computing Nash

Artus, P. and Guvenen, O. (eds.): International Macroeconomic Modelling for Policy Decisions.
© *1986. Martinus Nijhoff Publishers, Dordrecht/Boston/Lancaster.*
ISBN 90-247-3201-8. Printed in The Netherlands.

equilibrium strategies that are closed loop *between* decision makers within a dynamic noncooperative game. The benefits available from optimally coordinated policy choices are then compared with the cooperative policies and with the optimal policies where no allowance is made for the mutual dependence of trading economies.

For this exercise we use a model which was developed by Siebrand and Van der Windt (1982) and which contains three interdependent economic regions; the U.S., the European Economic Community (EEC) and the rest of the world. In a related study, Shishido et al. (1980) concluded that economic recovery depends crucially on finding policies for the OECD countries which are domestically manageable as well as mutually supporting. In contrast, Hickman and Schleicher (1978) found that international cooperation only moderately improves national targets, and that international growth is actually steadier with unsynchronised policies. Studies such as these have relied on simulation techniques, and the divergence of their results may well appear because simulation is an unsystematic search procedure for locating the best policies and also because it is an incomplete search since rational expectations of the choices made by other countries cannot be constructed as part of the conditioning information for the choices facing each individual economy. Therefore we adopt an explicit optimisation approach, in which each policymaker's decision is determined jointly with rational expectations of what he expects other policymakers to do[1].

Recently several authors have begun to examine policy interdependence via game theory, but almost always using extremely simplified theoretical models (e.g. Canzoneri and Gray (1985), Miller and Salmon (1984))[2]. We deliberately chose not to follow this line because, for all the shortcomings of existing macro-econometric models, it is not clear that they will be inferior to models containing only two or three equations per economy as far as capturing the different policy responses between and within different economies is concerned. In addition we need to avoid three important features of the 'mini-model' approach: a) imposed coefficient values, (b) identical and symmetric policy responses in each economy, (c) deterministic relations so that the effects of uncertainty cannot be investigated. The severity of those restrictions means that such examples may usefully illustrate the mechanics of the game, but they do not illustrate the interactions in economic policymaking. The lack of uncertainty seems unrealistic, and it is hard to think of economies whose structures are even approximately mirror images of each other. Not surprisingly the results appear to be extremely sensitive to small changes in these restrictions. In contrast, our analysis uses an estimated multicountry model which, though strongly aggregated with respect to the number of countries, represents the typical linked country model employed by the policymakers themselves.

2. COOPERATIVE STRATEGIES

Consider an objective function involving a total of m targets. The outcomes of the corresponding variables can be influenced by the decisions of a number of policy-makers (denoted by $i = 1 \ldots p$) who may here be thought of as countries or blocks of countries having control over one or more instruments of economic policy. But, of course, the policymakers could also represent the economic decision units within a country or on a supranational level. They have n_i instruments at their disposal for $i = 1 \ldots p$ respectively, while all the noncontrollable and uncertain variables are gathered together in one composite stochastic variable. We let the planning period contain discrete decision intervals $t = 1 \ldots T$, and stack the target variables y_t in $y' = (y_1' \ldots y_T')$. Similarly, $x^{(i)'} = (x_1^{(i)'} \ldots x_T^{(i)'})$ for the instrument variables of block i, and $s = (s_1' \ldots s_T')$ for the stochastic variables s_t. Note that y either represents a common set of world objectives or the union of the individual target sets.

Each decision maker is supposed to have desired values for his own instruments; say $x^{(i)d}$. The ideal values for the target variables are y^d, so that a world objective function can be represented by the positive semi-definite quadratic form

$$w = \tilde{y}'B\tilde{y} + \sum_{i=1}^{p} \tilde{x}^{(i)'}A^{(i)}\tilde{x}^{(i)} \tag{1}$$

where $\tilde{y} = y - y^d$ and $\tilde{x}^{(i)} = x^{(i)} - x^{(i)d}$. The policymakers face a dynamic economic model which connects the target and instrument variables. For an extended vector of state variables z_t it can be written as (see Hughes Hallett and Rees (1983), pp. 127–130)

$$z_t = f_t(z_t, z_{t-1}, x_t^{(1)}, \ldots, x_t^{(p)}, e_t) \tag{2}$$

where e_t represents the noncontrollable exogenous influences. The model may be linearised as (in stacked form)

$$y = \sum_{i=1}^{p} R^{(i)}x^{(i)} + s \tag{3}$$

where the $R^{(i)}$ are lower block triangular matrices of dynamic multipliers evaluated numerically around suitable paths for $x_t^{(i)}$, $i = 1 \ldots p$, and e_t. For linear models (3) is just the final form, from which any rows corresponding to nontargets will be deleted.

The cooperative minimisation of (1) constrained by (3) is now a straightforward linear-quadratic control problem, and we will not go into the details of its solution here. In fact, the optimal decisions $x^{(i)*}$, $i = 1 \ldots p$, constitute a partitioning of an overall vector $x' = (x^{(1)'} \ldots x^{(p)'})$ and the solution x^* is reflected in the formulae below. At this point it is instructive to note that the same solution can be found by a method of decentralised control, which resembles the Gauss-Seidel technique for solving equation systems. Starting from a tentative solution x^0, which might coincide with x^d (both partitioned as before) the minimisation of (1) would give

$$\tilde{x}^{(i)k} = - [R^{(i)'}BR^{(i)} + A^{(i)}]^{-1}R^{(i)'}Bb^{(i)} \qquad (i = 1 \ldots p) \qquad (4)$$

for $k \geqslant 1$, where $b^{(i)} = s - y^d + R^{(i)}x^{(i)d} + \Sigma_{j \neq i}R^{(j)}x^{(j)k-1}$.

This produces the values represented by $x^k = \tilde{x}^k + x^d$, which are then used to start off the next iterative step by (4); and so on, until convergence is achieved.

The attraction of the above procedure is that one can easily imagine it being implemented as an interactive scheme of policymaking between interdependent economies. The problem is, of course, to decide on a suitable specification of the objective function which is acceptable to all parties. A well-known result in welfare economies is that as soon as such a world objective is agreed upon, all countries can gain by following the cooperative solution, but a redistribution of income over countries may be necessary to achieve this. This can easily be seen for the case where the world objective function is separable and each country equally weighted:i.e.

$$w = \sum_{i=1}^{p} w^{(i)} = \sum_{i=1}^{p} (\tilde{y}^{(i)'}B^{(i)}\tilde{y}^{(i)} + \tilde{x}^{(i)'}A^{(i)}\tilde{x}^{(i)}) \qquad (5)$$

where $\tilde{y}^{(i)}$ and $B^{(i)}$ are a partitioning of $\tilde{y}$ and B according to some allocation of targets over countries.

This partitioning of the set of targets, y, into sets of national targets between countries must be inserted into the model (3) to yield the constraint set

$$y^{(i)} = \sum_{j=1}^{p} R^{(i,j)}x^{(j)} + s^{(i)} \qquad (i = 1 \ldots p) \qquad (6)$$

The decision rule (4) could then be rewritten as

$$\tilde{x}^{(i)k} = - [R^{(i,i)'}B^{(i)}R^{(i,i)} + A^{(i)}]^{-1}R^{(i,i)'}B^{(i)}c^{(i)} \qquad (7)$$

where $c^{(i)} = s^{(i)} - y^{(i)d} + R^{(i,i)}x^{(i)d} + \Sigma_{j \neq i}R^{(i,j)}x^{(j)k-1}$.

Choosing each $\tilde{x}^{(i)}$ to minimise each $w^{(i)}$ will not generally minimise w since we assumed in (3) that $x^{(i)}$ not only influences $y^{(i)}$ but also the other target variables in y. There is an externality in each private solution which, if it could be eliminated by the joint or cooperative optimisation of (5), offers the possibility of all-round gains of the Pareto type. Partitioning the x^* by $x^{*'} = (x^{*(1)'} \ldots x^{*(p)'})$

shows that the optimal cooperative solution will only by coincidence be individually optimal for all i in terms of their own objectives $w^{(i)}$. Hence the desire to default while other countries maintain their components in x^*, and the obvious difficulty of persuading policymakers of the credibility and superiority (for them) of implementing x^*. This difficulty appears perhaps most clearly in the Da Cuhna and Polak (1967) result that the set of all nondominated (i.e. Pareto optimal) strategies will be generated by minimising $w = \Sigma_{i=1}^{p} \alpha_i w^{(i)}$, where $0 \leqslant \alpha_i \leqslant 1$ and $\Sigma \alpha_i = 1$, jointly with respect to all $x^{(i)}$ subject to (3). Evidently the question of distributing the gains to cooperation depends on setting the weights α_i, which reflect the relative priority given to country i's goals. For the purpose of this study, which deals with nationally determined intermediate targeting, it is convenient to impose separability in (5). But this would be a strong assumption if, for instance, one wished to formulate the target in terms of discounted world consumption.

3. NONCOOPERATIVE STRATEGIES

Noncooperation means that each country maximises its self-interest, subject to its perception of the constraints and conditional on the rational choices anticipated from other countries. The optimal decisions for this noncooperative game are $x^{(i)*}$, $i = 1 \ldots p$, satisfying

$$w^{(i)}(\tilde{x}^{(i)*}, x^{(j)*}) \leqslant w^{(i)}(\tilde{x}^{(i)}(\tilde{x}^{(i)}, x^{(j)*})) \qquad (8)$$

for $j \neq i$, and all feasible $\tilde{x}^{(i)} \neq \tilde{x}^{(i)*}$. The objective functions $w^{(i)}$ were already defined in (5), and each $w^{(i)}$ depends on $x^{(j)}$, $j \neq i$, via $y^{(i)}$. Note also the distinction between the noncooperative decisions, $x^{(i)*}$, and the partitioning of x^* in $x^{*(i)}$, $i = 1 \ldots p$, in section 2. For notational convenience we chose to write the conditions (8) one by one with respect to the other players in the game, although for more than two players some mathematical complications are involved. If (8) is satisfied for all i and $j \neq i$, neither player has any incentive to deviate unilaterally from his own choice, so the decisions constitute a Nash equilibrium solution.

If $x^{(j)}$ were fixed and known the optimal decisions would be given by (7). But rationality demands that $x^{(j)}$ should be replaced by $x^{(j)*}$, so that the optimal decision for $x^{(i)}$ is structurally dependent on, and must be determined simultaneously with, that for $x^{(j)}$. This can also be seen from the necessary conditions for (8), which allow for the consequences of the fact that $x^{(j)}$ will in fact react to the values anticipated for $x^{(i)}$:

$$\partial w^{(i)}/\partial \tilde{x}^{(i)} + [(\partial \tilde{y}^{(i)}/\partial \tilde{x}^{(j)})\partial \tilde{x}^{(j)}/\partial \tilde{x}^{(i)} + \partial \tilde{y}^{(i)}/\partial \tilde{x}^{(i)}]'\partial w^{(i)}/\partial \tilde{y}^{(i)} = 0 \quad (9)$$

for $i = 1 \ldots p$ and $j \neq i$. It is not possible to write down analytic expressions for the optimal decisions, since $\tilde{x}^{(i)}$ and $\tilde{x}^{(j)}$ are mutually dependent implying that (9) is nonlinear in these decision variables. But it is possible to insert trial values for the reaction matrices $D^{(j)} = \partial \tilde{x}^{(j)}/\partial \tilde{x}^{(i)}$. Let $p = 2$ for notational convenience. Starting from $D_0^{(1)}$ and $D_0^{(2)}$, new values may be generated by

$$
\begin{bmatrix} I & -D_k^{(1)} \\ -D_k^{(2)} & I \end{bmatrix} \begin{pmatrix} \tilde{x}^{(1)k} \\ \tilde{x}^{(2)k} \end{pmatrix} = \begin{pmatrix} F_k^{(1)}c^{(1)} \\ F_k^{(2)}c^{(2)} \end{pmatrix} \tag{10}
$$

where $F_k^{(i)} = - [G_k^{(i)'}B^{(i)}R^{(i,\,i)} + A^{(i)}]^{-1}G_k^{(i)'}B^{(i)}$ for $G_k^{(i)} = R^{(i,\,i)} + R^{(i,\,j)}D_{k-1}^{(j)}$, $j \neq i$, and $D_k^{(i)} = F_k^{(i)}R^{(i,\,j)}$. The partitioning of the rows of the matrix $R^{(i)}$ between $R^{(i,\,i)}$ and $R^{(j,\,i)}$ corresponds to the partitioning of the targets, y in (3), between $y^{(i)}$ and $y^{(j)}$. Again (10) defines an iterative process, since $D_k^{(i)} \neq D_{k-1}^{(i)}$. In fact, we are trying to construct a fixed point, say $(D_*^{(1)}, D_*^{(2)})$ and $(x^{(1)*}, x^{(2)*})$, satisfying the first order conditions (9). We can be sure that such a point exists, although it is not certain if it is unique in this linear-quadratic framework (Aubin (1979), pp. 270–271). But, because of its nonlinearity, the key iteration in (10) is not guaranteed to converge automatically on the required fixed point. One way of conducting a search is to make sure that (8) is strictly satisfied at each step (Hughes Hallett (1984)). At the end of the search for a Nash solution, the optimal decisions must also satisfy

$$
\tilde{y}^{(i)} = (R^{(i,\,i)} + R^{(i,\,j)}D_*^{(j)})\tilde{x}^{(i)} + d_*^{(i)} \tag{11}
$$

for $i = 1$, 2 and $j \neq i$; where $d_*^{(i)} = c^{(i)} + R^{(i,\,j)}F_*^{(j)}c^{(j)}$ and $F_*^{(j)}$ is defined below (10) if $D_k^{(j)}$ is replaced by $D_*^{(j)}$. Indeed (11) is just a reformulation of the final form (6), in which $x^{(j)}$ has been substituted out by its Nash solution.

Formulating noncooperative decisions in terms of (10) is convenient because the standard solution concepts of game theory can all be obtained directly as special cases of that iteration. If the iteration is completed without restrictions closed loop Nash decisions are obtained. However one step, with $D_0^{(1)} = 0$ and $D_0^{(2)} = 0$ as starts, yields open loop Nash decisions. Similarly if policymakers follow feedback rules, such as $x_t^{(i)} = K_t^{(i)}y_{t-1} + k_t^{(i)}$, the implied reaction matrices $D^{(i)}$ can be the starts for one step of (10). Open loop or feedback Stackelberg strategies are obtained similarly from two steps of (10) where, in each case, the restriction $D_1^{(1)} = 0$ is imposed when player 1 is the leader. The nesting of these solutions within (10) is examined in detail by Brandsma and Hughes Hallett (1984b).

4. THE INFORMATION PROBLEM

Uncertainty enters the problem through s in (3). We assume that the matrices $R^{(i,\,j)}$ are known in order to avoid the additional complications of dynamic stochastic optimisation with parameter uncertainty. First order certainty equivalence then implies that the decisions which minimise the expectations of $w^{(i)} = \tilde{y}^{(i)'}B^{(i)}\tilde{y}^{(i)} + \tilde{x}^{(i)'}A^{(i)}\tilde{x}^{(i)}$, subject to (6), are

$$\tilde{x}^{(i)*} = - [G_*^{(i)'}B^{(i)}G_*^{(i)} + A^{(i)}]^{-1}G_*^{(i)'}B^{(i)}E_{ti}(d_*^{(i)}) \tag{12}$$

where $G_*^{(i)} = R^{(i,\,i)} + R^{(i,\,j)}D_*^{(j)}$. Let $E_{ti}(\cdot) = E(\cdot|\Omega_{ti})$ denote the expectation of a stochastic variable given the information of player i at time t contained in the information set Ω_{ti}. The certainty equivalence theorem states that in order to minimise $E_{ti}(w^{(i)})$ it is sufficient to replace the uncertain variables in s by their expectation.

Given complete information, each player can evaluate his own decision and that of the other player(s) in (12) without further assumptions. In practice one seldom has accurate knowledge about the contents of the information set employed by one's rivals, and player i's perception of the optimal decisions may not coincide with player j's evaluation. To allow for heterogeneous information, we have to insert $E_{ti}(s)$ into $d_*^{(j)}$ for $j \neq i$ as well as into $d_*^{(i)}$ for player i's determination of the decisions. The computed versions of (12) then minimise $E_{ti}(w^{(i)})$. Uncertainty has thus been reduced to just two terms in (12); $d_*^{(i)}$ contains both the direct uncertainty over s within $c^{(i)}$ and the indirect uncertainty over the evaluation of the other players' decisions (i.e. over s within $c^{(j)}$). Different estimates of the preferences in $Q^{(i)}$ and the multipliers in the $R^{(i)}$ matrices can be similarly handled. Of course, the differences between ex ante expectations $E_{ti}(w^{(i)})$ and ex post values will now be partly due to errors in i's perception of $\tilde{x}^{(j)*}$ for $j \neq i$. But any policy revisions will depend solely on Ω_{ti}, and hence on the innovations in the policymaker's expectations of the noncontrollable variables which will also determine his anticipations of future behaviour of the other participants (Brandsma and Hughes Hallet (1982), (1984a)).

We can now try to capture the differences between the cooperative decisions of Section 2 and the noncooperative solution described in Section 3. First, it is trivial that the cooperative and the noncooperative solution are identical if there are no cross-effects of any country's instruments on the target variables of the other countries (i.e. $R^{(i,\,j)} = 0$ for all $i \neq j$), for then the constrained optimisation problem would be completely separable. Secondly, it can also be seen that the noncooperative decisions are Pareto optimal if all countries happen to have objective functions in which the targets and their priorities are the same across countries[3]. In both cases the information sets are supposed to have the same contents. The main features of our approach can now clearly be distinguished: (i) it allows for individual objectives, (ii) no ex ante compromise of objectives − or leap of faith with respect to cheating − has to be made, and (iii) it can handle heterogeneous information among countries.

5. THE MODEL

The mutual dependence between the U.S. and EEC economies, and its implications for policymaking in those economies, has been explored empirically using a model related to the COMET multicountry model (Barten, d'Alcantara and Carrin (1976)). This is a typical representative of the models which are used for analysing economic interdependence and the potential for policy cooperation. The associated model describes the U.S. the EEC, and the Rest of the World and their trade flows. The real sectors of these economies have been augmented with financial sectors in such a way that the Rest of the World's accounts are forced to balance. A more detailed description will be found in Van der Windt *et al.* (1984), but for our purposes the important features are: (a) aggregation into three economic blocks, to give a systematic specification across the U.S. and EEC economies; (b) consistent accounts for the Rest of the World; and (c) the introduction of financial sectors, international capital movements, and endogenous exchange rates.

The U.S. and EEC blocks, some 200 equations in total, form the backbone of the model. The two real sectors have similar structures, based on a conventional Keynesian demand system covering consumption, investment, and foreign trade. Furthermore, Cobb-Douglas production functions determine labour demand and investment. The supply sides of both blocks are modelled by similarly specified potential output functions; potential and actual outputs are then reconciled by a capacity utilisation index. In each sector, prices are related to import prices and the GDP deflator. The GDP deflator in its turn depends on unit labour and capital costs and the utilisation index, while wages are a function of consumption prices, productivity, unemployment, taxes and social security contributions. The Rest of the World is modelled by a rudimentary macro-system explaining how export revenues are devoted to increasing international reserves, lent to one of the other two regions, or spent on imports.

Each monetary sector describes the financial relations between the central bank, commercial banks, the government, the private sector, and the foreign sector. Private and government financial surpluses are the main input from the real sector. Interest rates, which in turn affect both real spending and international borrowing, are determined by those surpluses and by the behaviour of the banks. There is an important difference between the U.S. and the EEC here. Government expenditure in both blocks is financed to a large extent by loans from the private sector. In the EEC, this involves selling bonds to the banks which adjust their portfolios and offset any upward pressure on interest rates. Meanwhile the extra government expenditure passes through the banking system and, both directly and via credit creation, tends to reduce interest rates and increase activity domestically and abroad, until inflation and wage increases set in to reverse that some periods later. Government expenditure in the U.S., on the other hand, is mostly financed by borrowing savings directly from the private sector or by tax measures. With a comparatively low propensity to save and less opportunity for the banks to maintain the term structure of their portfolios, this leads to the crowding out of private investment which is sensitive to interest rate changes in the U.S. Activity levels are falling and at the same time prices are rising due to higher capital costs. This crowding out process sets in after one year, and it is sustained because there is no offsetting expansionary pressure or credit creation. Government expenditure just displaces investment and new savings go into new government programmes.

Although American and European policies may ultimately have the same effects, policy responses in the U.S. are usually more powerful than those in the EEC. That appears to be due partly to the differences in reaction speeds, and partly because the impacts of those differences are accentuated by international capital movements which depend on relative interest rates, domestic (public and private) savings, changes in the trade balances, and relative growth rates. The interdependence of interest and exchange rates makes the U.S. and the EEC react similarly to a rise in the domestic discount rate of either one of the economies, but the U.S. balance of payments is the only variable affected positively in both instances. The latter reflects both the (endogenous) exchange rate adjustments and the fact that the dependence of EEC on U.S. interest rates is greater than the other way round. So monetary policy in the U.S. tends to be reinforced by its international consequences. This greater responsiveness explains why the U.S. has pursued a more active monetary policy, and also why the European governments fear higher interest rates, which, if induced by the need to protect their balance of payments and exchange rates in the face of high U.S. rates, lack any compensating credit creation effects.

In fact most government policies lead to quicker and stronger responses in the U.S. than in the EEC. This difference stems principally from reactions of the real quantities to price and interest changes; their effects spread more rapidly to other variables in the U.S. economy because the real and monetary sectors are more closely connected. The upshot is more powerful impact multipliers (which can be seen in the diagonal blocks of $R^{(i,\,i)}$ in (3)) but less powerful interim multipliers (which appear in the lower triangle of $R^{(i,i)}$).

6. THE POLICY PROBLEM

The choice of the planning period 1974–78 implies that we are interested in the policy responses of the U.S. and the EEC to the oil price shock of 1973–74. The observed responses have been classified by Van Wijnbergen (1982) as follows.

Western Europe experienced a large rise in unemployment, which proved to be persistent. Aggregate demand policies resulted in high inflation, supported by real wage rigidity. At the same time investment collapsed and remained low throughout the 1970s. The oil importing countries saw the balance of their current account become negative, although the deterioration of the balance of payments was short-lived. While the U.S. deliberately let their current account deteriorate to shield their economy from supply effects, investment did not slow down as dramatically as in Western Europe. Unemployment reached a postwar peak but, in the U.S., responded quickly to tax cuts. Alternatively, some countries in the third world tried expansionary fiscal measures and an accomodating monetary policy. In striking contrast to what happened in the OECD, private investment accelerated there together with the rise in government expenditure.

In the exercises below both the U.S. and the EEC are assumed to have the same target variables, but the priorities which the policymakers attached to these targets are different in accordance with the policy stance just described. The planning period implies a horizon of 5 years which is the length of medium term plans in most countries. Nevertheless, the planners are supposed to be interested in governing the supply conditions in the final year and thereafter. To that effect, the targets combine the conventional stabilisation objectives (1.5% less unemployment, 3% less inflation, 3% more production growth, 1% improvement in the balance of trade) with indicators of potential supply (a 3% increase in the real investment/production ratio and a similar increase in the ratio of gross operating surplus of companies to net national income). A representation of the differences in policy stance is provided by giving inflation a relatively high weight in the U.S. objective function and weighing the position of the current account more heavily in case of the EEC.

Van Wijnbergen's analysis concluded that induced unemployment after the oil price shock was of a Keynesian nature in the U.S., but more neoclassical in Western Europe. That would explain the quick responses of the U.S. economy to the tax cuts of 1975, and it would also provide a rationale for the contractionary aggregate demand policies in Europe. But the actual policies were more erratic during the period 1974–78. Chouraqui and Price (1983) give a description for the OECD area in this period. Growing inflationary pressures caused monetary conditions to be tightened in 1973, and they became even more restrictive in response to the oil price shock. While budgetary policies started cautiously in 1974, they grew more expansionary towards the end of that year and through 1975 as several countries accepted the need to compensate for their external deficits by public expenditure. With monetary restraint also easing, the mutually reinforcing fiscal and monetary policies of the late 1960s seemed to be restored, but in 1976–77 most countries turned towards fiscal retrenchment. As output growth continued to stagnate, unemployment increased, and inflationary expectations persisted, the combined fiscal and monetary expansion of the early 1970s was perceived to have adverse effects in terms of stabilisation. Although greater stability in monetary conditions was found to be positively correlated with better economic performance in the cross-section study of Chouraqui and Price (1983), the historical record of U.S. and EEC policies from late 1975 up to the second oil shock shows increasing divergencies and an unsynchronised pattern. The smaller EEC economies apparently resorted to unstable fiscal and monetary actions. A large cut of government expenditure in 1976 was followed by a rise in 1977 and a shift from social outlays to government consumption in 1978. During these years changes in the discount rate were alternating. This erratic and unsynchronised pattern of policy adjustments suggests that coordination between the U.S. and EEC might bring important benefits.

In this paper the relationship between economic goals and the variability of monetary and fiscal instruments is examined with the help of the following instrument variables, which are the same for both blocks:

CGO : government consumption;
SBH : social outlays;
DTH : direct taxes on households;
DTC : direct taxes on firms;
RCB : discount rate;
LCG : loans of the central bank to the government;
LBG : loans of commercial banks to the governments.

In comparison with an earlier study (Brandsma and Hughes Hallett (1983)) the last variable has been added to this list, while social security premiums disappeared as an instrument since in the new version of the model they are coupled with SBH by strict budget balancing in the social sector. All instruments are treated as discretionary adjustments to the policies which were actually implemented. They are given in percentage changes, except for the discount rate for which multipliers were based on level changes. The penalties on deviations of the instrument variables from their historical values were equally distributed in order not to prejudice the policy mix as long as the instrument changes remain within acceptable bounds.

7. THE RESULTS

Table 1 presents optimal cooperative and noncooperative policies for the U.S. and the EEC over the years 1974–78. The Cournot-Nash solution represents the case where each country assumes ideal values for the instruments of other countries.

Table 1. Optimal certainty equivalent policies and the coordinated respectively cooperative solution of the policy problem

Variables	CN		CLN		CP	
	US	EEC	US	EEC	US	EEC
1974						
CGO	− 1.33	1.88	0.31	1.99	0.78	2.04
SBH	− 2.83	0.29	− 1.20	− 0.86	− 0.62	0.28
DTH	− 0.44	− 1.74	− 0.62	− 2.91	− 0.53	− 1.60
DTC	− 0.87	− 0.21	− 0.70	− 0.50	− 0.37	− 0.19
RCB	− 1.44	− 1.01	− 1.33	0.60	− 0.39	− 0.57
LCG	0.39	− 0.02	0.22	0.18	0.10	− 0.01
LBG	0.76	− 0.53	0.35	0.88	0.28	− 0.53
1975						
CGO	− 1.78	0.84	− 0.07	0.87	0.37	1.44
SBH	− 2.80	0.39	− 1.22	0.75	− 0.55	0.42
DTH	− 0.56	− 0.94	− 0.59	0.00	− 0.42	− 1.05
DTC	− 0.62	− 0.03	− 0.35	0.01	− 0.26	− 0.06
RCB	0.37	− 1.41	0.99	− 2.22	− 0.29	− 0.55
LCG	0.19	0.03	0.11	− 0.12	0.04	0.01
LBG	0.89	0.09	− 0.20	− 1.61	− 0.18	− 0.20
1976						
CGO	− 0.88	0.31	0.06	0.81	− 0.24	1.00
SBH	− 2.20	0.39	− 0.95	0.28	− 0.56	0.39
DTH	− 0.78	− 0.08	− 0.63	− 1.14	− 0.24	− 0.47
DTC	− 0.36	0.03	− 0.15	− 0.02	− 0.08	− 0.03
RCB	0.67	− 1.32	− 0.27	− 0.44	− 0.13	− 0.38
LCG	0.09	− 0.01	0.07	0.09	0.07	− 0.01
LBG	0.19	− 0.33	− 0.92	0.71	− 0.20	− 0.20
1977						
CGO	− 0.32	− 0.19	− 0.26	− 0.03	− 0.14	0.38
SBH	− 2.13	0.11	− 1.09	0.54	− 0.61	0.31
DTH	− 0.97	0.24	− 0.58	0.63	− 0.29	0.07
DTC	− 0.26	0.03	0.02	0.07	− 0.01	0.00
RCB	0.04	− 0.28	− 0.35	− 1.47	− 0.78	0.29
LCG	− 0.11	0.02	− 0.07	− 0.02	− 0.01	0.01
LBG	− 1.64	0.02	− 1.43	− 0.23	− 0.53	− 0.00
1978						
CGO	− 0.49	− 0.26	0.86	− 0.22	0.38	0.20
SBH	− 1.96	0.10	− 1.08	− 0.06	− 0.72	0.22
DTH	− 0.91	0.46	− 0.93	0.32	− 0.53	0.10
DTC	− 0.11	0.02	0.03	− 0.04	0.01	− 0.01
RCB	− 0.69	− 0.01	− 1.49	0.97	− 0.58	0.44
LCG	− 0.09	0.00	− 0.10	0.00	− 0.05	− 0.00
LBG	− 1.39	− 0.02	− 1.40	0.03	− 0.71	− 0.02

Note: CN stands for the Cournot-Nash decisions which minimise $w^{(i)}$, i = 1, 2, in (5) given the reference path $\tilde{x}^{(j)} = 0$ for j ≠ i; CLN refers to the closed loop Nash solution given by (10); and CP is the cooperative solution minimising w in (5) for p = 2.

Unilateral decision rules of this kind are sometimes called open loop Nash solutions (e.g. Oudiz and Sachs (1984)). Obviously this is only appropriate in a limited sense because the assumption of fixed instrument values for other policymakers is clearly inconsistent with the fact that they are also optimising their decisions. In other words, the Cournot-Nash solution takes the decisions of the other countries as known, rather than just taking their reactions to be fixed at zero (apart from the responses already present in the model). It is included here as a benchmark representing the result of optimising behaviour which ignores the game aspects of interdependent policymaking; and it is distinguished from the Nash solutions described by (12) which recognise the game even if the behavioural reactions imputed in (10) are restricted.

The closed loop Nash solution[4] allows unrestricted policy reactions by each player, including anticipations terms, and estimates the conclusion of the conjectural variations process given by (10). The right hand column of Table 1 gives the cooperative solution, which is the result of optimising the weighted sum of U.S. and EEC objectives as described in Section 2. These three solutions represent the three fundamental approaches to interdependence which policymakers might wish to adopt: to ignore the strategic aspects of interdependence; to play an unrestricted game; or to pick an equitable compromise by cooperation.

Consider first optimal policies when the mutual economic dependence is ignored. Inspection of the Cournot-Nash policies in Table 1 reveals a cut in government expenditure and social security benefits in the U.S., while there is a rise in both quantities in the EEC and a small negative adjustment of government expenditure in the last two years. That contrast reflects the speed of policy responses in the U.S. The financing of public expenditure induces contractionary pressure on output plus upward pressure on prices and interest within a year; so reductions of expenditure (compared to the historical path) are necessary to start with, but can be eased towards the end of the planning period. Social security benefits are adjusted downwards by 2% a year but lack the short run flexibility displayed by government consumption. This fiscal disengagement is matched by tax cuts, mainly favouring the corporate sector to start with but ultimately benefiting households by more. Contrarily, fiscal expansion in the EEC goes together with tax reductions which almost completely accrue to the household sector. This pattern is reversed in the final 2 years (expenditures being cut and taxes increased) in order to offset the gradual build up of adverse effects of the initial expansion. Substantial financing of the budget would be necessary in the EEC as, overall, tax cuts complement the extra expenditures.

The monetary variables show that the change in European government budgets is not financed by loans from the central banks (LCG) and that the loans from commercial banks (LBG) cause no extra money creation, while the main instrument, the discount rate, is lowered throughout the period. After a few years, balance of payments problems and the undesirability of monetary financing lead to the switch in fiscal policy already noted above. In the U.S. the dependence of budget financing on savings requires a more sophisticated strategy. First a lowering of the discount rate has to induce a fall in interest changes to stimulate economic activity. A rise of the discount rate (RCB) is then used to acquire savings until the loans from the banks to the government start to decline, after which the discount rate is lowered again. The base policy position is therefore one of standard Keynesian deficit financing in Europe to stimulate aggregate demand and output, with monetary control and falling interest rates to reduce inflation. Meanwhile policies which have come to be associated with 'supply side' economies operate in the U.S.; a reduction in government intervention, especially in social security outlays and taxes, is coupled with an actively pursued monetary policy.

Turning to the noncooperative policies which recognise joint economic dependence, the closed loop Nash solution is rather different from the Cournot-Nash case. Both economies would now experience rising government expenditures, although this is more marked in the U.S. The U.S. social security cuts are halved, while in Europe SBH is still positive but only in 1975–77. Once again tax cuts appear in both economies, although in this scenario they are more variable than before in Europe and they are relatively more beneficial for households in the U.S. The changes in monetary policy are more complicated. An initial rise in European discount rates attracts American capital, as witnessed by lower loans to the U.S. government. The latter necessitate the Federal Reserve Board to resort earlier to negative discount rate adjustments. As a result of the policy interaction process described in Section 3, rational expectations together with the destabilising interim effects of U.S. discount rate changes then lead to larger adjustments in both monetary and fiscal policy in Europe. Indeed Table 1 shows that the main changes are in the monetary variables. The U.S. follow a more restrictive policy in 1977–78, but interest rates are reduced; the EEC intervenes more actively both with loans and the discount rate, and now pursues a more active monetary policy than the U.S.

In summary, recognising policy interactions had led to some convergence in the national policies. The U.S. have dropped most of their 'supply side' stand in favour of demand creating measures; and the EEC is partly able to overcome the inertia of its own policy responses as indicated by more flexible interventions, using particularly the discount rate and the money supply. Finally, excepting the discount rate, U.S. interventions are smaller and more consistent, while European interventions run at the same level but have become more active.

Cooperation between the U.S. and the EEC takes the optimal policies a step further towards convergence. Government expenditures rise rather faster in both economies, and the U.S. social security cuts are halved once again. Tax cuts are still in evidence, although less prominent in the U.S. The activism of monetary policy has vanished – particularly the sharp restrictions on money supply and interest rates which appeared in the closed loop Nash solution of the EEC. In fact both loans to the government and the discount rates now follow constant or steadily changing paths. This suggests that it may be important to coordinate monetary policies, and the gains to cooperation may be significant when that is done. However, the convergence pattern does show that cooperation may require individual policies to be surrendered for the sake of concerted action, as seen in the expenditure variables here. Overall the cooperative policies call for reduced intervention in the U.S., and for more consistent policies in both economies. The exceptions to this pattern are the rise in government expenditure in the first 2 years, followed by a drop in 1976–78. European countries benefit from this initial rise in government expenditures and from the continuous U.S. discount rate reductions. The induced stability provides the opportunity to follow more consistent aggregate demand policies in the EEC. These policies are much like the Cournot-Nash solution for the first two years. In 1976 they are similar to the closed loop Nash solution, except for a cut in the loans to the government, and the last 2 years of the planning period show an increase in the EEC discount rate. This break in the concerted action of discount rate changes between the EEC and the U.S. is necessary for Europe to attract capital imports which then compensate for the balance of trade deterioration induced by the growth in government outlays. In their turn, higher government expenditures in the EEC are beneficial for the U.S. economy.

Table 2 shows the average expected changes in the target variables compared to those values which could have been expected by simulating the historical instrument choices. These expected outcomes are better for all variables in both economies, except for the U.S. balance of trade. The EEC does relatively better in the Cournot-Nash solution, and in raising investment and profits in all solutions. But it does badly with the employment target, indicating that European unemployment is a very persistent problem. In contrast to the associated instrument changes, the U.S. target changes become more favourable as we move from the Cournot-Nash to the cooperative solution (especially for production, balance of trade, and investment). The EEC targets however are not much affected by the type of strategy chosen. Once again we have evidence of the asymmetry in U.S.-EEC economic relations. The gains to cooperation for the U.S. take the form of smaller interventions and improved expected target outcomes. But in the EEC those gains arise from a redistribution of intervention effort.

8. THE GAINS FROM POLICY COORDINATION

Finally, we turn to the evaluation of the policy schemes in which each decision maker has the choice of four policies. On the reference path both decision makers

Table 2. Effects of the different policy schemes on the target variables of the US and the EEC in average annual percentage changes

Variables	Desired change	CN	CLN	CP
US targets:				
Inflation	− 3.0 (4/12)	− 1.6	− 2.2	− 2.3
Production	3.0 (4/12)	1.9	2.3	2.7
Balance of trade	1.0 (1/12)	− 2.1	− 0.5	− 0.2
Employment	1.5 (1/12)	0.9	1.2	1.2
Investment ratio	3.0 (1/12)	1.5	1.8	2.0
Profit ratio	3.0 (1/12)	1.2	1.5	1.3
EEC targets:				
Inflation	− 3.0 (1/12)	− 2.2	− 2.3	− 2.1
Production	3.0 (4/12)	2.4	2.3	2.4
Balance of trade	1.0 (4/12)	− 0.1	0.3	0.4
Employment	1.5 (1/12)	0.8	0.8	0.9
Investment ratio	3.0 (1/12)	3.8	3.3	3.7
Profit ratio	3.0 (1/12)	3.4	3.6	3.6

Note: The parenthesised figures are the relative weights attached to the diagonal of $B^{(i)}$ in (5); CN, CLN and CP refer to the policy schemes of Table 1.

stick to the desired values of their instruments, while the CN policy just assumes ideal values for the other player's instruments. Knowing that the opponent has the same options, the latter constitutes an inconsistent strategy and that is why we introduced the closed loop Nash solution which implies optimal reactions and anticipations by the policymakers in the EEC and in the U.S. given their own objectives. The fourth option is cooperation in which the economies agree upon a common objective. Tables 3 and 4 present the evaluations of the individual objective functions, normalised on the outcome when both economies stick to their reference paths. Thus, if the U.S. were to default and follow the certainty equivalent policy instead of the cooperative solution they could expect to worsen the expected cooperative outcome by doubling it to 40% of the reference solution. Of course, in view of the other expected outcomes the US would only be tempted to do so if they suspected the EEC of doing nothing. Adhering to the cooperative policy in spite of U.S. suspicions, the EEC in its turn could only expect an outcome of 36 instead of 16% (see Table 4).

A few other observations can be made with regard to the contents of these tables. By assumption the certainty equivalent and the coordinated choice should lead to the minimum entry in the RF and CLN column, respectively. Here we find that the noncooperative policies also produce minima in the CN column of both tables. On the other hand, cooperation is not guaranteed to lead to a stable solution in terms of the individual objectives. This may be illustrated using the proximity of

Table 3. Objective function evaluations for the U.S. under various policy schemes

EEC policies U.S. Options	RF	CN	CLN	CP
Reference path (RF)	1.00	0.29	0.42	0.33
Certainty equivalent policy (CN)	0.48	0.81	0.69	0.40
Coordinated policy rule (CLN)	0.94	0.28	0.22	0.32
Cooperative policy scheme (CP)	0.71	0.39	0.41	0.20

Table 4. Objective function evaluations for the EEC under various policy schemes

US policies EEC options	RF	CN	CLN	CP
Reference path (RF)	1.00	0.92	1.50	0.89
Certainty equivalent policy (CN)	0.19	0.39	0.88	0.16
Coordinated policy rule (CLN)	0.84	0.33	0.24	0.69
Cooperative policy scheme (CP)	0.22	0.36	0.84	0.16

the CN and CP entries in the last column of Table 4. Suppose the EEC is tempted to choose its Cournot-Nash policy. If this switch is perceived by the U.S., they might implement their noncooperative policy rule, and so on. It is interesting to recognise that this process, which is started by a small perturbation only, actually ends up in the closed loop Nash solution. This clearly confirms the Nash property that, for given objectives, neither player has any incentive to deviate unilaterally from the correctly 'coordinated' decisions.

The diagonal entries of both tables reveal that the gains to 'playing the game' are larger in the U.S. than in the EEC, but the reverse is true for the incentive to cooperate. In other words, this result shows that, although the gain of coordination relative to the CN policy scheme is large enough for the U.S. to choose a not completely agnostic strategy, the additional gains of cooperation are small and unevenly distributed in favour of the EEC. Furthermore, we find that not altering EEC policies with respect to their reference values is not only bad for the EEC itself but also for the opportunities of the U.S. This holds for whichever option the U.S. choose but especially if they implement the CLN policy on the unrequited assumption that the EEC would simultaneously follow the coordination solution. On the other hand, choosing the CLN option would be risky for the EEC in the same sense. Disregarding the possibility that no active policy is pursued in either one of the economies, the EEC is distinctly more sensitive to the selection strategy adopted in the U.S. than vice versa. That is, the differences between the lowest and highest value in the last three columns of each row are much larger for the EEC. So, adequate knowledge of the policy rule followed in the other economy proves to be an essential part of the information problem.

9. CONCLUSION

In this study we apply dynamic game theory to the problem of policy coordination between the U.S. and the EEC in a strongly aggregated model of the world economy. The method allows for rational expectations of the other player's policy selections to be part of the conditioning information of each policymaker. We argue that the advantages of following this approach, instead of trying to find a cooperative solution, are that the parties do not have to surrender their individual objectives and that no decision about the weighing of each other's targets has to be negotiated beforehand. The outcomes of the different approaches are compared in the empirical part of the study. Our results lead to the following conclusions.

(i) Individual policies, which ignore the influence of actions pursued in the other economy, show fiscal retrenchment in the U.S. but stimulation in the EEC. In all policy schemes considered here, the U.S. has to cut social benefits and reduce taxes. In the individual policy of the EEC it is optimal to lower the discount rate throughout the planning period. No evidence exists that such policies were implemented in the period concerned. In fact, most instrument changes prove to be reversals of historical values.

(ii) There is also no empirical evidence that correctly 'coordinated' policies have been followed, nor that the EEC policy adjustments should be smaller and the discount rate changes closer to their historical values than in the uncoordinated case. However policymaking in both economies is now supposed to be interconnected, and it might well be that the erratic historical pattern is actually caused by unpredictable American discount rate changes. The adjustment of U.S. policy in the closed loop Nash solution would, if combined with the actual values, lead to a more stable evolution of discount rates.

(iii) At first sight the coordinated policy scheme confirms the conclusion of other studies that unsynchronised policies may stabilise the world economy. Furthermore, the outcomes in terms of objective function evaluations are close to the results of cooperation, so it should not be difficult to persuade countries to discard their individual uncoordinated policies.

(iv) The choice between coordination and cooperation needs some more consideration. The cooperative solution implies concerted action in the form of raising government expenditures, reducing taxes and lowering the discount rates in both economies. No active policy of the central banks is implied and in both the U.S. and the EEC a tight money policy is used to control the commercial banks. On the other hand, the implication that government expenditure grows slower in the U.S., and that social outlays are lowered there while they are raised in the EEC, might prove less acceptable to the U.S. and might be one reason for not cooperating.

(v) The EEC is very sensitive to which strategy is selected by the U.S., but in their turn the U.S. would not much care which policy the EEC chooses so long as it follows an active policy in pursuit of its own or common objectives. These results are certainly consistent with the recent history of American-European economic relations, and as such they provide one rather plausible explanation of why the Europeans have repeatedly argued for more cooperative policies from the U.S. and why those requests have fallen on deaf ears. We think that the (closed loop Nash) game solution is therefore an attractive form of policy coordination because it requires no mutual interference with policymaking but only the exchange of information about the determinants of each other's plans for achieving economic recovery.

NOTES

Supported by the Netherlands Organisation for the Advancement of Pure Research (ZWO).
  We also thank J.R. Pijpers for his cooperation.
1) The technique is widely used elsewhere (e.g. Kydland (1975), Van der Ploeg (1982), Hughes Hallett and Brandsma (1983)). It is reviewed in Section 3.
2) An exception is Oudiz and Sachs (1984), although their decision analysis is restricted to a single time period.
3) An explicit demonstration is given by Hughes Hallett and Rees (1983), p. 294.
4) Recall this solution is 'closed loop' *between* decision makers because the iteration in (10) is completed. It is not necessarily closed loop for successive intervals of time.

REFERENCES

Aubin, J.P. (1979), *Mathematical Methods of Game and Economic Theory*, North Holland, Amsterdam.

Barten, A.P., G. d'Alcantara and G.J. Carrin (1976), 'COMET: A medium-term macroeconomic model for the European Economic Community', *European Economic Review*, 7, pp. 63–115.

Brandsma, A.S. and A.J. Hughes Hallett (1982), 'The impact of noncausality on noncooperative strategies for dynamic games', *Economics Letters*, 10, pp. 9–15.

Brandsma, A.S. and A.J. Hughes Hallett (1983), 'Optimal policies for interdependent economies: risk aversion and the problem of information', in: T. Basar (ed.), Proceedings of the 4th

228

IFAC/IFORS/IIASA Conference on *The Modelling and Control of National Economies*, Pergamon, New York.

Brandsma, A.S. and A.J. Hughes Hallett (1984a), 'Noncausalities and time inconsistency in dynamic noncooperative games: the problem revisited', *Economics Letters*, 14, pp. 123–130.

Brandsma, A.S. and A.J. Hughes Hallett (1984b), 'Economic conflict and the solution of dynamic games', *European Economic Review*, 26, pp. 13–32.

Canzoneri, M. and J.A. Gray (1985), 'Monetary policy games and the consequences of non-cooperative behaviour', *International Economic Review* (forthcoming).

Chouraqui, J.C. and R. Price (1983), 'Medium term financial strategy: the coordination of fiscal and monetary policies', Working paper no. 9, OECD Economics and Statistics Department, Paris.

Da Cuhna, N. and E. Polak (1967), 'Constrained minimisation of vector-valued criteria in finite dimensional spaces', *Journal of Mathematical Analysis and Applications*, 19, pp. 103–124.

Hickman, B.G. and S. Sleicher (1978), 'The interdependence of national economies and the synchronization of economic fluctuations: evidence from the LINK project', *Weltwirtschaftliches Archiv*, 114, pp. 642–708.

Hughes Hallett, A.J. (1984), 'Noncooperative strategies for dynamic policy games and the problem of time inconsistency', *Oxford Economic Papers*, 36, pp. 381–399.

Hughes Hallett, A.J. and A.S. Brandsma (1983), 'How effective could sanctions against the Soviet Union be?', *Weltwirtschaftliches Archiv*, 119, pp. 498–522.

Hughes Hallett, A. and H. Rees (1983), *Quantitative Economic Policies and Interactive Planning*, Cambridge University Press, Cambridge.

Kydland, F.E. (1975), 'Noncooperative and dominant player solutions in discrete dynamic games', *International Economic Review*, 16, pp. 321–335.

Miller, M. and M. Salmon (1984), 'Dynamic games and the time inconsistency of optimal policy in open economies', *Economic Journal* (Supplement 1984), pp. 124–137.

Oudiz, G. and J.D. Sachs (1984), 'Macroeconomic policy coordination among industrial economies', *Brookings Economic Papers* (1), pp. 1–64.

Shishido, S., H. Fujiwara, A. Kohno, Y. Kurokawa, S. Matsuura and H. Wago (1980), 'A model for the coordination of recovery policies in the OECD region', *Journal of Policy Modeling*, 2, pp. 35–55.

Siebrand, J.C. and N. van der Windt (1982), 'The case for international cooperation', Erasmus University, Rotterdam (mimeo).

Van der Ploeg, F. (1982), 'Government policy, real wage resistance and the resolution of conflict', *European Economic Review*, 19, pp. 181–212.

Van der Windt, N., J.C. Siebrand, J. Swank and J.R. Pijpers (1984), 'RASMUS: an annual model of the US and EEC economics', Discussion papers 8405/G and 8411/G, Institute for Economic Research, Erasmus University, Rotterdam.

Van Wijnbergen, S. (1982), 'Oil price shocks, unemployment, investment and the current account: an intertemporal disequilibrium analysis', World Bank Development Research Department, Washington DC (mimeo).

CHAPTER 10

SIMULATING ECONOMIC POLICY WITH THE COMET MODEL

A.P. Barten and G. d'Alcantara
Katholieke Universiteit van Leuven and Center for Operational Research and Econometrics (CORE), Belgium

1. INTRODUCTION

Over the years an increasing number of forecasts and alternative simulation experiments have been made with versions of COMET. These involved discussions with various members of the Staff at the Commission of the European Communities which have enriched later versions of the model. In particular Messrs. Castermans, Ranuzzi, Robinson, Schubert, Rohaert, Charpin, Toft Nilson, and recently Dramais and Sfiroeras have in this way contributed to the development of the project. This has given COMET the possibility to acquire maturity and credibility resulting in its recognition as a useful tool in the design of economic policy.

In this spirit we present here some new results obtained with COMET IV. A number of alternative simulations are made in two different ways: for one individual country separately and for the countries of the European Community (Belgium, Denmark, Germany, Greece, France, Ireland, Italy, The Netherlands and the United Kingdom) all jointly. It is interesting indeed to check whether policies followed by individual countries are either offset or reinforced when all European countries follow the same policy.

The first three sets of simulations, each time a simulation A for an individual country and a simulation B for all EEC countries, are related to policies aiming at an improvement of international competitivity. The fourth set of simulations is related to public investment policies. Simulations of type B will be referred to as coordinated actions.

2. NOMINAL WAGE RATE DECREASE IN GERMANY AND IN THE
   EUROPEAN COMMUNITY

The effects of a nominal wage rate decrease are obtained as the difference between two simulations: the alternative simulation which includes a sustained wage rate

Artus, P. and Guvenen, O. (eds.): International Macroeconomic Modelling for Policy Decisions.
© *1986. Martinus Nijhoff Publishers, Dordrecht/Boston/Lancaster.*
ISBN 90-247-3201-8. Printed in The Netherlands.

decrease and a free reference simulation. The alternative simulation is obtained by keeping the wage rate exogenously at a level which is below the level of the reference simulation by an amount which reduces the wage bill by 1% of the 1983 GDP at current prices. This is done for Germany separately and for all European countries jointly. This corresponds to an exogenous decrease of the German wage rate by -1.71% in 1983 and by decreasing percentages up to -1.02% in 1988. For the European Community the exogenous wage shifts are -1.8% in 1983 up to -1.0% in 1988.

The effects are presented in Table 1 for the percentage differences in the following variables:

WR — wage rate
PC — consumers price index
YO — gross domestic product
IPO — gross investments in fixed assets
N — employment
UR — unemployment rate (over active population)
TBR — current trade balance ratio (over total exports)
SGR — current government balance ratio (over total government receipts)

The results are deflationary in the short run: in 1983 in Germany the GDP decreases by 0.16 in the German wage rate simulation and by 0.23 in the European wage rate simulations. In the long run, after 6 years, the German GDP increases by 0.44 and by 0.35 respectively. In terms of employment, the long term elasticities resulting from the simulation are 0.45 and 0.37 respectively. The individual German wage policy is offset by the joint European wage policy by only 0.08. In other words, the fact that all European neighbours follow the same wage policy as Germany reduces its long term efficiency in terms of employment by only 8% out of 45%. It is also interesting to notice that the increased employment is obtained with only a temporary loss in real wage rate (-1.49 and -1.45 respectively) and a small gain in real wage rate after 6 years ($+0.06$ and 0.11 respectively). This is due to the long term gain in the volume of value added.

The deflationary effects disappear after only 1 year. GDP results to be 0.05 higher than the reference after 1 year as can be seen from the bottom lines of Table 1.

One would ask whether this result is not typical for a large EEC country and whether a small country would not be able to benefit more from a solitary wage policy and lose these benefits when all other European partners compete with similar wage cuts. This does not seem to be the case as can be seen from the next set of simulation results where the gross wage rates are decreased via a reduction of the employers' social security contribution rates.

Table 1. Wage rate decrease ($-$ 1% of GDP)

	WR	PC	YO	IPO	N	WR	TBR	SGR
A in Germany								
effects on Germany								
1983	-1.71	-0.22	-0.16	-0.55	-0.15	0.14	0.22	-0.28
1988	-1.02	-0.96	-0.44	0.38	0.45	-0.28	-0.22	0.53
effects on the EEC								
1983	-0.5	-0.1	-0.1	-0.2	0.0	0.0	0.1	-0.1
1988	-0.4	-0.4	0.2	0.2	0.1	-0.1	0.1	0.3
B in the EEC								
effects on Germany								
1983	-1.71	-0.26	-0.23	-0.60	-0.18	0.17	0.29	-0.34
1988	-1.02	-1.13	0.35	0.36	0.37	-0.23	-0.16	0.46
effects on the EEC								
1983	-1.8	-0.4	-0.2	-0.4	-0.1	0.1	0.2	0.0
1988	-1.0	-1.1	0.3	0.2	0.3	-0.2	0.1	0.8

change in Germany; effects on German GDP (YO)					
1983	1984	1985	1986	1987	1988
-0.16	0.05	0.19	0.33	0.42	0.44
change in the EEC; effects on German GDP (YO)					
-0.23	0.03	0.13	0.29	0.38	0.35

3. EMPLOYERS' SOCIAL SECURITY CONTRIBUTION RATE DECREASE IN BELGIUM AND IN THE EUROPEAN COMMUNITY

In COMET IV the employers social security contribution rate is an exogenous component of the gross wage costs per employee. This exogenous contribution rate is used as a policy instrument to decrease the wage rate cost by the amount which decreases the wage bill by 1% of the 1983 GDP at current prices. This is done first for Belgium separately where one reduces the contribution from 16.7% to 14.5% and then for the European Community where the rates are decreased by 2.2% in Germany, 3.1% in France, 2.7% in Italy, 2.8% in the Netherlands, 2.2% in Belgium, 2.2% in the United Kingdom, 1.9% in Ireland, 1.9% in Denmark and 3.4% in Greece.

These interventions result in instantaneous changes of the wage rate by $-$ 2.09% in the Belgian case and $-$ 2.23% in the European case. The effects are presented in Table 2.

In the very short run, the current period, the effects are positive for GDP only and for employment slight but negative on the current trade balance and the current government balance. One year later all objectives benefit from the measure. In the Belgian experiment, employment increases by 1.23% after 3 years and by

Table 2. Employers social security contribution rate (in wage cost)

	WR	PC	YO	IPO	N	UR	TBR	SGR
A in Belgium								
Effects on Belgium								
1983	− 2.09	− 0.30	0.44	− 0.21	0.12	− 0.12	− 0.38	− 0.86
1985	− 2.02	− 0.62	1.00	0.37	1.23	− 1.12	0.09	0.51
1988	− 0.17	0.42	0.24	− 0.58	0.63	− 0.74	0.27	0.87
Effects on the EEC								
1983	− 0.10	− 0.02	0.04	0.02	0.02	− 0.02	0.02	− 0.01
1985	− 0.10	− 0.06	0.05	0.03	0.06	− 0.05	0.03	0.04
1988	− 0.02	− 0.01	0.01	0.01	0.02	− 0.02	0.00	0.04
B in the EEC								
Effects on Belgium								
1983	− 2.15	− 0.43	0.80	− 0.12	0.28	− 0.27	− 0.02	− 0.32
1985	− 2.21	− 0.94	1.11	0.50	1.39	− 1.25	0.28	0.74
1988	− 0.65	− 0.19	0.45	− 0.30	0.68	− 0.79	0.49	1.03
Effects on the EEC								
1983	− 2.23	− 0.57	0.48	0.25	0.22	− 0.20	− 0.15	− 1.24
1985	− 2.06	− 1.47	0.86	0.77	1.11	− 0.77	− 0.07	− 0.70
1988	− 1.60	− 1.69	1.12	0.50	1.19	− 0.76	− 0.06	− 0.18

Effects on the government balances (SGR) in % of GDP

	1983	1985	1988
DB	− 1.53	− 0.72	− 0.23
FR	− 1.02	− 0.18	0.82
IT	− 1.36	− 0.59	0.09
NL	− 0.37	0.12	0.51
BE	− 0.32	0.74	1.03
UK	− 0.79	− 1.21	− 1.46
IR	− 1.05	− 1.14	− 1.44
DK	− 1.26	− 1.17	− 0.86
HE	− 1.32	− 1.29	− 1.01

0.63% after 6 years with favourable effects on the current trade balance and government balance. In the joint European action case one can see that the Belgian economy does not lose its benefits, on the contrary. Employment increases more, and this results from a global improvement of activity in Europe; the trade balance does not deteriorate significantly by the first year and improves by 0.49 points while the government balance gains more than one full point after 6 years. After only 2 years the initial decrease of social security returns of the government (− 0.32) are more than compensated by an improvement (0.74) of the government balance. This leaves net gains after more or less 1.5 year. Instead of offsetting each other these policies reinforce each other at the European level as can be seen from the performances of European employment. In Belgium, the initial increase of the government deficit, which directly goes to the enterprises, is a small cost to be paid for a large medium term benefit for the government finances, for the trade balance, for employment and for growth. For some other countries the improvement of government finances, is much more slow to obtain. Their government balances react as shown in the bottom lines of Table 2. According to their structures the countries with large external trade proportions in GDP and larger supply deter- mined competitivity effects of domestic costs on exports are able to achieve a much larger self financing of social wage cost reductions.

As compared to the previous policy which showed weak neutralizing effects of direct decreases of the wage rates from other countries, in the case of social wage cost reductions, the European policies reinforce each other.

4. EXCHANGE RATE CHANGES

And the exchange rate changes? How do they modify the competitive positions and what are the resulting short term and long term effects on employment (N), growth (YO), the current trade balance (TBR), the current government balance (SGR) and prices (PC)?

In the first simulation, the French franc is devalued by 10% with respect to all other currencies. In the second simulation all European currencies are devalued by 10% with respect to all other world currencies. The results are presented in Table 3. Let us note that the ECU has been devaluing by more than 40% wrt. the US $ since 2 years.

The effects are very different in the short run and in the long run. In the short run there exists a competitive or profitability advance for France which in all cases increases output investment and employment, but to a much larger extent (the effect is more than double) when the European Community devalues. In the short run there is a perverse effect on the current trade balance in France (J curve) while this is not the case for Europe as a whole. In the long run, however, the trade balance on the one hand improves relatively more in France in the case when France devalues alone. Inflationary pressures on the other hand offset the devaluations. The final result after 6 years shows lower activity, lower investment, lower em- ployment in all cases. One can say that the high $ and the high Yen have provided a temporary relief for the European economy, with up to 0.8% more employment after two years. Simultaneously, however, more expensive raw materials cause inflationary pressures which are progressively transmitted into the domestic price systems. Benefits from the devaluations could even turn into dramatic inflationary episodes, depending on the price wage spirals and related effects.

Table 3. Exchange rate change (+ 10%)

	WR	PC	YO	IPO	N	UR	TBR	SGR
A in France								
Effects on France								
1983	1.0	1.3	0.5	0.3	0.1	− 0.1	− 1.4	0.2
1984	2.3	2.9	1.1	0.6	1.1	− 0.9	1.4	2.6
1988	8.5	8.8	− 1.1	− 1.9	− 0.6	0.4	2.8	1.0
Effects on the EEC (in US $)								
1983	− 1.8	− 1.8	0.2	0.1	0.0	− 0.0	0.0	0.1
1984	− 1.6	− 1.6	0.2	0.1	0.2	− 0.1	0.1	0.4
1988	− 0.6	− 0.7	− 0.3	− 0.5	− 0.2	0.1	0.3	0.1
B in the EEC								
Effects on France								
1983	0.6	0.8	1.1	1.4	0.5	− 0.4	− 0.5	1.0
1984	1.5	2.0	0.7	− 0.2	1.0	− 0.6	1.7	1.7
1988	6.4	6.7	− 1.1	− 1.8	− 1.0	0.7	1.4	0.0
Effects on the EEC (in ECU)								
1983	0.9	0.8	1.1	1.1	0.5	− 0.4	− 0.0	1.0
1984	1.9	2.0	0.6	− 0.2	0.8	− 0.6	1.0	1.6
1988	5.3	5.9	− 0.8	− 1.5	− 0.3	0.2	1.1	− 0.5

5. PUBLIC INVESTMENT MULTIPLIER

The Keynesian public investment expenditure remedies are still alive as can be seen in the report to the European Parliament by Albert (1983). His basic idea was that a concerted action generates more return than the simple sum of the individual actions. We will illustrate this with COMET IV in the same way he has done it with COMET III. The order of magnitudes of the multipliers and their dynamic patterns are different in both models. COMET IV includes a more refined factor demand system where each component of final demand has specific production factor and import contents. COMET IV also comprises financial and monetary feedbacks as a result of increased investment demand by the government.

Table 4 presents the effects of an exogenous and sustained shift of the exogenous public investments volume by amounting to 1% 0f 1983 GDP in current prices deflated by the investment price index in the United Kingdom and in the European Community. The effects on the GDP of the United Kingdom, which can be directly interpreted as multipliers are 0.6 and 0.8 in the short run and 0.0 and 0.1 in the long run (after 6 years) in the case of an individual and of a joint European action, respectively. It is worth noting that the multipliers are significantly lower and decrease significantly faster than in what is shown by Albert (1983), nl. in the case

Table 4. Public investment (+ 1% of GDP)

	WR	PC	YO	IPO	N	UR	TBR	SGR[1]
A in the U.K.								
Effects on the U.K.								
1983	0.0	−0.0	0.6	0.2	0.3	−0.3	−1.9	0.7
1988	0.3	−0.3	0.0	−0.4	0.5	−0.5	0.0	1.7
Effects on the EEC								
1983	−0.0	−0.0	0.2	0.2	0.1	−0.1	−0.1	0.3
1988	0.2	−0.1	0.0	−0.1	0.1	−0.1	0.1	0.6
B in the EEC								
Effects on the U.K.								
1983	−0.0	−0.0	0.8	0.3	0.5	−0.4	−1.1	1.0
1988	0.6	−0.1	0.1	−0.5	0.6	−0.5	0.6	1.9
Effect on the EEC								
1983	0.0	−0.1	1.2	1.1	0.7	−0.6	−0.9	1.4
1988	1.6	0.8	0.4	−0.9	0.5	−0.4	−0.1	0.8

Effects over time						
	1983	1984	1985	1986	1987	1988
A. YO UK	0.55	0.23	0.20	0.68	0.55	0.02
YO EU	0.24	0.12	0.12	0.27	0.18	0.01
B. YO UK	0.83	0.36	0.30	0.84	0.64	0.09
YO EU	1.21	0.74	0.62	0.92	0.68	0.44
COMET III Albert (1983)						
A. YO UK		0.9	1.1			
B. YO EU		1.6	1.5			

[1] Does not include the additional investments themselves.

of the individual action of the United Kingdom 0.9 after 2 years and 1.1 after 3 years and in the case of concerted action of all European countries 1.6 after 2 years and 1.8 after 3 years. It is also interesting to note the cyclical nature of the new multipliers showing a periodicity of 4 years. For the European Community the multiplier goes from 1.21 the current year to 0.62 the third year, increases again to 0.92 the fourth year and decreases to 0.44 the sixth year. Still, the employment effects are not unimportant. It also remains true that in the long run, the trade balance constraint is much easier in the case where the United Kingdom participates in a joint investment action.

6. CONCLUSION

A conclusion should start with a word of caution. The simulation results shown are valid for the 'research version' of the COMET IV model which includes a given set of mechanisms and coefficient values which are open for discussion. It would be of interest to compare alternative simulations of the model using alternative mechanisms to determine sets of variables. As an example one could mention the acceleration and the profit version of the investment equations, different regimes on the financial markets . . . .

The importance of the results, however, is their demonstration of the comparative advantage of COMET as a policy instrument in the possibility to cover the world economic mechanisms without losing the information about the individual countries of the model.

The measurement of the effects of joint actions as compared to the sum of individual actions may lead to the measurement of quantitative arguments for co-operation.

The exact cooperation argument is that the individually rational actions could in certain cases lead to a stable suboptimal solution for all players. This solution can be replaced by a Pareto optimal solution if all players can agree to act jointly in view of a fully informed collective rationality. They can all increase their returns compared to the returns of a Nash equilibrium. In practice no such cooperative solutions were found in the simulations shown in this paper when employment is considered as the objective. Coordinated actions as defined above should not be considered as cooperative actions in the sense of game theory.

What the simulations did show is that joint policy actions do not end up with neutralizing competitive effects.

The policies which have been simulated, when yielding positive results, followed by an individual country, yield comparable results when all countries follow them jointly. This means that coordination cannot be justified on just these types of arguments.

NOTES

The authors gratefully acknowledge the computational assistance of Jan Duerinck.
Note of the editors: the version given here consists of Section II of the paper presented at the workshop of the AEA. The first section, which has been omitted, was a brief presentation of the COMET model.

REFERENCES

Barten, A.P. (1971), 'An import allocation model for the Common Market', *Cahiers Economiques de Bruxelles*, 50, pp. 3–14.
Barten, A.P. and G.J. Carrin (1972), 'A medium-term model for the European Economic Community', Some first results, Paper read at the European Meeting of the Economic Society, Budapest, September 1972.

Barten, A.P., G. d'Alcantara and G.J. Carrin (1976), 'COMET, a medium-term macroeconomic model for the European Economic Community', *European Economic Review*, pp. 63–115.

Alcantara, G. and A.P. Barten (1984), 'Explaining factor demands in COMET', *Journal of Economic Modelling*, 1.

Albert, M. (1983), *Un Pari pour l'Europe*, Seuil, Paris.

PART IV

THE USE OF INTERNATIONAL MACROECONOMIC MODELS

CHAPTER 11

MAKING INTERNATIONAL ECONOMIC FORECASTS

John Llewellyn, Lee Samuelson and Nick Vanston
OECD, Paris, France

1. INTRODUCTION

The OECD publishes in July and December each year in the *Economic Outlook* a set of economic forecasts covering each OECD country and major world zones. A key feature of these forecasts is that they are internationally consistent as regards both volumes and prices. The forecasts are accompanied by detailed text describing the forecasts and analysing economic developments in the OECD and elsewhere, and a broad description is given, at the back of the *Economic Outlook,* of how the forecasts are made. Nevertheless, there are periodic requests for greater detail about the forecasting exercise, and this paper is a response to those requests.

2. BACKGROUND

The forecasting round exercise is the largest single coordinated exercise regularly performed by the OECD Secretariat. Most of the Economics Department's professional economists are involved in it. Co-ordination is assured throughout via advance planning, a flow of written information among the participants, regular meetings and informal contacts. International consistency at all stages is assured via pre-determined iterations feeding through the Secretariat's INTERLINK world economic model, followed by discussions between country and international trade and financial experts. It is recognised that experts have primacy in their own domain: nevertheless, they have to argue their case before their peers and superiors, and if necessary, modify their forecasts accordingly.

Thus when the Secretariat makes forecasts for the whole world economy, activity and prices in each country or zone impinge on all others through international trade and finance. This raises problems which national forecasters do not have to face, namely the sparseness of exogenous variables. For an individual

Artus, P. and Guvenen, O. (eds.): International Macroeconomic Modelling for Policy Decisions.
© *1986. Martinus Nijhoff Publishers, Dordrecht/Boston/Lancaster.*
ISBN 90-247-3201-8. Printed in The Netherlands.

country, demand for its exports and the prices of its imports are essentially exogenous, even if the economy of the country is large. With foreign trade accounting on average for a quarter of GNP for the typical industrialised country, a national forecaster is in the happy position of finding twenty-five per cent of demand and prices pre-determined, or fixed by assumption. For the world as a whole, this is not true. The world economy is very nearly a simultaneous system. In the last analysis, the only truly exogenous variables are the stock of goods and productive resources at the beginning of the projection period, and the state of the weather world-wide during it. These are obviously not enough to determine the course of economic events world-wide even if the first were known with precision and the second predictable. In practice, assumptions have to be made.

The most important such assumption underlying the Secretariat forecasts is that announced economic policies remain unchanged in OECD countries over the projection period. This is not merely a matter of convenience, although it does simplify the forecasting task. The main reason for making forecasts in the OECD is precisely to explore the implications of the existing set of policies in order to inform and advise policy makers in individual OECD countries. This is why a preliminary version of the Secretariat forecasts is discussed in detail with national forecasters shortly before the meeting of the Economic Policy Committee, in which the participants are senior economic policy advisers from Member countries.

Other major assumptions concern oil prices and exchange rates. The level and development of oil prices became significant after the first oil shock, and the Secretariat typically adopts the technical assumption that crude oil exported by OPEC would sell at nominal dollar prices in accordance with known OPEC intentions as far as they are scheduled to last, and at a constant 'real' price thereafter. 'Real' in this context means changing at the same rate in dollar terms as those of manufactured goods exported by OECD countries.

Nominal exchange rates are assumed to remain constant at the levels they averaged just before the forecasts are finalised, except for countries which have a well-defined publicly-announced exchange rate policy. The reasons for this are twofold. For many years, forecasts of exchange rates were politically very sensitive, and remain so in several countries. Secondly, acceptably accurate forecasts of short-run exchange rate movements have so far proved technically impossible to make. And in practice, 'naive' forecasts based on, for example, constant 'real' exchange rates (i.e. adjusted for differences in inflation rates) have not proved more accurate or useful than those based on constant nominal rates when the forecast period is 18 months or less.

INTERLINK – the OECD Secretariat's model of the world economy – helps ensure the coordination and smooth functioning of the multi-country forecasting Round, which necessarily involves thousands of data series, and in which all

Divisions in the Economics and Statistics Department participate. It provides a focal point for the interchange of information, helping co-ordinate the contributions of staff involved. It ensures that domestic and international accounting identities are respected as forecast components are revised, and that the economic consequences of a revision to a given forecast component are appropriately reflected through the entire forecast set.

3. THE INTERLINK SYSTEM

In its present form, INTERLINK consists, basically, of:

1) medium-size structural models (approximately 150 equations each) for each of the 23 OECD countries,[1] which broadly reproduce the simulation properties of larger econometric models well-known to, and used by, national administrations;

2) reduced-form models for each of eight non-OECD regions, established on the basis of empirical evidence available both within the Secretariat and in research centres and institutions specialising in the economies of non-OECD countries;

3) world trade and financial linkage models, which link the OECD economies and the non-OECD regions through merchandise and services trade volumes and trade prices, international capital flows and other factors such as cross-country wage emulation.

Exchange rates, factor payments, and net transfers are, at this stage, treated as exogenous, as is customary in the OECD Secretariat's semi-annual forecasting exercises, although in simulation work the model is often used in 'floating rate mode', whereby exchange rates are determined endogenously.

3.1. The OECD country models

The OECD country models are basically demand-determined, income/expenditure models, in which blocks of equations determine the main components of demand; wages and prices. foreign trade prices and volumes; the distribution of income; output and employment; and financial variables. Supply effects operate primarily through the effects of labour market conditions on wage rates and hence prices, as well as the effects of varying levels of capacity utilisation on prices.

Each country model consists of approximately 150 equations, of which about 50 are behavioural equations, and around 100 are identities. Given that there are models for 23 OECD countries, it would be impractical to attempt to describe here the more than three thousand equations involved. The features that broadly characterise the country models of the INTERLINK system, however, are summarised below.

(i) Domestic expenditure

Three broad categories of *domestic expenditure* are distinguished: consumption, investment, and government. Depending on the country, some further disaggregation may be involved. Private consumption is typically related to real disposable income and the long-term real interest rate, with due allowance given for adjustment lags. Other financial variables and measures of 'consumer confidence' are not at present included, although current OECD empirical research is being directed towards the modelling of possible 'real wealth' effects and the role of consumer uncertainty (proxied by variables such as unemployment and changes in the inflation rate).

Investment expenditure is, in most of the country models, divided into at least three components: business fixed investment, residential construction, and stockbuilding. Business fixed investment is determined on the basis of changes in private sector output and long-term real interest rates. The dynamics of the investment function are typically more complex than those of consumption behaviour and in general involve a second-order lag adjustment process. Equations for the major economies, involving an integrated factor demand system based on explicit underlying production technology, are being incorporated to supplement the existing accelerator-based investment equations.

Given its volatility, residential construction does not, for some OECD economies, lend itself readily to econometric 'explanation', whilst in others it may be so heavily influenced by government policy that it may be more appropriately viewed as a policy instrument. For most OECD economies, however, the model treats residential construction as a function of real household disposable income, and the long-run real interest rate, again subject to lagged adjustment. Inventory investment (stockbuilding) series are so volatile and/or prone to measurement error, that this variable is typically treated as exogenous in forecast mode.

Government expenditure, which is typically sub-divided into consumption and investment components, is treated in the model as being exogenous in nominal terms for most countries. For some countries, however, the nature of the national budget process is such that government expenditure is treated as exogenous in real terms, and this is readily accomodated by use of corresponding policy targeting facilities in the model.

(ii) Wages and domestic prices

Wage rates are determined primarily as a function of labour market conditions, in the form of linear and non-linear unemployment terms, trend productivity, and prices. In some of the smaller, open OECD economies, wages in larger neighbouring economies are also used as a determinant of domestic wage trends. Prices (deflators for private consumption and other expenditure components) are determined via a mark-up on costs — of which labour and imported materials are the most important — and trend productivity. In some cases the mark-up process is variable, reflecting variations in product market conditions as measured by capacity utilisation or the 'gap' between actual and potential output. The relative weights attached to various cost components are derived from information contained in input-output tables. Changes in labour costs and in import prices are typically assumed to be shifted into domestic prices within 12—18 months.

(iii) Foreign trade — prices and volumes

Six trade categories are distinguished, of which five are endogenous: manufactures, energy, food, raw materials, and private non-factor services. A sixth category, consisting of government services and factor payments, is treated as exogenous, as are net foreign transfers.

Import volumes for each of the five commodity groups treated endogenously are determined by changes in the level, and composition of, aggregate demand, with expenditure components weighted according to their import content. Expenditure elasticities for manufactured goods generally lie in the range of $1\frac{1}{2}$ to 2, and around unity for non-manufactured trade components. Relative prices of imported and domestically-produced goods are also an important determinant of countries' imports. Price elasticities typically lie in a range of -0.7 to -1.1 for manufactures and private non-factor services (lagged over 2—3 years), around -0.6 for oil (lagged over 6—7 years), and close to zero for food and raw materials.

Export prices for manufactures are determined through a variable mark-up on costs — of which unit labour costs and import-content-weighted average import prices are the most important elements — with allowance for changes in competitors' export prices. Export prices for internationally-traded raw materials and food vary according to fluctuations in world activity and the world price level. In the case of food prices, allowance is made in the context of forecasting applications for the effects of the EEC's Common Agriculture Policy. While responses are dependent both on baseline conditions and on the pattern of changes in activity, the model assumes broadly that a 1% change in OECD area GNP will induce, over a period of 1 to 2 years, an increase of about 3% in the prices of internationally-traded raw materials, and an increase of about 2% in the prices of internationally-traded food. Export prices of oil move, by technical assumption, in line with the average OECD export price of manufactures, though in some simulation applications the price of internationally-traded oil may be determined as that which equilibrates world demand and supply.

For the commodity groups treated endogenously in the system, export volumes are determined primarily on the basis of changes in market growth (a weighted average of changes in partner countries' imports) and in relative price competitiveness. The market growth elasticity is usually assumed to be unity for commodity groups other than manufactures trade where, for some countries, this elasticity may be slightly above or below unity. Price elasticities for manufactures and non-factor services (export prices relative to those of competitors) typically lie in the range of -1.0 to -2.0 (lagged over 3 years). For other commodity groups (oil, food, raw materials) relative export price elasticity effects play little role over the short to medium-term simulation horizon for which the system is used. For a given country, import prices for each of the five commodity groups treated endogenously are determined primarily as a weighted average of partner countries' export prices to that country. The trade linkage block, described below, ensures the international consistency of countries' trade volumes and prices.

(iv) Distribution of income

Appropriation accounts for households, business and government for most OECD economies are constructed by identifying first the different sources of income on the revenue side, while the disposition of each sector's income is determined in the expenditure account.

Income of households consists primarily of compensation of employees, income of the self-employed, and transfers received. These income elements, together with property and other income, are adjusted for direct taxes and transfers paid to derive households' disposable income. Consumption – and hence household saving – is a function of this variable. Households' net lending is then determined by further subtracting exogenously-given capital transactions.

Business taxes are a lagged function of business income. The remaining components of the business appropriation account are derived as residuals: business income is GDP minus the net income of the three other sectors (households, government and foreign); business net lending is determined residually as the difference between the foreign balance and net lending of the other two domestic sectors.

Current receipts of government are the sum of direct taxes on households and business, indirect taxes, various transfers received, and property income of government. Current disbursements of government are the sum of government consumption and investment expenditure, and various transfers, subsidies, and property income paid, including interest payments on government debt. Net lending of government is given by government saving (current receipts less current disbursements) net of investment and other capital transactions.

(v) Supply

Private sector dependent employment is determined as a function of current and lagged activity and real wage rates, though for the major economies this is being reviewed in the light of recent factor demand/supply block research. Self-employment is typically assumed to move in line with private sector dependent employment, while government employment is exogenous. Unemployment is defined as the difference between labour force and total employment. Industrial production, unit labour costs, productivity, and capacity utilisation measures are also determined by identity in the supply block. Supply effects currently manifest themselves in the country models primarily through the influence of labour market conditions on wage rate determination, and the influence on prices of capacity utilization terms.

(vi) Financial

The transmission of monetary influences – whether within a given economy or internationally – is a particularly complex area. Further, surveying the empirical literature does not reveal a measure of consensus as to the relative importance of the channels through which monetary influences operate, and the lags involved. In view of the strength of the monetarist/Keynesian debate in recent years, such a lack of consensus is perhaps not surprising. Further, the widely differing institutional arrangements in Member countries preclude making a common approach to modelling financial mechanisms.

For most country models, however, short-term interest rates are given via an inverted demand-for-money function, with the money supply either given exogenously, or, for example, determined via unsterilised changes in net foreign asset holdings of the central bank. For countries where interest rates are administered directly by the central bank, this variable may be treated as exogenous. In the case of a number of small countries, considerable weight is also given to the influence of overseas short-term interest rates which are determined consistently through the international linkage mechanism. The short-term interest rate is the immediate response variable, and influences, inter alia, international capital flows. The long-term rate, which typically feeds into the expenditure equations, is determined through a distributed lag of short-term interest rates, with allowance for the expected inflation rate. The influences on the money supply of a country's balance of payments, and of alternative means of financing public sector deficits, are represented explicitly in most of the country models, although these can be modified by suitable choice of policy targeting rule.

International capital flows are determined on the basis of changes in interest rate differentials, expected exchange rates, world wealth, and other factors, such as trade-related credit, recycling of OPEC surpluses, and so on. The financial linkage block, described separately below, ensures the global consistency of international capital flows and exchange rates, in both fixed and floating exchange rate models.

3.2. Non-OECD regional models

The eight non-OECD regional models included in the INTERLINK system represent countries which are not members of the OECD. These countries are grouped broadly according to similarity of economic characteristics, as follows:

OPEC

LOP: Les absorptive OPEC countries:
Kuwait, the Libyan Arab Jamahiriya, Oman, Qatar, Saudi Arabia, and the United Arab Emirates

HOP: More absorptive OPEC countries:
Algeria, Ecuador, Gabon, Indonesia, Iran, Iraq, Nigeria and Venezuela

Developing countries

OOP: Oil producing developing countries:
Angola, Argentina, Bahrein, Bolivia, Brunei, Burma, Cameroons, Colombia, Congo, Egypt, Guatamala, Malaysia, Mexico, Peru, Syria, Trinidad and Tobago, Tunisia and Zaire

NIC: Newly industrialising countries:
Brazil, Hong Kong, Korea, Singapore and Taiwan

LMI: Low and middle income developing countries:
All other developing countries

Other non-OECD countries

SOV: USSR and Eastern European countries:
Albania, Bulgaria, Czechoslovakia, Germany (Dem. Rep.), Hungary, Poland, Rumania, and the Union of Soviet Socialist Republics

SIN: China and selected other Asian countries:
China, Dem. Kampuchea, Lao People's Dem. Rep., Mongolia, North Korea and the Socialist Republic of Vietnam

OTH: Other:

Malta, South Africa and Yugoslavia (also includes trade not specified in terms of origin or destination).

The non-OECD regional models are much less detailed than the models for OECD countries. They do not, for example, include structural equations for determination of domestic expenditure, domestic wages and prices, and income distribution. Rather, they are cast in the form of reduced-form equations characterising import volume and export pricing behaviour.

Import volumes in each non-OECD regional model are expressed as a function of changes in each region's foreign exchange resources, (export earnings, transfers, borrowing), adjusted for changes in the terms of trade. The rationale underlying this approach is that the foreign exchange resources of most non-OECD countries are limited; hence, changes in export earnings, whether the result of price changes or volume changes, tend to be closely associated with changes in imports. In cases where export earnings fall, for example, import restrictions tend to be tightened, in order to protect the foreign exchange resource position. Conversely, an increase in export earnings tends to give rise to a loosening of import restrictions.

In simulation applications with the system, capital flows for non-OECD regions are assumed simply to be the counterpart of current balance positions, such that international reserves are unchanged. In forecasting applications, however, this is not necessarily the case, with changes in net capital flows expected to have effects in non-OECD countries' imports analogous to those of a change in export earnings. A decrease in net capital flows might, for example, tend to result in tightening of import restrictions, and an increase in net capital inflow would tend to induce a loosening in import restrictions.

Debt interest payments account for a large proportion of the current account deficits of non-OECD regions (excluding OPEC). Because much of this debt is floating rate debt, with interest payments periodically marked to changes in world short-term interest rates, fluctuations in these short-term rates should also play an important role in determining the foreign exchange resources of non-OECD regions. Their effects are not yet explicitly represented in the system, however, so that the effects of changes in financial conditions affecting the non-OECD regions have to be taken into account via add-factor adjustments.

For most non-OECD regions, it is assumed that any changes in real foreign exchange resources will be fully spent in the course of a year or two, depending on the region. The lags involved are assumed to be shortest for low- and middle-income developing countries (which have an assumed spending propensity of 1.0, distributed over 1 year), and longest for OPEC low-absorbers (spending propensity of 0.7, distributed over 2 years).

The non-OECD regions are assumed to be 'price takers' for trade in manufactures: their export prices of manufactures are assumes to follow the average of the OECD area. As with the country models for OECD countries, real export prices of food and industrial raw materials respond to changes in demand conditions in the OECD area. Also, as with the OECD country models, the export price of internationally-traded energy is customarily assumed to move in line with OECD countries' average export price of manufactures, though in simulation applications the price of inter-nationally-traded oil can be determined through a market-clearing mechanism which balances total OECD area oil requirements with indigenous energy produc-tion, non-OECD energy production (OPEC and non-OPEC), and changes in inventories.

3.3. International linkage

World trade and financial models link the OECD country models, together with those of the non-OECD regions, to provide internationally-consistent projections of trade volumes and prices; and, in 'floating rate mode', of international capital flows also. For some countries, other linkage channels can be important, such as wage rate determination in small open economies, and interest rate determination, where the course of United States interest rates has a strong influence elsewhere.

(i) Trade volume and price linkage

Within each country and non-OECD regional model, import volumes and export prices are endogenously determined for given values of, inter alia, exchange rates, import prices and export volumes. When the system is used in fully linked mode, these individual country projections are passed to the central world trade block where a consistent set of export volume and import price estimates is determined. These are in turn passed back to the country models as revised inputs into the determination of domestic demand and costs, so that on repeated iteration a convergent and internationally-consistent model solution is achieved. The linkage process therefore consists of allocating country-model-based estimates of global import demands between individual exporting countries, while also determining individual country import prices, given a global view of export prices, exchange rate movements, and the emerging patterns of international trade.

(ii) Financial linkage

The main considerations underlying the design of the financial linkage block and the organisation of related information flows are similar to those for international trade linkage. In both cases an essential operational requirement is that the system should be solveable both in single country and internationally-linked modes. For this reason it is again useful to decompose the main features of the financial linkage system into domestically- and internationally-determined components. The relationships for the former category of variables have been described in the block structure of individual country models. Those for the latter group are computed in the financial linkage block, which may operate in either fixed or floating exchange rate mode.

Consistency of international capital flows in the international financial linkage is achieved as the result of appropriately-defined weighting procedures for interest rates and exchange rates and a related set of cross-country parameter restrictions embodied in the net capital flow relationships. Taken together these ensure that, for given changes in interest and expected exchange rate differentials, the net capital flow resulting for any one country is exactly matched elsewhere in the system either by capital flows, of the reverse sign, or changes in overseas currency holdings.

4. THE FORECASTING ROUND IN PRACTICE

The following is a description of how the work of the forecasting round is carried out at present, i.e. in 1984. No two Rounds are identical, but all share the same broad features.

Before the Round proper gets underway, the INTERLINK 'machinery' is over-hauled. The tracking performance of the equations in INTERLINK is analysed by those responsible for the various blocks (demand, supply, wages and prices, trade, fiscal and monetary) and any necessary modifications tested and incorporated into the structure.

The Round then begins with an exchange rate assumption for each OECD country put into the computer files and circulated. Next, the simultaneous world economic system is broken into at its most nearly exogenous components, namely non-OECD zones, and the largest OECD countries. This is potentially risky, because the exogeneity is far from complete. In principle, those who have to prepare these forecasts must at this stage 'second-guess' the forecasts of the rest of the system.

The Balance of Payments Division (BoP), in co-operation with other Directorates, makes an initial assessment of how much non-OECD deficit countries are likely to receive in the form of loans and transfers, and how much non-OECD surplus countries (in practice OPEC) will be willing to run down their surpluses. The various country experts, at this stage, form preliminary views about economic policy developments (government expenditure, money supply, interest rates).

These variables, together with technical assumptions concerning exchange rates, form the new values of 'exogenous' variables in the INTERLINK model for a first-stage 'Climate run'.

This first stage climate run is essentially the previous set of forecasts (i.e. those published in the previous *Economic Outlook*) incrementally updated by INTER-LINK for changes in exogenous variables of the types mentioned above. The system is run in linked mode, thereby ensuring international consistency of the new set of preliminary forecasts, which retain all the add-factors from the previously-published set of forecasts. The climate run set of forecasts is circulated to country specialists and to BoP, who examine them to see how their previous forecasts should be modified in the light of new exogenous information.

The next step is to generate preliminary forecasts of real demand and price developments in the United States. The United States is by far the most important single OECD country, its GDP being about two-fifths of the OECD total, and its import demand has a substantial impact on other OECD (and non-OECD) countries. Furthermore, U.S. interest rates play a key role in determining interest rates elsewhere. Notwithstanding its importance for the rest of the world, the rest of the world is not very important for the United States. Although foreign trade as a proportion of U.S. GDP has doubled since the early 1960s, it still remains well below the OECD average, and the United States is in this respect more nearly exogenous than other countries. Furthermore, nearly half of its exports go to non-OECD countries, whose import demand has already been determined provisionally. The preliminary forecasts for the United States are put on computer file and circulated to participants.

Shortly after the preliminary forecast for the United States is circulated, one is prepared and circulated for Germany, the major trading partner for other European countries. A second 'Climate run' is then made. Again this uses the INTERLINK system in linked mode. In this run, the revised exogenous assumptions from the first run are retained, and are supplemented by new and revised historical data, and, through modified add-factors, initial judgemental revisions for key forecast components. Further, at this stage, INTERLINK 'locks on' to the preliminary forecasts for the United States and Germany. The model is then solved for all other countries. This run thereby enables country and subject specialists to examine the impact on their 'own' country or variables not only of revisions to exogenous assumptions, but also the revised outlook for the United States and Germany. As with the first climate run, the results for all countries and variables are necessarily as globally consistent as the previously-published set of (baseline) forecasts. The object of splitting up the climate runs into two distinct steps is to obviate the difficulty of interpreting the results of runs where too many variables are changed simultaneously.

Preliminary forecasts for the five other major countries are then prepared and circulated, and discussed together with other material at the General Internal Meeting, which is usually held ten days or so after the beginning of the Round proper.

5. THE GENERAL INTERNAL MEETING

The General Internal Meeting is attended by nearly all in the Economics Department administration including the Head of Department and Directors. The meeting has changed in nature over the years. At one time, it was an informal discussion of the economic 'climate', held very early in the Round. Country desks made oral summaries of recent developments in major countries and gave their impressions of likely future prospects. Subject specialists did likewise. Over the years the meeting has become more formalised. The Monetary and Fiscal Policy Division (MFPD) circulates notes on policy developments in major countries and a quantitative assessment of them. The preliminary forecasts for the United States and Germany are discussed. The Economic Prospects Division circulates a note which details the economic factors affecting the forecasts and summarises the main features of the Climate runs. The Statistics Division also circulates a note on their latest leading indicators of OECD countries, and their interpretation. At the meeting, the outlook for the United States is discussed in some detail, and that of other major OECD countries more briefly. BoP and MFPD make oral interventions. The discussion is wide-ranging, and all present may participate in it.

After the General Internal Meeting, Country Desks of the major countries revise their preliminary forecasts after discussing them with the Balance of Payments Division (BoP). These forecasts are put in the computer and circulated, usually 2 or 3 working days after the meeting. Four or 5 days subsequently, forecasts for smaller OECD countries are put in the computer file and circulated. The time lag is for two reasons. Major Country Desks are also responsible for one or more minor countries, and would find it difficult to work on several country forecasts simultaneously. More importantly, the export market growth of smaller countries is heavily influenced by developments in the major countries, and in the non-OECD zones. At the same time, export market growth for major OECD countries is not greatly influenced by developments in the smaller countries; in aggregate, smaller OECD countries are equivalent in economic importance to one major OECD country. It is therefore desirable that smaller country forecasts be prepared after those of the major countries, especially as activity in smaller countries is particularly dependent on foreign trade. At one extreme, there is the United States, where exports are equivalent to about 12% of GDP, at the other is Belgium where the ratio is 65%.

On the basis of these detailed domestic forecasts for all OECD countries, BoP generates revised foreign trade goods volume and price forecasts, using the INTER-LINK system. Also at about this time (some 4 or 5 working days after the domestic forecasts for smaller countries have been put on file, and 6 or 7 working days after the General Internal Meeting), BoP prepares preliminary forecasts of trade by volume and price in services by country, circulates them and puts them on computer file. The method used for forecasting trade in non-factor services is similar to that used for goods. The INTERLINK system is used to generate import volumes by country as a function of forecast total domestic demand volume, and export prices by country are a function of forecast GDP deflators. The system also converts import volumes into export volumes via a share matrix, and export prices are converted into import prices likewise. Trade in factor services is forecast by a mixture of extrapolation and specialist knowledge (e.g. financing the level of outstanding external debt). Forecasts of private and official transfers are largely extrapolations, and these flows are forecast on a net basis. The detailed goods (and sometimes service) trade forecasts are discussed with individual Desks, who modify the external and possibly domestic aspects of their forecasts accordingly. These revised detailed forecasts are put on computer file, circulated and form the basis of discussion at the Intradepartmental Meeting, which typically takes place about 2 weeks after the General Internal Meeting, or 5 weeks after the beginning of the Round.

6. THE INTRADEPARTMENTAL MEETING

This meeting lasts 2 days. The morning of the first day is usually mainly devoted to a detailed discussion and analysis of the forecast of the United States economy. The other major countries are examined during the remainder of the first day. Comments are expected from the subject specialists, but all Round participants are free to comment and criticise. The smaller countries are examined on the second day. As on the first day, subject specialists attend and are expected to comment. Generally speaking, the subject specialists, BoP especially, will have had bilateral discussions with the Desks prior to the meeting, but any outstanding differences of opinion are aired and settled at the meeting.

Subsequently, Desks revise domestic demand components in the light of comments received, and BoP converts these into revised trade forecasts. At the same time, BoP circulated an updated exchange rate assumption, and discusses details of trade and current balance forecasts with Desks. The finally-revised forecasts by Desks and by BoP form the basis of the Short Term Forecasters' document (STF document), to be discussed by the national forecasting experts.

7. THE SHORT-TERM FORECASTERS' MEETING

Approximately 2 months after the beginning of the Round, and 2 weeks after forecasts are finalised, the Short-Term Forecasters (STF) meeting is held. The majority of participants are short-term forecasting experts from each of the OECD countries. If they have official forecasts for their own countries they are given to the meeting and discussed. The national experts also comment on the Secretariat's forecasts which have been circulated to them in advance. Their comments, and other points, are taken up during the meeting by Desks and Heads of Country Studies Divisions. This meeting document typically contains a hundred pages or so of tables and charts of Secretariat forecasts in some detail (more detail than eventually published in the *Economic Outlook*) and (usually) some brief text outlining and analysing the forecasts. Early in the meeting, the Secretariat collects details of the national official forecasts and later circulates comparative tables of Secretariat and national expert forecasts. The meeting is also attended by representatives of the World Bank, the IMF and the European Common Market. Representatives from the Economic Prospects and BoP divisions also make oral interventions of a summary nature. The afternoon of the second day is frequently devoted to a general discussion of the world economic outlook, with particular emphasis on the technical uncertainties in the situation.

If the Secretariat is convinced by the national and international experts that the Secretariat forecasts for individual countries or global variables (e.g. developing countries' import demand) should be revised, then these revisions are made. The Secretariat is not obliged to align its forecasts with those of Member Governments, however, and often does not. Any revisions that are made are subjected to a final iteration and discussion between BoP and Desks, and these final, consistent forecasts are published in the *Economic Outlook* some weeks later.

8. THE ECONOMIC POLICY COMMITTEE AND THE ECONOMIC OUTLOOK

The object of the forecasting Round is not simply to publish forecasts in the *Economic Outlook*. And, conversely, the Outlook contains a good deal more than short-term forecasts. Rather, the Outlook is a summary version of the work of the Secretariat for the Economic Policy Committee (the EPC). The EPC is one of the two committees served by the Economics and Statistics Department. The other is the Economic and Development Review Committee (EDRC). The EDRC meets about 20 times a year to examine each Member country. The examination is based on a draft survey of the country in question, prepared initially by the Desk concerned. These surveys are revised in the light of the Committee's comments and then published by the Committee. The EPC meeting (which lasts 2 days) is attended by senior policy advisers and by senior members of the Secretariat, including the Secretary-General. The Chairman is elected from the national representatives. Discussion is normally centered around documentation prepared by the Secretariat. A main purpose of the meeting is to allow Member Governments to discuss and explain their economic policies, considered individually and in relation to those of partner countries. In addition, the summer meeting of the EPC paves the way for the ministerial meeting at the OECD, held usually in June, of Ministers of Finance.

Much of the documentation presented to the EPC meeting, together with selected material submitted to Working Parties, is revised and published in the *Economic Outlook,* along with the final revised forecasts. Preparing the Outlook text, tables and charts for the printers is the responsibility of the Economic Prospects Division. The Outlook is usually published five or six weeks after the EPC meeting.

9. THE ROLE OF COMPUTERISATION

It can be seen from the description above that the development of the forecasting process at OECD over the past 5 years or so owes much to computerisation. This is as it should be, and certainly is in common with developments in probably the majority of forecasting institutions. But it is worth emphasizing that while the term 'computerisation' is often taken in this context as synonymous with 'modelling', in fact the scope that computerisation has opened up is much wider than that, and has brought particular benefits to the process of making international forecasts.

Word processing, photocomposition directly from computer memory, automatic table generation routines, the on-line entry of forecast data and other such advances have all helped speed up the production process, while simultaneously helping ensure global coherency of the exercise, and significantly reducing error. This is very important. But perhaps the most striking feature of computerisation over the last 5 years has been the increase it has brought about in the speed and accuracy with which the participants in the forecasting process can communicate with each other, and hence the quickness with which the centre of action in the forecasting process can be passed from one group of participants to another. To use a football analogy, the ball now spends much less time out of play.

This has meant that it is now possible to do rather more, in fact considerably more, in the course of the 6-week forecasting Round than used to be the case. This is just as well, because the task has unquestionably got harder. The forecasting difficulties associated with large oil shocks, sharply fluctuating exchange rates, unusually high interest rates and sharp changes in the volumes of non-OECD imports are just some examples of some of the problems that have had to be wrestled with over the last 5 years. Small wonder, then, that the increased time made available has been used rather to provide the forecasting Round participants at OECD with more time to think and reflect their thought in further iterations of the global forecast, than to shorten significantly the overall length of the forecasting Round. This increased thinking time has potentially been a key feature in maintaining, and perhaps increasing, overall forecasting accuracy in recent years.

On the other hand, perhaps one further area where computerisation is opening up a potential which so far has been largely unexplored, both within OECD and outside, concerns the frequent and timely conducting of post mortems on forecast accuracy. Post mortems are useful: it is always as well to know not only by how much a forecast went wrong, but also why. It is even more useful to know why in time to do something about it. But post mortems are hard to do, and are all the harder when part at least of the reason for error in the projection for any given country lies in error in the forecast for, or assumptions made about, other countries. For example, the OECD Secretariat is required to make its forecasts on the basis of a 'no policy change' assumption, so as to provide an appropriate basis for policy discussion. The INTERLINK system can be drawn on to help adjust an internationally-consistent set of forecasts to find out what would have been forecast for each country, had policies been entered as they actually turned out.

At the OECD work is just starting in this area, with the methods being developed as the work proceeds. Preliminary findings were put before forecasting experts earlier this year, and are to be published in due course. If developed appropriately, this exercise may teach some important lessons. In that way, the computerisation that is described in this paper may prove to be leading not only to better forecasts, but also perhaps to better policy.

NOTES

Views expressed in this paper are those of the authors and should not be interpreted as necessarily representing official views of the OECD Secretariat.

1)   Belgium and Luxembourg are, at this stage, considered together as one 'country'.

CHAPTER 12

INTERNATIONAL MACROECONOMIC MODELLING FOR POLICY DECISIONS: SOME PROPOSALS

Orhan Guvenen
University of Paris IX-Dauphine, France

1. INTRODUCTION

The structure of economic and social fluctuations since the 1970s necessitates a reconsideration of international macroeconomic modelling.
The aim of this chapter is:

1) to evaluate the main characteristics of international macroeconomic modelling through three generations of models, and the analysis presented in the previous chapters;
2) to discuss some proposals for reconsidering international modelling.

2. INTERDEPENDENT SYSTEMS MODELLING

The evolution of macroeconomic modelling follows the evolution of international economic phenomena. Main phases in world economy since 1950s have been:

1) 1950–1972 (a period of reconstruction and rapid economic growth);
2) 1973–1985 (oil shocks, fluctuations on raw material and financial markets);
3) present and potential problems (the increasing importance of socioeconomic factors and social protection expenditures, unemployment; inflationary potential, fluctuations in financial, oil and raw material markets, a shift of final demand towards services, external debt, difficulties in coordinating economic policies).

Three generations of international macroeconomic modelling coincide with this evolution:

1) neo-keynesian macroeconomic models linked through trade flows;
2) linkage of energy and raw material models and financial blocks to the first

Artus, P. and Guvenen, O. (eds.): International Macroeconomic Modelling for Policy Decisions.
© *1986. Martinus Nijhoff Publishers, Dordrecht/Boston/Lancaster.*
ISBN 90-247-3201-8. Printed in The Netherlands.

generation-type models;

3) modelling the world as a single economy and linkages through satellite modelling.[1]

This book has presented some recent developments in the construction and use of international macroeconometric models. It covers theoretical and empirical research by model builders and users aiming to improve economic policy decisions through a better understanding and forecasting of complex and interdepdenent systems.

In Part I on the analysis of trade linkages and exchange rate determination, A. Italianer and G. D'Alcantara's study has shown how the sectoral disaggregation of bilateral trade flows in a model that links several national models and zone models to a world model can bring a value added to econometric analysis and decision-making.

It has shown how different economic policies that a priori have the same macro-economic impact, in fact generate differential macroeconomic patterns due to the disaggregated channels through which the policy measures are propagated. The analysis was applied to European Economic Community (EEC) which represents strongly integrated markets with differential sectoral developments and some scope for co-ordinated policy.

From a demand and supply equation on each bilateral market, a system of disaggregated bilateral trade flows was derived for five categories of goods. The estimated trade flows were introduced in the linked macroeconomic model Comet IV. Through policy simulations, it was demonstrated that shocks in different final demand components of all EEC countries, according to the category of goods which is directly attributed, generate different trade effects.

An alternative form of import demand function by allowing for commodity and country disaggregation was presented by J.M. Viaene.

The various stages of country interdependence were analysed in a theoretical and empirical context with various stages of country interdependence:

— interdependence between the importing country and the supplying nations through the trade flows of various commodity groups;
— within a commodity group the possibility of substitution or complementarity between the supplying countries;
— among commodity groups the substitutive or complementary relationships which are based upon the characteristics of the underlying domestic cost and utility functions.

The estimation results provided the evidence of substitution between sources of supply of food products, and of energy. In contrast they supported the hypothesis of complementarity between bilateral flows of raw materials, and of manufactures.

Chapters 3 and 4 dealt with exchange rate determination. The study by P. Masson and P. Richardson implemented a strategy for treating exchange rate expectations in the OECD Interlink model. It was focused on alternative specifications for exchange rate expectations, and calculating the rational expectations solution for the expected exchange rate.

A. Murfin and P. Ormerod's research developed an operational system which allows the analysis of more direct and more powerful effects of a change of any of the countries on the economies of other countries. The described framework demonstrated that economic models of national economies can be linked in a coherent way via the exchange rate.

In Part II on modelling and simulating the international economy, it was interesting to see the differences between the model building approach chosen by P. Artus and those of G. Kirkpatrick (Globus model), Interlink, Project Link, Comet, Atlas, EPA model approaches, i.e., national models linked together by commercial and financial flows. P. Artus considered the world as a whole to be modelled as a single country. A similar approach was chosen by Parkin-Zis (1976), B. Piganiol (1979), Beenstock-Dicks (1983).

The advantage of this approach is that commercial and financial flows between countries as well as exchange rate fluctuations disappear. But, on the other hand, data is difficult to construct on such an aggregate basis.

To evaluate the efficiency of different policies and the consequences of the changes in the prices of raw material and in money supply occurred after 1973, an aggregate econometric model for the world economy taken as a whole was estimated and simulated.

The disequilibrium estimates induced the choice of a neo-keynesian model to represent the functioning of the world economy. The model gave significant results in spite of the complexity of the economy to be described, and represented a central block to which satellite models of energy and raw material markets, financial markets, and models dealing with social protection expenditures or some specific socioeconomic problems can be linked.

In the study by G. Kirkpatrick the same model was used for groups of countries. The differences between countries of a group being parametric models were estimated using continuous time econometric estimation techniques. They are intended to be used for scenario analysis, and to provide a method for examining complex dynamic processes for which no analytical solution is possible in an interdependent system.

The evolution of competitivity and employment in some industrialised countries and the international differences were analysed by E. Kremp and Le Dem. Their conclusion was that the competitiveness depends on the overall macroeconomic performance and that the overall impact of changes in productivity on macroeconomic performance can be inflationary, neutral or deflationary.

The current account of the United States, Japan and Germany, a cyclical analysis by P. Hooper and R. Tryon focused on the cyclical factor, analysed the quantitative importance of the recent and expected current account positions in the three countries, and considered the relative importance of the drop in exports to developing countries by using the MCM model (Federal Reserve Board's Multi-country Model).

In our interdependent economies international policy co-ordination is a key factor for national and international policy decisions. This topic was covered by Chapters 8 and 9.

A.S. Brandsma and A.J. Hughes Hallett adopted an explicit optimisation approach in which each policy maker's decision is determined jointly with rational expectations of what he expects other policy makers to do.

Dynamic game theory was applied to the problem of policy co-ordination between the US and the EEC in a strongly aggregated model of the world economy. The originality of the approach is that the parties do not have to surrender their individual objectives and that no decision about the weighting of each other's targets has to be negotiated beforehand. The method allows for rational expectations of the other player's policy selections to be part of the conditioning information of each policy maker.

A.B. Barten and G. d'Alcantara described the evolution of Comet model since 1969 to the present day. Alternative policy simulations were presented on various subjects such as: nominal wage decreases, social security contribution rate decreases, public investment multiplier, exchange rate changes.

J. Llewellyn, L. Samuelson and N. Vanston, as model builders and users, presented the OECD Interlink model, and related the Organisation's experience in making international forecasts. This was a stimulating contribution concerning the use of a world model, and the functioning of forecasting round experience which is the largest single coordinated exercise regularly performed by the OECD Secretariat.

3. SOME PROPOSALS FOR RECONSIDERING INTERNATIONAL MACROECONOMIC MODELLING

Through the state of art in international modelling in 1980s, and studies presented in this book, what appears as possible proposals in reconsidering international macroeconomic modelling could be summarised as follows:[2]

1) the need for further theoretical and empirical studies on the interdependence of world economy, transmission of fluctuations, and internationally co-ordinated policies;

2) the impact of structural changes on the capacity of international macro-economic models in exploring and forecasting the economic phenomena; and a closer link between micro- and macroeconomic considerations;
3) determinants of international specialisation;
4) more emphasis on medium-term modelling;
5) identification of institutional, national, regional, behavioural specifications, and of some economic behavioural changes;
6) short- and medium-term exchange rate determination;
7) to introduce the impacts of stocks with the traditional flow approach in modelling;
8) more international coherence on the trade of goods, services, and financial flows;
9) better understanding of energy and raw material markets, the linkage of energy and commodity models with world models;
10) identification of the socioeconomic behavioural changes, and the increasing importance of social protection and public expenditure;
11) regime shifts and policy making;
12) policy-oriented problem-solving approach through sectoral disaggregation of structural models on the one hand, and on the other hand central and satellite modelling, exploration modelling, and valid reduced forms for policy analysis.

Complementarity of various modelling and quantification techniques (statistical analysis, econometrics, operations research, input-output analysis, systems analysis, game theory, optimal control, mathematical programming), and application of decision theory to economic policy making are the key factors in the objective of a policy-oriented problem-solving approach. Modelling of the historical probability structure can be used in an appropriate way to make conditional projections that will be useful in policy analysis.

As remarkably mentioned by E. Kuh in his address to Applied Econometric Association on its tenth anniversary: 'Technology-driven progress of the past three decades can be viewed as computerization of intellectual capital'.[3] This makes it more critical than ever to balance computational opportunities with real-world problems in applied econometrics and in international modelling.

NOTES

1) Guvenen, O. and B. Piganiol (1984), 'Modélisation internationale sous contrainte des modèles de produits et des modèles financiers', Université de Paris IX-Dauphine, CEPRI, pp. 7–15.
2) A stimulating discussion on this subject could be found in:
   – Lambelet, J.C. (1983), 'Crise économique et modèles économétriques internationaux,

réfléxions dubitatives sur l'utilité de ceux-ci pour éclairer celle-là', Applied Econometric Association International conference on the use of International Models in the context of Economic Crisis, EEC; Brussels.
- Ullmo, Y. (1983), 'Les modèles internationaux et la crise; quelques reflexions', AEA Conference cited, EEC, Brussels.
3) Kuh, E. (1983). 'A Perspective on Applied Econometrics', Address to Applied Econometric Association on its Tenth Anniversary, Lyon, France.

REFERENCES

Aoki, M. (1980), 'Dynamics and Control of a System Compared of a Large Number of Similar Subsystems', in: P.T. Lin (ed), *Dynamic Optimization and Mathematical Economics*, Plenum Press, New York, pp. 183–203.

Artus, P., M. Deleau and P. Malgrange (1984), *Modélisation macroéconomique quantitative*, ENSAE, Paris.

Balasko, Y. (1984), 'The Size of Dynamic Econometric Models', *Econometrica*, Vol. 52, No. 1.

Beenstock, M. and G.R. Dicks (1983), 'An Aggregate Monetary Model of the World Economy', *European Economic Review*, May.

Courbis, R., ed. (1981), *Commerce international et modèles multinationaux*, Economica, Paris.

Dramais, A. (1981), 'Le modèle Desmos' in: R. Courbis (ed.), *Commerce international et modèles multinationaux*, Economica, Paris.

Guvenen, O. and B. Piganiol (1984), 'Modélisation internationale sous contrainte des modèles de produits et des modèles financiers', Cahiers de CEPRI, Université de Paris IX-Dauphine.

Guvenen, O., B. Piganiol and F. Pinto (1980), 'Linkage of International Macroeconomic and Commodity Models: Mondeco, Simlink, World Bank Global Model', Econometric Society World Congress, University Aix-Marseille III.

Helliwell, J.F. and T. Padmore (1982), 'Empirical Studies of Macroeconomic Interdependence', in: *Handbook in International Economics* by R. Jones and P. Kenen, North Holland, Amsterdam.

Kaneko, T. and N. Tasuhara (1983), 'An Analysis of the Dynamic Properties of the EPA World Economic Model – A Simulation Approach', Economic Research Institute, Economic Planning Agency, Japan.

Klein, L.R. and A. Tishler (1979), 'Long-run projections of the Link World Trade Model', in: J.A. Sawyer (ed.), *Modelling International Transmission Mechanism*, North Holland, Amsterdam, pp. 73–94.

Kuh, E. (1983), 'A Perspective on Applied Econometrics', Address to Applied Econometric Association on its Tenth Anniversary, Lyon, France.

Lambelet, J.C. (1983), 'Crise économique et modèles économétriques internationaux, refléxions dubitatives sur l'utilité de ceux-ci pour éclairer celle-là', Applied Econometric Association International Economic Crisis, EEC, Brussels.

Llewellyn, J. and H. Arai (1984), 'International Aspects of Forecasting Accuracy', *OECD Economic Studies*, No. 3 (Autumn), pp. 73–117.

Malgrange, P. and P.A. Muet, eds (1984), *Contemporary Macroeconomic Modelling*, Basil Blackwell, Oxford.

Malinvaud, E. (1981), 'Econometrics Faced with the Needs of Macroeconomic Policy', *Econometrica*, Vol. 49, No. 5, November, pp. 1363–1376.

Parkin, M. and G. Zis (1976), *Inflation in the World Economy*, Manchester University Press and University of Toronto Press.

Piganiol, B. (1979), 'Le Modèle Mondeco', CEPRI, Université de Paris IX-Dauphine.

Ranuzzi, P. (1981), 'The Experience of the EEC Eurolink project in Modeling Bilateral Trade Equations', *Journal of Policy Modeling,* Vol. 3, No. 2, pp. 153–173.

Samuelson, L. (1976), 'International Transmission of Economic Fluctuations', Economic Contributions to Public Policy, International Economic Association.

Sawyer, J.A. (1979), *Modelling the International Transmission Mechanism,* North Holland, Amsterdam.

Ullmo, Y. (1983), 'Les Modèles internationaux et la crise: quelques reflexions', Address to Applied Econometric Association, Brussels.

Waelbroeck, J., ed. (1976), *The Models of Project Link,* North Holland, Amsterdam.

Ward, M.D. and H. Guetzkow (1979), 'Toward Integrated Global Models: From Engineering to Social Science Modeling', *Journal of Policy Modeling,* Vol. 1, No. 3, September, pp. 445–464.

INDEX

ADVANCED STUDIES IN THEORETICAL AND APPLIED ECONOMETRICS
VOLUME 5

Paelinck J.H.P. (ed.): Qualitative and Quantitative Mathematical Economics, 1982.
ISBN 90 247 2623 9.
Ancot J.P. (ed.): Analysing the Structure of Economic Models, 1984.
ISBN 90 247 2894 0.
Hughes Hallett A.J. (ed.): Applied Decision Analysis and Economic Behaviour, 1984
ISBN 90 247 2968 8.
Sengupta J.K.: Information and Efficiency in Economic Decision, 1985
ISBN 90 247 3072 4.
Artus P. and Guvenen O. (eds.), in collaboration with Gagey F.: International Macro-
economic Modelling for Policy Decisions, 1986.
ISBN 90 247 3201 8.
Vilares M.J.: Structural Change in Macroeconomic Models, 1986
ISBN 90 247 3277 8.